Social Tourism in Europe

ASPECTS OF TOURISM

Series Editors: Chris Cooper, *Oxford Brookes University, UK*; C. Michael Hall, *University of Canterbury, New Zealand*; and Dallen J. Timothy, *Arizona State University, USA*

Aspects of Tourism is an innovative, multifaceted series, which comprises authoritative reference handbooks on global tourism regions, research volumes, texts and monographs. It is designed to provide readers with the latest thinking on tourism worldwide and push back the frontiers of tourism knowledge. The volumes are authoritative, readable and user-friendly, providing accessible sources for further research. Books in the series are commissioned to probe the relationship between tourism and cognate subject areas such as strategy, development, retailing, sport and environmental studies.

Full details of all the books in this series and of all our other publications can be found on http://www.channelviewpublications.com, or by writing to Channel View Publications, St Nicholas House, 31–34 High Street, Bristol BS1 2AW, UK.

Social Tourism in Europe

Theory and Practice

Edited by

Scott McCabe, Lynn Minnaert and Anya Diekmann

CHANNEL VIEW PUBLICATIONS
Bristol • Buffalo • Toronto

Library of Congress Cataloging in Publication Data
A catalog record for this book is available from the Library of Congress.
Social Tourism in Europe: Theory and Practice/Edited by Scott McCabe, Lynn Minnaert and Anya Diekmann.
Includes index.
1. Tourism – Social aspects – Europe. 2. Heritage tourism – Europe. 3. Europe – Cultural policy.
I. McCabe, Scott, Ph.D. II. Minnaert, Lynn. III. Diekmann, Anya.
G155.E8.S64 2012
338.4'7914–dc23 2011035555

British Library Cataloguing in Publication Data
A catalogue entry for this book is available from the British Library.

ISBN-13: 978-1-84541-233-3 (hbk)
ISBN-13: 978-1-84541-232-6 (pbk)

Channel View Publications
UK: St Nicholas House, 31–34 High Street, Bristol BS1 2AW, UK.
USA: UTP, 2250 Military Road, Tonawanda, NY 14150, USA.
Canada: UTP, 5201 Dufferin Street, North York, Ontario M3H 5T8, Canada.

The policy of Multilingual Matters/Channel View Publications is to use papers that are natural, renewable and recyclable products, made from wood grown in sustainable forests. In the manufacturing process of our books, and to further support our policy, preference is given to printers that have FSC and PEFC Chain of Custody certification. The FSC and/or PEFC logos will appear on those books where full certification has been granted to the printer concerned.

Typeset in Schneidler by R. J. Footring Ltd, Derby.
Printed and bound in Great Britain by Short Run Press Ltd.

05713084

Contents

Figures

Tables

Acknowledgements

The editors are indebted to many people who assisted in the production of this book. Chief among those to whom we would like to extend many thanks are the chapter and case study contributors, for whose hard work, attention to the detail of our requests and criticisms and continuing support in the face of time pressures we are extremely grateful. There are many other people who assisted us in the process, too many to name here, but we wish to extend our grateful thanks to all of you. However, we would especially like to thank Thea Joldesma at the Family Holiday Association, Charles Etienne Belanger at ISTO, Małgorzata Aleksiejuk at the Polish Ministry of Sport and Tourism, and Anne Mette Hjalager at Advance 1 Consulting in Denmark. We would also like to thank Sarah and Ellie at Channel View for all their support throughout the process, and Ralph Footring for his fine copy-editing. This project has been hard work but was made a great deal more enjoyable by the collegial, fun and supportive working relationships between the editors. Finally, we would like to thank those closest and dearest to us (for Scott: Lisa, Kieran and Harry; Lynn: Pierre and my loving family in Belgium; Anya: Patrick, Alexandra, Felix and Hannah) for giving us the support to enable us to complete this work.

Contributors

Sheela Agarwal is Associate Professor (Reader) in the School of Tourism and Hospitality, University of Plymouth. She has written and co-authored numerous journal articles and book chapters and more recently co-edited a book on various aspects of coastal resort tourism, including the impact and consequences of globalisation, economic restructuring and social exclusion. Her research interests include discourses of globalisation, economic restructuring, conceptualisations of place and space, local governance and social exclusion. s.agarwal@plymouth.ac.uk

Christian Baumgartner is Secretary-General of Naturefriends International, Vienna, Austria. He studied landscape ecology. He gives lectures in Austria and China, is a member of the Tourism Sustainability Group within the European Commission and a member of several national and international tourism-related advisory boards. Being a specialist in development and monitoring of sustainable tourism, he has guided several tourism development projects in Europe and south-east Asia. christian.baumgartner@nf-int.org www.nf-int.org

Frances Brown is the former editor of the journal *Tourism Management* and the author of *Tourism Reassessed: Blight or Blessing?* (Butterworth Heinemann, 1998). Currently editor of the journal *Space Policy*, she has degrees in international relations and modern languages. fbrown.seabank@virgin.net

Gilles Caire is Maître de conférences in economic sciences in the Faculty of Law and Social Sciences at the Université de Poitiers. He is director of the professional Master's programme 'Droit et développement de l'économie sociale et solidaire' and researcher at the CRIEF (Centre de recherche sur l'intégration économique et financière) in tourism economics, social protection and sustainable development. gilles.caire@univ-poitiers.fr

Anya Diekmann is Associate Professor and co-director of the research centre LIToTeS (Laboratoire interdisciplinaire Tourisme, Territoires et Sociétés) at the Université Libre de Bruxelles (ULB). Her publications include work on social tourism and aspects of cultural tourism, with a particular focus on heritage, urban and ethnic tourism. She recently published together with Kevin Hannam *Tourism and India: A Critical Introduction* (Routledge, 2010). adiekman@ulb.ac.be

Derek Hall has been professor of regional development, head of a leisure and tourism management department, and a part-time tour manager in Eastern Europe and the Far East. Together with Frances Brown he co-authored *Tourism and Welfare: Ethics, Responsibility and Sustained Well-being* (CABI, 2006). derekhall.seabank@virgin.net

Kevin Hannam is Associate Dean (Research) and Head of the Department of Tourism, Hospitality and Events, University of Sunderland, Faculty of Business and Law. He holds a PhD in geography from the University of Portsmouth. He is the co-author (with Dr Dan Knox) of *Understanding Tourism* (Sage, 2010), co-author (with Dr Anya Diekmann) of *Tourism and India* (Routledge, 2010) and co-editor (with Professors Mimi Sheller and John Urry) of the journal *Mobilities* (Routledge). kevin.hamman@sunderland.ac.uk

Freya Higgins-Desbiolles is a lecturer in tourism at the University of South Australia. Her research has included a focus on the concerns of host communities, the impacts of tourism, indigenous tourism and justice through tourism. She has recently worked with indigenous Australian communities and Palestinians on projects fostering the use of tourism for community benefit. freya.higginsdesbiolles@unisa.edu.au

Tess Kay is Director of the Brunel Centre for Sport, Health and Wellbeing (BC-SHaW). She has a special interest in the role of family relationships and wellbeing and has served on family-related social policy research networks for the European Commission. She edited the international research collection *Fathering Through Sport and Leisure* (Routledge, 2009). tess.kay@brunel.ac.uk

Scott McCabe is Associate Professor in Tourism Management/Marketing at Nottingham University Business School. His research interests are in marketing communications in tourism, tourist experience, consumption and participation. He has published a number of articles on the sociology of tourism, including social tourism and social justice, socio-linguistics and rhetoric of tourism. scott.mccabe@nottingham.ac.uk

Lynn Minnaert is a lecturer in tourism and events at the University of Surrey. She has published a series of research and consultancy papers on the impacts and conceptualisation of social tourism. She is co-editor of a special issue on social tourism of *Current Issues in Tourism*. l.minnaert@surrey.ac.uk

Gareth Shaw is Professor of Retail and Tourism Management in the Business School, University of Exeter. He has co-authored a number of books on tourism, including (with Allan Williams) *Critical Issues in Tourism: A Geographical Perspective*, Wiley-Blackwell, 2002) and *Tourism and Tourism Spaces* (Sage, 2004). He is an Innovation Fellow at the Advanced Institute of Management. g.shaw@exeter.ac.uk

Liz Such is Senior Lecturer of Leisure, Sport and Physical Activity at the University of Bolton. Her research interests centre on the relationships between individuals in family settings and the role of leisure in lifestyle. She has worked as a research analyst for the UK government and continues to work in the field of social policy. liz.such@bolton.ac.uk

1 Introduction

Scott McCabe, Lynn Minnaert and Anya Diekmann

Social tourism is an established part of the tourism sector in many European countries. Early manifestations date back to the 19th century, and in the 20th century social tourism played a large part in the democratisation of travel for the masses. Today, there is a wealth of organisations involved in the supply of social tourism to a diverse range of groups. Social tourism schemes across Europe involve billions of euros of spending and help to provide access to tourism for millions of citizens. Social tourism is diverse, innovative and collaborative, and often at the cutting edge of sustainable practice in the tourism sector. Social tourism provides opportunities for social inclusion in European society; it not only delivers important benefits for individuals but also helps to create stronger families, improves wellbeing and delivers a fairer Europe for all.

Considering its importance and rich history, its linkages across sectors of the industry and government policies, its orientation to social goals, and its implementation across Europe in many different ways, it is surprising that social tourism as a concept has been largely neglected in the tourism literature, at least in the English language, until fairly recently. Somewhat less surprisingly, but no less of an issue, social tourism is not represented at all in the English language literature on social policy. The tourism industry is often described as a hidden industry because of its intangible characteristics, but within the sector social tourism is very often totally invisible. Moreover, because great variations exist across Europe in the scale, emphasis and direction of social tourism practice (as well as the lack of translated research or policy across European languages), it is difficult to generalise about social tourism as a phenomenon. What is certain, though, is that social tourism has not received the attention which it deserves in terms of either conceptual debate or an understanding of practices, systems and contexts.

This book aims to address the peripheral position that social tourism has been afforded by the literature. It offers a multidisciplinary perspective that seeks:

- to develop our understanding of what social is and how it is structured and organised in Europe;
- to set out the role that tourism plays in society generally, problematising the conception of tourism as 'just an industry' and social tourism's role in the emerging restructuring of a 'social economy';
- to establish the links between tourism as a feature of social and welfare policies (incorporating social inclusion agendas) and the sustainability agenda;
- to highlight the ways in which tourism is affected by social policies that relate to changing family structures and disability issues.

The book also aims to connect academic discussions with practical examples of how social tourism operates in Europe today, identifying best practices across a broad range of European contexts. The purpose is to set a context for future debate and research, to outline the range of challenges and opportunities for social tourism in the future and to assess the contribution that social tourism can make to an inclusive Europe.

The timing of this book is particularly apt, as social tourism is presently being discussed with renewed interest. Over the past 15 years, there has been a seismic shift in consumer practices in the developed world. The consumer society, heralded by the great social theorists in the late 1960s, has truly come to pass. European economies have witnessed a massive transformation from production to consumption; they are now dominated by the service and public sectors, and are driven by huge leaps in technological advances. The most recent economic crisis and global recession, triggered by the collapse in global investment banking businesses in late 2007, demonstrates both the interconnectedness of global economies and also the fragility of European capitalism's dependence on the financial and other service sectors. The impacts of the crisis in the financial services sector and the high levels of public debt in many European countries may have a lasting and profound effect on consumer practices, even well established norms in areas such as holidays and leisure travel.

Tourism is one area of consumption that has come to epitomise the processes of development and economic growth of the past decades: European travel has been democratised as a consequence of a deregulated market which has aligned cheaply available accommodation, combined with mass transport infrastructure, to an exploding market demand. This has positioned Europe as the leading generating and receiving region for global tourism over the last 30 years. Europeans have become addicted to travel and holidays have become an increasingly essential aspect of social life. In terms of academic position, the new mobilities paradigm, 'enabling "the social world" to be theorised as a wide array of economic, social and political practices, infrastructures, and ideologies that all involve, entail or curtail various kinds of movement of people, or ideas or information or objects'

(Urry, 2007: 18) appears most apt in highlighting the centrality of travel as an organising construct.

The growing importance of the concept of the 'visitor economy' has heralded a hegemonic shift in thinking about travel and tourism, from a crude sectoral perspective to being considered a central force driving economic and social regeneration in many regions of Europe. For these economies, the tourism sector represents an important component of the service sector, which is threatened by the fiscal tightening caused by the economic crisis, important enough for many key players in the industry to call for stimulus actions on the part of governments because of its resilience and potential to help drive recovery (see UNWTO, 2010). The extent to which European national governments and the European Commission (EC) take up this opportunity remains to be seen. In fact, the level of government focus on, and willingness to develop policy for, the travel and tourism sector are uneven, partially depending on whether international travel is a negative or positive factor in balance of payments, and the relative contribution of tourism in each country's gross domestic product (GDP) among a range of other factors. But the growth of mass tourism (and its growing importance as an economic driver) masks great inequalities across Europe in access to its products, as well as differences in cultural practices. Despite increases in the opportunities for and take-up of leisure travel over the last 40 years, many people across Europe cannot access or participate in travel at all, whether holidays, short breaks or even day trips.

It is at this point that debates about the purposes and outcomes of tourism need to be addressed. Some people argue that tourism is just one aspect of discretionary consumer practice, not a fundamental human need, and therefore not a priority for social policy. This view is epitomised by the press coverage which accompanied the launch of the European Union's Calypso programme in 2010. In many examples available on the blogosphere, the announcement was interpreted as a move by Brussels to spend taxpayers' money on subsidies for holidays for the poor. The argument is that holidays are luxury consumer goods that are 'earned' as a reward for work. This rather one-dimensional position appears to have been driven more by an anti-interventionist approach to European politics per se rather than a critical assessment of the role and purpose of holidays in people's lives.

However, others believe travel and tourism to be a social right. The United Nations (1948) Universal Declaration of Human Rights enshrines in its article 24, 'Everyone has the right to rest and leisure, including reasonable limitation of working hours and periodic holidays with pay'. And although this article is about the right for leisure time and does not mention the right to travel or to tourism activities, article 13(2) of the Declaration insists on the right that 'Everyone has to leave any country, including his own, and to return to his country'. While this article clearly is about free mobility and goes far beyond 'tourism' issues, it still is part of a general conception of a new perceived right to mobility among large proportions of European society. The article is not expressly concerned with social equality of access to travel, however. It is indeed only in the Global Code of Ethics for Tourism of the United Nations World Tourism Organization (UNWTO, 1999: article 7) that tourism is considered to be a right, accessible to all. The semantic backdrop to this debate originates in the European Council Treaty of Nice in 2000, where the right to holidays formally for all people was linked in title IV:31 to work (see Chauvin, 2002). While these two views represent opposing perspectives, it is certainly true that over the last 10–20 years a lack of an ability to take a holiday once per year has become embedded in social indicators of relative poverty, and demonstrates the increasing social importance attached to holidays.

There has also been renewed recent interest in the potential for tourism beyond its economic value as a discretionary consumer activity served by a group of connected service industries. Higgins-Desbiolles (2006; and Chapter 4 in this volume) has argued powerfully that tourism can and should be seen as a social force capable of assisting with development goals as well as providing intrinsic benefits to users. Recent research has reflected on: the potential for tourism to contribute to development goals, particularly as a tool to alleviate poverty through what has become known as pro-poor tourism (Briedenhann & Wickens, 2004; Meyer, 2007); the welfare of people in destination communities (Hall & Brown, 1996, 2006); the links between holiday participation and subjective wellbeing (Gilbert & Abdullah, 2004; McCabe et al., 2010); and the potential for tourism to increase social and human capital (Minnaert et al., 2009), especially in the context of disadvantaged families facing difficult personal, social and environmental circumstances.

Research on the benefits of tourism for tourists, however, is limited and lacks comprehensive analysis. Much more focus has been placed on developing the research case for tourism in terms of the development and widespread application of consistent and universal metrics to measure tourism activity and to understand its impacts upon host (destination) communities than on trying to develop a more systematic understanding of the effects of participation on tourists. There is no denying that these effects are not always positive. People on holiday have, for example, been reported to drink more alcohol, take less care with diet and engage in risky sexual behaviour (Hughes et al., 2009; Josiam et al., 1998; Uriely & Belhassen, 2006), but also, at perhaps the more mundane level of family life, the stress of organising family travel coupled with the financial investment in a short, concentrated time can produce severe tensions. Nevertheless, tourism participation is also reported to have a range of positive effects on tourists, which can be seen as responses to a range of psychological, social and physical needs.

Holidays, for example, offer an escape from routine, commitments and social norms and roles. They can represent important opportunities for rest and recuperation from work. Leisure travel (which, in addition to holidays, may take the form of visiting friends and relatives, or religious pilgrimage) provides new experiences, leading to a broadening of horizons and the opportunity for learning and intercultural communication, thereby promoting of peace and understanding, as well as personal and social development and health (McConkey & Adams, 2000; UNWTO, 1980). Relatively little is known about these potential benefits, or indeed the challenges presented by leisure travel. We intuitively accept that holidays are 'good for you' and yet we have very little idea how, or to what extent. Because of this lack of research there is hardly any general understanding of how tourism could be used to improve the lives of those people who are currently disadvantaged and unable to participate in tourism, or indeed how to recognise and maximise benefits and minimise the negatives among wider society.

The quest to understand the transformative role of tourism is not new, however. Many scholars across the social sciences and within the tourism academy have noted the potential of tourism to have a lasting impact in terms of identity, personal development, career shifts and worldview. And while there has been much useful recent research focusing specifically on evaluating the impact of government and third-sector support, particularly for disadvantaged groups and people living with disability, this research is atomised, resulting in piecemeal findings that are not connected or which coalesce around an overarching conceptual area. A useful framework does exist, however, in the form of social tourism, especially in relation to its benefits to people, economies and society. But although social tourism is well established in some parts of the world, it is hardly known in others. Even across Europe there are myriad interpretations and understandings given to this term, with multiple definitions and a varying range of applications across national boundaries, despite the existence of the International Social Tourism Organisation (ISTO, formerly BITS – see Case Study 1), based in Brussels, and an increasing importance attached to social tourism through the European Union's Tourism Unit (Diekmann & McCabe, 2011). Also, there is a lack of academic focus on social tourism in the European university curricula, to the extent that no specific high-level programmes are currently available. There are few academic study materials available in English: the current book aims to address this, to put social tourism on the educational agenda in tourism studies.

The rationale for attempting to provide a comprehensive analysis of social tourism stems partially from the lack of attention given to the subject by the various stakeholders, but also from a recognition that tourism has come full circle from its origins as an activity which was acknowledged to bring important social and personal benefits for individuals in the early days of the development of mass tourism in the 19th century. After a long period in which tourism was seen solely as an aspect of conspicuous consumption, it is being considered once again for its merits for individual and social growth, partially through recognition of tourism's role in modernisation and development in the poorest countries of the world, but also through social tourism.

European societies have undergone dramatic structural changes: increasing inequalities between the poor and the better-off (see for example Organisation for Economic Co-operation and Development, 2008); restrictions on mobility placed by soaring fuel prices; the 'ghetto-isation' of disadvantaged people in high-density, urban, deprived neighbourhoods; and greater differences in health, education and work opportunities between communities. Coupled to these problems is a recognition that government interventions are perceived to have been unable to achieve a real difference in the quality of people's lives. This has left governments across Europe to reassess their policies to tackle material deprivation, health, education and wellbeing. Our impetus with this book is to make the case that social tourism does have the potential to make a real difference to people's lives, that there is a need for social tourism in Europe and that the adoption of a pan-European social tourism policy can be a realistic goal. The need for further research and policy is also highlighted, as this book aims to provide a theoretical overview of the scope for social tourism, to outline the issues and to place them in the context of a broad range of case studies that illuminate a wide range of practices across Europe.

Structure of the Book

This book combines an exploration of the theoretical underpinnings of social tourism with examples of practical implementations. The more conceptual chapters draw upon different fields in the social sciences, such as economics, mobilities studies, politics and sociology. The key issues raised in each chapter (apart from the concluding one) are highlighted in the case study that follows it.

In contrast to recent interest in research on social tourism, many governmental organisations, federations, unions, health insurance companies, ecclesiastic movements as well as private enterprises have been important key actors since the introduction of paid holidays back in the 1930s. These actors have shaped the development of social tourism in Europe and have contributed to its diverse evolution. Chapter 2 discusses the various definitions of social tourism and places it in its historical context. The chapter examines the development of social tourism since the 19th century and explores how this history informs current practices and systems. We highlight how conceptions of social tourism are still evolving today, in response to a rapidly changing socio-economic and political environment. This discussion provides a context for later chapters and we conclude by adopting a definition of social tourism for the purposes of this book.

Social tourism's diverse historical development is a consequence of the various political systems in Europe taking social tourism in different directions. Different actors in different countries developed a range of approaches to supplying social tourism to various consumer groups, which created systems that are still very much in place. While in some countries social tourism was a politically motivated and thus a government activity, as in the former Eastern European countries, in other countries, such as the UK, social tourism was (and still largely is) a third-sector activity (i.e. one undertaken by charities and community organisations). In other countries it was the trade union movement that developed social tourism. Many of these organisations drafted regular activity reports and policy papers; until recently, these were virtually the only reflections on the social tourism phenomenon. Chapter 3 describes the current supply and demand factors driving social tourism in Europe. The chapter reviews the different systems and organisational structures of social tourism. It introduces management systems, and indicates the demand for social tourism. It highlights the different stakeholders, such as trade union organisations, local, regional and national government, the European Union, public–private partnerships and third-sector organisations.

Chapter 4 discusses the political economy of tourism in the context of the current hegemonic supremacy of neoliberalism, to argue that a more balanced, interdependent systems approach be adopted to reposition tourism as a social force through social tourism. Freya Higgins-Desbiolles describes how, through neoliberal political processes and a desire to be taken more seriously as a legitimate economic activity, tourism has become marketised, adopting the practices, languages and systems of the market economy. This, she argues, has not achieved the desired result of greater political recognition; instead, industrialisation through mass tourism has become exploitative and caused political problems in some cases. Higgins-Desbiolles identifies that the drive to position tourism purely as an 'industry' limits the understanding of tourism to its corporate attributes, thus privileging industry interests while marginalising the many social and other attributes. These other interests, she goes on to argue, could play a much more powerful role in the emerging political discourse following the fallout from the recent global recession, and she argues for a repositioning of tourism, such that it can be understood and valued for its role in human development, where social tourism can make important contributions to the social fabric.

In Chapter 5, Gilles Caire offers an alternative approach to the neoliberal hegemony, in the form of the 'social economy' perspective adopted in France, and outlines how this has been successfully implemented in the development of social tourism as a mainstream aspect of the tourism economy. Caire describes the characteristics of organisations in the social economy, and provides a historical overview of the development of social tourism in France as a context for the analysis of the ways in which social tourism has become a major force in the tourism industry. He identifies how social tourism was initially developed through a rationale based on hygiene factors, enabling workers to rest and recuperate to ensure their contribution to society could be maintained. Social tourism rapidly emerged as part of the trade union movement and the mass support of leisure opportunities based on social solidarity. Caire highlights the evolution of the system for social tourism in France: how it has had to adapt to a changing political context and market. The French model, marked by its plurality and a steadfast refusal to target only the disadvantaged to ensure that social tourism encourages social integration for all sections of society, has contributed to the success of the system (social tourism remains central in the French tourism economy) but also to current challenges.

Chapter 6 assesses the contribution that the mobilities paradigm can offer in respect of its focus on exclusion. The aim of this chapter is to explore the sociological perspectives underpinning current social practices of travel. Kevin Hannam argues that mobility has become a pervasive feature of society and has shaped socio-economic and political discourses and interactions. He argues that physical mobility, an ability to travel, is linked to social mobility and human capital. Hannam identifies that tourism studies have failed to develop theoretical linkages between travel and its consequences for social structures (work, family life and leisure). He outlines the differences in this respect between leisure studies scholars, who have variously sought to understand how leisure participation can be more readily understood in relation to social inequality and human development. The potential for the mobilities paradigm to be applied to social tourism is illustrated with an example of an emerging discourse on children's mobility. Different perspectives on mobility and how that creates social exclusion and cohesion issues among those who experience barriers to travel are discussed.

By contrast, in Chapter 7 Derek Hall and Frances Brown apply the concepts of the 'welfare society' to social tourism. They turn to the concept of tourism as a human right (see above) to argue that access to tourism can be shaped significantly by government's position on welfare. Hall and Brown link different trajectories of welfare among European countries and show how these have affected the different types and systems of social tourism and consequentially differential rates of participation in it. Hall and Brown provide a useful summary of the development of tourism in the former Soviet-controlled Eastern European states. Importantly, they identify the links between welfare provision, social tourism and wellbeing.

Chapter 8 focuses on the role of family structures, relating social class and family situations to access to tourism, and thus provides a context for an examination of research on the family in tourism more generally and an agenda for social tourism for families in particular. Liz Such and Tess Kay define the significance of tourism in family life, drawing on the wider leisure studies literature as well as the meagre research on the benefits of tourism to family relationships. However, across Europe families are very diverse in terms of their size, structure and the nature of relationships between members, their histories and traditions. Underlying these differences are ideological structures of social class and culture which mediate individual experiences. Such and Kay map out the contemporary diverse structures and assess the implications for tourism research and social tourism itself. It is important to recognise that tourism provides opportunities to bring family members together to 'be' a family and to develop skills in sustaining the productive social relationships on which inclusive family life is based.

Gareth Shaw and Sheela Agarwal in Chapter 9 focus on the policy context surrounding the provision of supported access for people with disabilities and explore the reality of access within the policy contexts of the European legislative framework. They discuss the notion of 'empowerment' for people with disabilities, highlighting the lack of adequate research on the perspectives of disabled people themselves, despite the fact that recent European research has shown that people with disabilities are among the most discriminated against citizens in the European Union. They point out that physical access remains a key barrier and that there are wide variations in the levels of empowerment among people with disabilities and (more positively), that able-bodied members of society are generally aware of less-abled people and their circumstances. Shaw and Agarwal go on to describe the experiences of tourism for people with disabilities, including a critical discussion on the representation of disabilities in the media and tourism discourses. The chapter concludes by arguing that there is a need to include disabled people in the development of new social tourism offers and programmes, and that a 'co-creation perspective', which is becoming established in mainstream marketing, is particularly relevant in the context of the provision of services for people with disabilities.

We end the substantive chapters with a discussion of the links between social tourism and sustainability. Christian Baumgartner returns to the issue of the focus for social tourism raised in Chapter 2 and that Higgins-Desbiolles touches upon in her discussion of an interdependent systems approach in Chapter 4. This concerns the recent shift by the European Commission to make social tourism coterminous with sustainable tourism. Baumgartner unpacks the links between the two concepts, identifying how they developed closely together, defining sustainable tourism and showing how the two approaches can be compared. Using the example of Naturefriends (an Austrian non-governmental organisation), he shows how social tourism and sustainability can be mutually reinforcing. However, there are critical challenges to the wide-scale interpretation of social tourism as sustainable tourism and Baumgartner concludes with a discussion of the factors and policy decisions which will determine the extent to which social tourism can truly reflect the principles of sustainable tourism.

The final chapter summarises the main contributions of the book, looking back on the main themes outlined, and identifying critical issues. We seek to take forward these issues and challenges in a framework for further research and outline the opportunities going forward. We organise this framework into three thematic areas: The book concludes with an agenda for taking social tourism forward as an area of academic study, social policy, and inter-disciplinary research.

The Case Studies: Social Tourism Practices

The practitioner case studies presented in this book aim to reflect the wealth of organisations and initiatives that exist in social tourism practice today. They include international organisations working in social tourism (such as the ISTO, formerly the BITS), represent different forms of funding structures (such as the Labour Market Holiday Fund of Denmark and the charity-funded Family Holiday Association in the UK), providers of services for particular target groups – people with disabilities (Family Fund in the UK and COIN in Italy) and children from low-income families (the Sunshine Fund in Ireland, and Floreal in Belgium) and young people (EUFED) – and include public–private partnership schemes (such as that operated by Tourism Flanders). They also represent the diverse geographic regions of Europe and the political and social systems, through the inclusion of Eastern Europe, Mediterranean countries, Scandinavia and Western Europe. The case studies all follow a structured template, showing the historical development of the organisations, their key activities and examples of good practice. By incorporating theoretical reflections and practical implementations side by side, the book aims to start a dialogue between academic researchers and practitioners – a dialogue that has hitherto been largely non-existent.

The case of ISTO is important, since it is the main example of a supranational network involved in promoting social tourism and solidarity among organisations working in the delivery of social tourism. It is currently the largest social tourism membership organisation, with members in Europe, Africa and the Americas. The organisation is actively involved in the shaping of social tourism policies and plays a major role in the current development of European Union policies for improving and developing social tourism.

The Holiday Participation Centre, run by a government department, Tourism Flanders (Belgium), is a good example of how government can have a direct role in the support of an inclusionary programme for tourism in a region. This is Case Study 2. The Centre plays an intermediary role, actively engaging with private sector operators, which voluntarily allocate discounts for social tourism target groups. The Centre also communicates the reduced tariffs available to social sector organisations (public and voluntary) and potential holiday beneficiaries. The system operates with minimal expense for the government and is based on voluntary cooperation and the goodwill of the private and social sector.

The Family Holiday Association is the focus of Case Study 3, which outlines the UK model of social tourism, based on charitable provision as one form of integrating social tourism into the welfare state. The UK-based charity provides holiday grants for beneficiaries on low incomes who are faced with different types of disadvantage. The Family Holiday Association is the only national social tourism charity in the UK, and plays a major role in the development of policy, linking the tourism industry to an emerging government agenda on tourism. The charity also sponsors research, as well as developing its own programme of activities tailored to a range of issues affecting low-income families.

The Labour Market Holiday Fund, based in Denmark, presented in Case Study 4, represents an innovative funding mechanism for social tourism. The history of the development of the Fund, established through the interest accrued on holiday stamps (vouchers), bought by employers to ensure that workers had access to holidays in the period following the Second World War, provides a novel example of the democratisation of social tourism through redistribution policies, not largely funded by government. The Danish social welfare system offers strong support to disadvantaged groups in society, and the Labour Market Holiday Fund does not discriminate in favour of social tourism initiatives, organisations or programmes. The Fund is used to help drive up quality across the entire tourism system as well as targeting specific actions towards social tourism projects.

Floreal is a Belgian organisation that provides holiday accommodation in coastal and rural areas via campsites and holiday centres, and is the focus of Case Study 5. Its historical roots lie in the socialist trade union movement. Floreal operates a social pricing strategy, with discounts for selected target groups, with the aim to make the benefits of holidays and recreation accessible to people in all layers of society. The case study highlights the commercial pressures many social tourism organisations face and is therefore particularly apt to follow the discussion in Chapter 5.

Case Study 6 presents the example of Sunshine Holidays in Ireland. The foundations of this initiative within a religious framework are noteworthy, as religious organisations played an important role in the early development of social tourism in many countries in Europe (as identified by Caire in Chapter 5) and continue to do so. Sunshine Holidays has a long history of providing holidays for disadvantaged children in the Dublin area.

Case Study 7 reiterates the sense of a historical perspective still driving social tourism activities in the present day. The Polish Tourist Country-Lovers' Society has its roots in a mission to provide opportunities for 'positive' recreation alongside a sense of citizenship and national identity. It provides another example of how a national organisation can be actively involved in providing activities and accommodation for the general population, together with opportunities for social inclusion through subsidy or specific activities at the local level.

Case Study 8 provides details of another charity in the UK, whose focus is on the provision of grants for families living with a severely disabled child.

The Family Fund is a national charity funded by a direct grant from the UK government, and so is a good example of an 'arms' length' organisation whose purpose is to respond directly to the needs and requests of its target group. The Family Fund has witnessed a large shift in requests towards holiday grants, and it now provides some 37,000 holiday grants to families with severely disabled children.

COIN, or Consorzione Sociale, in Italy, provides an example of how organisations can become involved in the provision of opportunities for people living with disabilities, in Case Study 9. The largely state-funded organisation recognises that there are barriers to disabled people's access to tourism, and that a fundamental cause of these barriers is insufficient information. COIN provides training, information and consultancy services to the tourism industry, as well as providing information for disabled people.

EUFED's main focus is on coordination, strategy and policy making and advocacy for the inclusion of young people in travel. It provides assistance through discounts for socially disadvantaged young people. It is the subject of the last case study. EUFED has a specific emphasis on sustainability and responsible tourism; it promotes social integration and a greater sense of citizenship, and policy coordination in terms of sustainable tourism in Europe and across the youth hostel network.

Conclusions

Social tourism is an emerging area of policy and practice in Europe. In this volume we hope to show how it is relevant to the current socio-economic and political issues and challenges facing Europe, both in terms of its position at the nexus of public, private and third-sector integration in the delivery of sustainable, fair and equitable tourism for all European citizens, and in terms of its relevance as an academic field of study. We hope to open up a dialogue between researchers in sociology and social policy, political economy, geography and the mobilities paradigm, leisure studies and those scholars whose primary interest is in pushing forward tourism as a legitimate subject of social science. We have sought to bring together a range of scholars and practitioners in this one volume but recognise that this is only a fraction of the range of activity being undertaken across Europe, as well as understanding that an equally wide range of practices are taking place outside Europe. In aiming to capture a great diversity there is the realisation that we may have overlooked or provided only a simple gloss on some key issues, but hope that the following work will provide a stimulus for further work in this critical field of research and theorising.

References

Briedenhann, J. and Wickens, E. (2004) Tourism routes as a tool for the economic development of rural areas – vibrant hope or impossible dream? *Tourism Management*, 25(1): 71–79.

Chauvin, J. (2002) *Le tourisme social et associatif en France*. Paris: L'Harmattan.

Diekmann, A. and McCabe, S. (2011) Systems of social tourism in the European Union: a comparative study. *Current Issues in Tourism*, 14(5): 417–430.

Gilbert, D. and Abdullah, J. (2004) Holidaytaking and the sense of wellbeing. *Annals of Tourism Research*, 31(1): 103–121.

Hall, D. and Brown, F. (1996) Towards a welfare focus for tourism research. *Progress in Tourism and Hospitality Research*, 2: 41–57.

Hall, D. and Brown, F. (2006) *Tourism and Welfare: Ethics, Responsibility and Sustainable Well-being*. Wallingford: CABI.

Higgins-Desboilles, F. (2006). More than an 'industry': the forgotten power of tourism as a social force. *Tourism Management*, 27: 1192–1208.

Hughes, K., Downing, J., Bellis, M.A., Dillon, P. and Copeland, J. (2009) The sexual behaviour of British backpackers in Australia. *Sexually Transmitted Infections*, 85: 477–482.

Josiam, M.B., Hobson, J. S. P., Dietrich, U.C. and Smeaton, G. (1998) An analysis of the sexual, alcohol and drug related behavioral patterns of students on spring break. *Tourism Management*, 19(6): 501–13.

McCabe, S., Joldesma, T. and Li, C. (2010) Understanding the benefits of social tourism: linking participation to subjective well-being and quality of life, *International Journal of Tourism Research*, 12(6): 761–773.

McConkey, R. and Adams, L. (2000) Matching short break services for children with learning disabilities to family needs and preferences. *Child Care, Health and Development*, 26(5): 429–444.

Meyer, D. (2007) Pro-poor tourism: from leakages to linkages. A conceptual framework for creating linkages between the accommodation sector and 'poor' neighbouring communities. *Current Issues in Tourism*, 10(6): 558–583

Minnaert, L., Maitland, R. and Miller, G. (2009) Tourism and social policy – the value of social tourism. *Annals of Tourism Research*, 36(2): 316–334.

Organisation for Economic Co-operation and Development (2008) *Growing Unequal: Income Distribution and Poverty in OECD Countries*. Paris: OECD.

United Nations (1948) Universal Declaration of Human Rights. Online at http://www.un.org/en/documents/udhr.

UNWTO (1980) Manilla Declaration on World Tourism. Online at http://www.unwto.org/sustainable/doc/1980%20Manila-eng.pdf.

UNWTO (1999) Global Code of Ethics for Tourism. Online at http://www.unwto.org/ethics/index.php.

UNWTO (2010) *Roadmap for Recovery*. Madrid: United Nations World Tourism Organization. Online at http://www.unwto.org/pdf/roadmap_EN.pdf.

Uriely, N. and Belhassen, Y. (2006) Drugs and risk taking in tourism. *Annals of Tourism Research*, 33(2): 339–359.

Urry, J. (2007) *Mobilities*. Cambridge: Polity Press.

Case Study 1:
International Social Tourism Organisation
(ISTO, formerly BITS)

Charles Belanger *Director*

Rue Haute 26–28
1000 Bruxelles
Belgium
Telephone: + 32 2 549 56 89/90 / Fax: + 32 2 514 1691
Email: info@bits-int.org
http://www.bits-int.org

Aims/Mission

The ISTO is an international non-profit organisation in order to promote access to leisure, holidays and tourism for the greatest number of people. It works with all stakeholders – states, social actors and operators. The ISTO's mission also includes promoting a tourism based on sustainability and solidarity, to encourage intercultural understanding between hosts and guests, and respect for both natural and cultural heritage.

History

The ISTO was created in 1963 (as the International Bureau of Social Tourism, Bureau International du Tourisme Social, or BITS). The main reference document of the ISTO is the Montreal Declaration, 'Towards a humanist and social vision of tourism', adopted by the organisation in 1996. It sets out the key objectives of social tourism: 'a shaper of society, a promoter of economic growth, a stakeholder of the regional and local development as well as a partner in global development programs'. The Declaration was reinforced in 2006 by the Aubagne Addendum, which put more emphasis on the international development and solidarity components of social tourism.

Location

The ISTO's secretariat and headquarters are in Brussels, Belgium. In order to better represent the interests of its members at a regional level, the ISTO created regional sections: ISTO Americas, with a secretariat based in Montreal; ISTO Europe; and ISTO Africa.

Current Activities/Programmes

The main component of the ISTO is the general assembly, which meets every year. The board of directors is elected every four years and the executive committee is the office in charge of implementing the decisions of the board and of the secretariat.

The regional sections (ISTO Americas, with a secretariat based in Montreal; ISTO Europe; and ISTO Africa) were created in 2004.

In 2006, the ISTO created a network of local and regional authorities in order to facilitate partnerships and exchanges of good practices between local and regional actors active in this field. The network helps with the implementation of projects that can benefit from European Union finance, by encouraging cooperation between network members, as well as cooperation with different associations and towns and regional networks, such as the Assembly of European Regions (AER) and United Cities and Local Governments.

At its 2010 world conference in Rimini, the ISTO decided to launch an Alliance for Training and Research in the field of social tourism. This Alliance constitutes a collaboration platform for universities and institutes for higher education that are members of the ISTO, in order to facilitate the following on an international scale: partnerships for research projects, professional and scientific publications, research and training conferences, and courses in distance education.

Beneficiaries

The ISTO does not work directly with the beneficiaries of social tourism initiatives, but acts instead as an umbrella organisation for organisations that do so. The ISTO's membership includes both public and private organisations (both for-profit and non-profit), such as tourism associations, holiday centres and youth hostels, travel agencies and operators, trade union organisations, cooperatives, non-governmental organisations, training institutions as well as official tourism organisations, all exercising an interest in or actively engaged in the provision of social tourism. Currently, the ISTO has around 165 member organisations spread across 35 countries. Member organisations are classified within three categories: active members, associate members and honorary members. The active members are divided into three boards: the Board of Social Tourism Actors, the Board of States and Federated States; and the Board of Local and Regional Authorities.

Funding Sources

The ISTO's main source of income are the subscriptions from its member organisations.

Role in Social Tourism Provision

The ISTO's actions mainly take the form of networking and the provision and dissemination of information to its stakeholders, in order to influence policy on social tourism on the world stage. Information is delivered via its website, its magazine and electronic newsletter, and policy development is through carrying out surveys and studies, as well as participation in joint projects and expertise missions. The ISTO organises its world conference every two years, as well as regional and thematic seminars, and workshops aimed at stimulating exchanges between members and partners.

Areas and Examples of Best Practice

The ISTO is playing an important role in representation. It is a member of the United Nations World Tourism Organization (UNWTO) and of the World Youth Student and Educational Travel Confederation (WYSE-TC), and it also has an advisory body status to UNESCO and maintains close relations with the European Commission.

The ISTO also maintains cooperation with other international bodies, such as the World Leisure Organization (WLO), the International Cooperative Alliance (ACI), the Global Partnership for Sustainable Tourism (GPST) and the Organisation for Economic Co-operation and Development (OECD).

In order to promote social tourism accommodation of its members, the ISTO launched the portal 'Holidays for All' in 2009 (http://www.holidays-for-all.com). The portal enables searches of a database of holiday centres.

The ISTO is also very active through its regional sections.

Americas

One of the most important initiatives that ISTO Americas launched in 2009 is a research project aiming at drawing a map of social tourism in the Americas. The first part of this research, carried out in partnership with the Université de Québec à Montreal (UQAM), yielded an inventory and analysis of laws regarding annual holidays, stretching over all the Americas. The second part of the research, which was launched in 2010, looks at the application of these laws. The aim of the third part will be to draw up an inventory of all the initiatives and programmes set up by authorities and social enterprises in order to make holidays more widely accessible.

Europe

The ISTO has been particularly active at European Union level during the last few years, with some key actions that have contributed to the adoption by the European Parliament in 2008 of a Preparatory Action for the development of social tourism in Europe named Calypso. The ISTO also contributed to: the opinion paper entitled 'Social tourism in Europe', which was adopted by the European Economic and Social Committee (EESC) in 2006; the organisation in 2006, 2007 and 2008 of three important conferences in partnership with the European Commission's Tourism Unit that allowed the presentation of best practices linked to different target groups in social tourism, such young people, senior citizens, low-income families and disabled persons; and the Tourism Sustainability Group set up by the Tourism Unit, which recognises that making holidays accessible for everyone is one of the eight key factors for the development of sustainable tourism in Europe.

At European level, the ISTO has also been involved with the trade union movement. In 2008, the ISTO realised, in partnership with the European Federation of Food, Agriculture and Tourism Trade Unions (EFFAT) and the Université Libre de Bruxelles (IGEAT-ULB), a 'Study on employment in the social tourism sector', which was financed by the DG Employment and Social Affairs of the European Commission. In 2009, a task force was set up with the European Trade Union Confederation (ETUC) that entailed consulting ETUC members in order to better understand the attitude and intentions of trade unions regarding social tourism. The results of this consultation served for the Declaration 'The right to holidays: reclaiming lost ground?', which was officially published by the ETUC.

Last but not least, the ISTO organises a European Forum every two years, each of which deals with specific issues. The Forum held in Malaga in 2009 was dedicated to the impact and opportunities of the economic crisis on social tourism. The Forum in Riva del Garda in 2007 had as its theme 'Social tourism: protagonist of economic and social development in Europe' and in Budapest in 2005 the theme was 'Social policy in the tourism of the EU 25'.

Africa

The finalisation and publication in 2007 of the 'Study on the concepts and realities of social and solidarity tourism in Africa', achieved under the coordination of the ISTO in collaboration with the French Foreign Ministry, the Union Nationale des Associations de Tourisme (UNAT) and with financial support from the UNWTO, is one of the most important initiatives realised by ISTO Africa. It has also been very active in the preparation and participation of the 3rd International Forum on Fair Tourism (FITS), in Bamako, in October 2008.

2 Defining Social Tourism and its Historical Context

Lynn Minnaert, Anya Diekmann and Scott McCabe

What is 'social tourism'? The answer is not straightforward. Social tourism is not a well known or well understood concept in tourism studies, or across large sections of the tourism industry, although it is more widely practised in some regions. The reasons why social tourism remains relatively obscure can in part be traced back to the origins of the concept and the way in which social tourism has developed in Europe as an area of social policy or as part of the social/third-sector economy. It is difficult to formulate a discrete and all-embracing definition for this distinct area of tourism since such a wide variety of activities can be classified as social tourism: diverse holiday types, activities at destinations, types of accommodation and client groups can be involved. Finally, there is a semantic barrier to the development of a common understanding of what social tourism comprises. A range of different labels – such as tourism for all, inclusive tourism, responsible tourism – can all include some elements of social tourism, for example.

Perhaps one single unifying element that brings all these concepts together is an aim to enable specific groups in society, who would otherwise not be able, an opportunity to have a holiday. However, in order to progress knowledge about as well as research and practice in social tourism, it is critical to be able to define and develop boundaries around this concept, and this is the aim of this chapter. However, this is not an easy task. 'Social tourism' can be interpreted in various ways, for example in terms of the main stakeholders involved in its provision. These often include commercial and non-commercial, governmental and private organisations, each often having a separate understanding of what social tourism means. Providers range from small charities organising holidays for children from low-income backgrounds to government departments responsible for improving accessibility in hotels, and to private tour operators offering holidays that can be seen as socially sustainable, such as community-based tourism, 'voluntourism' and senior tourism (these different organisational structures are discussed in

18

more detail in Chapter 3). Clearly, the size of organisation active in the field depends on the level and depth of the integration of social tourism into the mainstream structures of the tourism industry. In some European countries, as exemplified in this book, there is a high level of integration and therefore social tourism is a relatively well understood and well defined concept. In countries characterised by low levels of integration, there is less clarity and, as in the case of the UK, virtually no general understanding of the aims and practices of social tourism.

Generally, social tourism can be seen as an umbrella concept, incorporating many different types of initiative and public, private and third-sector stakeholders. The complexity of the concept has an impact on the level of specificity possible in defining social tourism. At the most basic level, one can discern two groups of social tourism initiatives, according to their target group. In both cases, the target group will be the economically weak or otherwise disadvantaged elements in society, but the term can apply to both the hosts and the visitors in the tourism context. Some initiatives will thus strive to help local (destination) communities through tourism (economically and/or ecologically), and concentrate on the hosts in the process, whereas others will highlight the needs of the visitors (such initiatives might aim, for example, to introduce non-travelling groups into tourism) (Minnaert *et al.*, 2007). In the case of the former, the emphasis is commonly placed on aspects of tourism as a means to development, and often refers to the activities of tourists in less developed communities or regions. While not wishing to deny the importance of this type of social tourism, the focus of this book is on the latter type: it focuses on social tourism in the European context, where social tourism is currently less used as a development tool, but more often in terms of exchanges in relation to social inclusion and cohesion for persons affected by low incomes and/or social exclusion. The coexistence of the two types, however, highlights the need to examine different definitions and to disentangle concepts in order to understand issues which inform subsequent chapters of this book. This is the main purpose of this chapter.

The field of social tourism is blighted by fuzzy definitions, despite the fact that it has existed as a concept for at least 60 years (Diekmann & McCabe, 2011). Due to the very diverse processes and organisational structures in which social tourism has developed and been implemented in the different countries of the European Union (including voucher systems, holiday grants and public–private partnership structures), the concept can be interpreted very differently in different countries. In the UK, for example, a survey of social workers in 2006 by the Family Holiday Association (Case Study 3) showed that 68% of 273 respondents had never heard the term 'social tourism'. A large majority were also not familiar with the mainland Europe system of holiday vouchers. In Germany, the term *Sozialtourismus* refers to the migration of populations from poorer countries, but has hardly any connotation with tourism practices (Diekmann & McCabe, 2011).

Therefore, in order to compare and understand the critical circumstances which had led to the current situation there is a need to examine the historical context in which different forms of social tourism have arisen in Europe. This is the second aim of the chapter. The different organisational structures that are in use in Europe will be discussed further in Chapter 3.

Definitions

Early definitions of social tourism tend to focus on the inclusion of low-income groups in travel and tourism. This is because of an ongoing – and largely unchanging, over many decades, in terms of proportion – lack of participation in holidaymaking among poorer European citizens. In Europe, on average around 60% of the population take a yearly holiday of at least four days (Eurostat, 2008). Although there are people who do not travel because they simply do not want to, or because their health or lack of mobility, the proportion is small (4%). The most common reason for non-participation is the inability to afford a holiday. Typically this is around 20–30% of the European population, although there are variations (in some Mediterranean countries, the level of holidaymaking is relatively low because there is no tradition of it).

In one of the earliest works on the subject, Hunziker defined social tourism as 'the relationships and phenomena in the field of tourism resulting from participation in travel by economically weak or otherwise disadvantaged elements in society' (Hunzicker, 1951: 1). In 1957, he added a comment regarding the nature of social tourism and defined the concept as 'a particular type of tourism characterised by the participation of people with a low income, providing them with special services, recognised as such' (Hunzicker, 1957: 12). Haulot (1982: 208) also adopted this view of social tourism, and identified an inherently social agenda, as follows: 'Social tourism … finds justification in that its individual and collective objectives are consistent with the view that all measures taken by modern society should ensure more justice, more dignity and improved enjoyment of life for all citizens'. Haulot thus proposes the links between participation in tourism and the role of the state in advancing the dignity and wellbeing of all its citizens, also linking social tourism to modernity – a view that still resonates and which underpins current European Union policy, as evidenced in its recent Calypso project (see Chapter 3).

From the 1970s, the development of mass tourism resulted in a democratisation of tourism, with ever-increasing numbers in society having the ability to travel. After the emergence of mass tourism, the social tourism landscape changed drastically. Many groups, such as manual labourers, who were unable to travel before, could now afford foreign travel due to lower prices. The growth in tourism did not always result in a more equitable society. While 'Many considered the tourism industry to be a virtually costless generator of employment and well-being, offering seemingly limitless opportunities for "real" economic development to countless communities away from the centres of global industry and financial power' (Deakin *et al.*, 1995: 1), it soon became clear that this view was wildly optimistic: tourism revenues did not always reach local populations, because of large-scale foreign ownership and leakages, and tourism could be detrimental to local cultures and environments. Communities could be excluded from the benefits of tourism in two different ways: either by lacking the opportunity to participate, or by not receiving an equitable share of the economic benefits of tourism.

More recent definitions of social tourism have often been extended to include these new developments. The ISTO (the International Social Tourism Organisation), for example, in its statutes defines social tourism as 'the effects and phenomena resulting from the participation in tourism, more specifically the participation of low-income groups. This participation is made possible or is facilitated by initiatives of a well-defined social nature' (ISTO, 2003). The participation of low-income groups in this case can refer to both the supply side and the demand side of tourism: the ISTO aims to encourage access to tourism for all layers of society, and to develop models of tourism that are more beneficial to the host community (Bélanger & Jolin, 2011). However, there is a new emphasis here on initiatives of a well defined social nature. This definition adopts an interventionist approach: the market fails to provide for all needs in society, and therefore some form of intervention is necessary to make tourism participation inclusive. Minnaert *et al.* (2009; see also Minnaert & Schapmans, 2009) take this a step further by focusing on the moral stance of social tourism, defining it as 'tourism with an added moral value, of which the primary aim is to benefit either the host or the visitor in the tourism exchange'. These definitions highlight the difference between social tourism and those commercial tourism initiatives that incorporate some sustainable elements: in social tourism, the *primary* aim is to benefit groups who would usually be excluded from tourism – their social nature is *well defined,* explicit and purposeful, in that it is directed to the achievement of positive outcomes for members of society, through redistributive practices or other means.

By extending the reach of the social tourism concept to host communities, social tourism starts to show similarities with the concepts of community-based and sustainable tourism: one could even argue the different concepts start to overlap. Almeida makes this link in his definition of social tourism: 'Social tourism is socio-politically promoted by the State with aims clearly defined for psychophysical recovery and socio-cultural ascension for individuals; according to the principles of sustainability, which must be extended to the places visited' (Almeida, 2011: 484). Almeida, from a Latin-American perspective, highlights the role of the state in the provision of social tourism, whereas Aguilar points more towards the role of the private sector in his definition: 'all activities generated by tourism demand that is mainly characterised by its weak economic resources, and in order to provide access to tourist facilities, there is a need for tour operators aiming at maximising collective benefits' (Aguilar, 2001: 146). Even though the two authors disagree on which stakeholders should be responsible, they both agree on the need to adopt sustainable practices in social tourism. This issue is taken up later on in this book by Baumgartner (Chapter 10).

Even though an extended definition of social tourism may have the benefit of covering a wider range of forms and structures, one could argue it now has the disadvantage of becoming too broad and general – by trying to incorporate too many aspects, the concept may become so diffuse that it is hard to identify core values. This is why subcategories of social tourism are now increasingly proposed. Minnaert *et al.* (2011; see also Minnaert & Schapmans, 2009) propose the terms 'host-related' and 'visitor-related' social tourism.

Although host-related tourism is not the focus of this book, the concept is discussed here to complete the overview of existing definitions. Social tourism can be seen as a stimulation tool for destinations, to encourage or maintain the generation of revenue and employment via tourism. The role of host-related social tourism may become more prominent in Europe, as its development has been encouraged by the European Commission for Enterprise and Industry in the Calypso project (see Chapter 3). Host-related social tourism is particularly beneficial to declining destinations, or destinations that are strongly affected by seasonality, with a large increase in unemployment outside of the main tourism season. Host-related social tourism can also refer to a more equitable and responsible approach to tourism in destinations in developing countries. Barkin gives the example of tourism in rural communities in Mexico: 'These rural communities can become well equipped to receive small groups, and ensure respect for the ecosystems they visit. Various forms of tourism catering to niche markets of foreign visitors and low-income travellers from within are proving most attractive to communities searching for ways of promoting profitable avenues to generate income and employment opportunities, while sacrificing as little [as possible] of their traditions and inherited production systems' (Barkin, 2000: 2). The term 'social tourism' is often deemed appropriate because it seems to refer to a deeper social interaction between hosts and visitors than pertains in the mainstream tourist industry, as the following definition illustrates: 'there is emerging a more convivial and interactive form of travel, a kind of social tourism, designed specifically to enhance and offer insight into the lives of people, which figures neither in the glossy brochures, nor in the media coverage of third-world countries' (Seabrook, 1995: 22).

Visitor-related social tourism refers to groups in society who, for economic or health reasons, are excluded from taking holidays. This implies that these groups are willing to take holidays: visitor-related social tourism is not aimed at people who are able to take holidays but choose not to. When it comes to visitor-related social tourism, two different 'disadvantaged' target groups are taken into account. On the one hand, there are tourism initiatives that are aimed at people with disabilities, which strive for equal opportunities for this group to enjoy a holiday in the commercial tourism sector. On the other hand, there are the initiatives for low-income groups, for people who cannot afford a holiday in the commercial tourism circuit. This is also the point of view of the European Union: 'social tourism is organised in some countries by associations, cooperatives and trade unions and is designed to make travel accessible to the highest number of people, particularly the most underprivileged sectors of the population' (European Economic and Social Committee, 2006: 3). A growing body of evidence highlights that social tourism can have various benefits on the tourists, such as an increase in self-esteem, improvements in family relations, an extension of their social networks, broadening of travel horizons and more pro-active attitudes to life (McCabe, 2009; Minnaert et al., 2009; Minnaert & Schapmans, 2009; Tourism Flanders, 2008).

Proponents of visitor-related social tourism sometimes refer to the practice as the exertion of a 'right to travel'. Haukeland, for example, defines social tourism as follows: 'the concept of "social tourism" means that everybody, regardless of economic or social situation, should have the opportunity to go on vacation. Seen in this light, holiday travel is treated like any other human right whose social loss should be compensated by the welfare state' (Haukeland, 1990: 178). The European Economic and Social Committee (2006: 68), in its 'opinion' on social tourism, also defines social tourism as a right:

Everyone has the right to rest on a daily, weekly and yearly basis, and the right to the leisure time that enables them to develop every aspect of their personality and their social integration. Clearly, everyone is entitled to exercise this right to personal development. The right to tourism is a concrete expression of this general right, and social tourism is underpinned by the desire to ensure that it is universally accessible in practice.

In the Calypso project the slogan chosen by the European Commission is 'You have the right to travel', reinforcing the above statements and the recent Madrid Declaration (see Chapter 3).

Although there is some level of consensus around the existence of different forms of social tourism, there is no semantic consensus, and different terms are currently in use. The ISTO, for example, has developed terms to distinguish between host- and visitor-related social tourism: host-related social tourism is referred to as 'solidarity tourism', whereas visitor-related social tourism is referred to as 'tourism for all'. Even though tourism for all can be seen as an effective term to refer to initiatives that aim to facilitate access to tourism for all layers of society, it has also given rise to confusion about its exact meaning: in the UK, for example, it is often used to refer to accessible tourism for persons with a disability. An early example was the Holiday Care Service in Britain, which describes its vision of social tourism, or 'tourism for all', as 'an invitation to the tourist industry to take a wholly positive attitude to what have conventionally become known as "special needs"' (see English Tourist Board, 1989: 13). To avoid confusion, this book thus proposes to use the term 'social tourism' to focus on visitor-related services.

Social Tourism in Europe: A Brief History

The origins of social tourism can be dated back to the emergence of industrialised societies at the end of the 19th century. It is difficult to identify a single factor, or set of factors, or one or more specific interests, which led to the uneven development of social tourism and the roles of different institutions in Europe. However, rapid industrialisation leading to overcrowded and unhealthy conditions in cities undoubtedly prompted a significant increase in interest in the health and social conditions of workers and their families at this time. Also, tourism was beginning to develop as a commercial sector as a consequence of increased mobility through the introduction of the rail networks. Even though most workers had to work six days a week and leisure time was often organised by the dominant class, holidays now became accessible to the highest earners in the working class. 'Although poverty was widespread in the rapidly expanding industrial cities, some working people were able for the first time to accumulate savings to pay for holidays' (Sharpley, 1999: 47).

The first isolated initiatives began to appear that allowed disadvantaged workers or their children to go on a holiday. The pioneers of social tourism in Europe were often socio-educational and religious organisations. Chapters 5 (Caire) and 10 (Baumgartner) highlight the origins of social tourism in France and Austria, for example. In the UK, 'following the impoverishment of the British aristocracy, a series of well-kept properties surrounded by big parks was put on the market at very low prices, representing only a small percentage of their former value. In this way several organisations, especially the "Co-operative Holiday Association" and the trade unions have acquired properties that were later turned into family holiday homes' (Lanquar & Raynouard, 1986: 14). Other initiatives concentrated on inner-city children, who were taken to the countryside or the seaside by charities, which was seen as beneficial to their health (CESR, 1999).

Social tourism thus emerged alongside 'traditional' or mainstream, commercial tourism. Not being a commercial product per se, however, social tourism expanded strongly in countries with a well developed social system, in particular in France, Belgium, Germany and Eastern European countries. Organised by unions and other social welfare and health structures, these initiatives aimed to provide access to holidays for all, based on a clear ideo-logical understanding of the place of holidays in the wellbeing of individuals in society (such as children) and people's rights to free time as a reward for providing their labour.

There were also the interests of private initiatives. In the second half of the 19th century holiday tourism was promoted by the middle classes as a beneficial activity in relation to sport and health (for example the Alpine Club, was established in Britain in 1857). These early initiatives were fol-lowed by the creation of youth movements and the development of specific types of accommodation, such as youth hostels (for example the Deutsches Jugendherbergwerk, in 1900). At the same time, in France and Switzerland, Christian movements ran the first holiday camps for disadvantaged children.

Social tourism was not yet a concern for the public authorities generally. A pivotal point in the development of popular tourism was the 1936 Holidays with Pay Convention, put forward by the International Labour Office in Geneva. Article 2.1 of this Convention states that 'every person to whom this convention applies shall be entitled after one year of continuous service to an annual holiday with pay of at least six working days'. The Holidays with Pay Convention is generally considered to be the starting point for social tourism in Europe (Chauvin, 2002; Lanquar & Raynouard, 1986), even though it took many countries a number of years to implement the terms of the Convention as national legislation. The UK is an example: 'Private holidays-with-pay agreements between employers and workers proliferated throughout the 1920s and 1930s, and despite the slump, holidays-with-pay became a major industrial negotiating point. It was appreciated however that for millions of working people this could only be attained through legislation. The resulting campaign did not succeed in pushing legislation through Parliament until 1938, and only after a Royal Commission' (Walvin, 1978: 143). Tourism now became desirable for a large number of people, and the holiday was on its way to becoming part of the national 'lifestyle'. During the Second World War this process slowed down, but the 'holiday with pay' legislation was implemented for most workers across Europe after the war ended. This is also when public authorities started subsidising social tourism, which was, and still is, in many countries controlled by associations, workers' councils, popular educational movements and collectives (Chauvin, 2002).

The years following the Second World War were the heyday for social tourism in Europe. The period between 1950 and 1980 is described in France as the *trente glorieuzes*, the glorious thirty. Traditional social tourism was based around the holiday centre in mainland Europe, and around the holiday camp in Britain. The holiday centres on the mainland (e.g. in France, Belgium and Italy) were a new, desirable and affordable product, and helped towards a democratisation of holidaymaking. They offered full board, with all en-tertainment and activities included (Caire provides a detailed history of the development of the French system in Chapter 5). In many cases, the sector had a socio-educational or even socio-political aspect. The organised activities on holiday were often inspired by the ideals of the popular educational movements, and sometimes had a strong militant character (Jolin, 2003). The holidaymakers stayed in rather basic accommodation at low rates and often helped with the daily chores. Most holiday centres were run by charities or unions. This might have been one of the reasons why, over the years, their management often became very bureaucratic. Still, they developed according to the changing needs of their public; many switched from full board to half board, the visitors had more freedom when choosing their activities, and help with the chores was no longer required (Chauvin, 2002: 67). It is certainly no coincidence that these changes occurred when commercial tourism became more accessible to people from poorer economic backgrounds.

During the same period, social tourism in the UK was also on the rise. The holiday camps in Britain show certain similarities with the holiday centres on mainland Europe (they offered basic accommodation, full board, with all entertainment included), but there are also great differences. Firstly, they were mostly run on a commercial basis. Camps built by education authorities, trade unions or charities did exist but were far less common. Another difference is that although the first large camps were introduced in the 1930s, the heyday of holiday camps came later, in the 1950s and the 1960s. A third difference is that whereas in Europe the camps had adaptable rates, depending on family size and income, the British camps had one fixed rate. 'During the 1930s, when the average weekly wage was about £3, some of the simpler camps were charging fifty shillings (£2.50) per head, a competitive rate though still beyond the means of the lowest paid and unemployed' (Hardy, 1990: 550).

During these *trente glorieuzes*, a number of international organisations were launched (e.g. the International Federation of Popular Travel Organisations, IFPTO, 1950; the Federation of International Youth Travel Organisations, FIYTO, 1956). Their creation was accompanied by the launch of different declarations and the organisation of conferences on social tourism. In 1963, a number of bodies that aimed to provide a permanent platform where social tourism issues could be discussed at an international level established, the Bureau International du Tourisme Social (BITS; the International Bureau of Social Tourism). According to its website (http://www.bits-int.org), its goal was to 'further the development of social tourism within an international framework, by coordinating the tourist activities of its members, and informing them on all matters relating to the evolution of social tourism around the world'. The organisation changed its name to ISTO (International Social Tourism Organisation) in 2010 (see Case Study 1).

Following the *trente glorieuzes*, social tourism went through a period of transformation and reorientation. This was mainly due to changes affecting the traditional target group for social tourism, manual workers: they were increasingly able to take holidays in the commercial circuit, because of the low prices mass tourism could offer. In many cases, it transpired that traditional social tourism establishments found it hard to match the low price offered abroad. Manual workers were now no longer by definition excluded from the commercial tourism industry, and other groups took their place: the unemployed, one-parent families, young families on low incomes etc. Since the 1980s, tourism for persons with disabilities or restricted mobility has also received more attention.

As mass tourism grew in importance, its negative effects on local ecosystems and cultures received increasing attention, and a desire for more sustainable forms of tourism became apparent. Social tourism organisations such as the ISTO acknowledged the benefits the tourism industry can bring, and expressed the aim to transfer these benefits to communities either who can gain economically from tourism, or who are at risk to be negatively affected by the commercial tourism circuit. The ISTO for example has introduced the concept of 'solidarity tourism' as a part of social tourism, 'introducing a sense of solidarity between the tourist and the host population, confirming that social tourism is opposite to invasive mass tourism that overburdens local resources' (Bélanger & Jolin, 2011: 477). This sought to make the connections more explicit between the concepts of host- and visitor-related social tourism. The extent to which this can be achieved is not clear, however, as much social tourism currently depends on the mass tourism resorts and infrastructure.

All this shows that social tourism is not a static but a dynamic concept. To avoid becoming obsolete, social tourism organisations had to face the challenges new socio-economic factors posed, and adapt to address them successfully. In recent years, interest in social tourism has steadily increased, as Mignon points out: 'We have gradually evolved, in just a few years, from a period in which social tourism was perceived as, let's be frank, obsolete, negative or reductive, to a situation in which the notions of social policy, solidarity and durable development are, in contrast, viewed very positively – an evolution which, at the same time, puts the concept of social tourism back at the heart of the most up-to-date initiatives' (Mignon, 2002: 1).

Conclusions

This chapter has aimed to provide an overview of the definitions and the history of social tourism, focusing on the European context. It is clear that both aspects go hand in hand: how social tourism is defined has developed over time – both from the point of view of the providers and from the point of view of the visitors. The groups in society for whom social tourism was originally developed – factory workers and manual labourers – now often do not require a specific product for their holiday needs. The democratisation of travel and the development of cheap mass tourism led to holidays being accessible to many workers, regardless of their job role.

New groups have since taken the place of the manual workers, and recent developments in the tourism industry have led to social tourism organisations extending and revising their definition of what social tourism should be concerned with. Social tourism has become more connected with commercial tourism, as will be discussed further in the following chapter. Many social tourism organisations today face the challenge of competing with commercial establishments and becoming more economically self-sufficient while still fulfilling their social objectives. The evolution of the concept of social tourism can be clearly noted in the case of the ISTO. Its Vienna Charter, of 1972, proposed that social tourism is a 'fundamental social fact of our times', and emphasised that no social policy should be without a social tourism element – thus placing the responsibility for social tourism firmly with the public sector. In the period that followed, a number of profound social changes took place, with the growing importance of a liberal ideology, an emphasis on free competition and a reduced role of the state. The economic downturn of the 1980s led to far-reaching reductions in public investment and budget cuts. As a result of these developments, the ISTO developed the Montreal Declaration in 1996. This document proposes a humanistic and social vision of tourism, with a greater emphasis on sustainable and responsible management strategies. The Declaration clearly moves away from a previous emphasis on the public sector, by declaring that 'it is not the legal statutes or the procedures that are used that make sure businesses classify as social tourism, but it is the actions they take towards a clearly defined and pursued goal' (Bélanger & Jolin, 2011: 477). This view allows for associations and social enterprises, even private companies, to classify themselves as social tourism providers. Ten years later, in 2006, a new text was adopted, the Addendum to the Montreal Declaration. This document places greater emphasis on the role of (host-related) solidarity tourism as a fundamental aspect of social tourism.

As the concept has developed, it has become richer and more inclusive – by being dynamic it has kept up with the changing socio-economic environment. From an academic perspective, there has been a growing interest in the concept, and the recent Calypso project financed by the European Union has emphasised social's tourism current validity even further. The next challenge for academics and the industry alike is to make sure the concept does not become vague instead of inclusive. Most recent definitions highlight the contribution that social tourism can make to the long-term sustainability of the European tourism industry, a topic that is discussed in more detail in Chapter 3. There are clear overlaps between sustainable tourism and social tourism; nevertheless, the two terms need to be distinguished, as outlined above, in terms of host- or visitor-oriented social tourism. Social tourism can benefit the economies of destination regions, through income and employment creation. However, the main rationale for social tourism is that there must be a *primary* aim to benefit disadvantaged social groups – persons who cannot travel because of financial and/or health reasons or other constraints. Therefore, for the purposes of this book, we define social tourism as:

> All activities, relationships and phenomena in the field of tourism resulting from the inclusion of otherwise disadvantaged and excluded groups in participation in tourism. The inclusion of these groups in tourism is made possible through financial or other interventions of a well defined and social nature.

Because the advancement of the wellbeing of these groups is a *primary* aim, the initiatives, schemes and practices need to have a *well defined and social nature*. This distinguishes social tourism initiatives from commercial tour operators who make donations to charity or operate other sustainability practices – these projects are of course to be applauded, and can be included as part of a corporate social responsibility policy, but are in themselves not social tourism. This does not mean the commercial tour operator could not act simultaneously as a social tourism provider for some projects – only in this case the social aims of the project need to be of primary importance, fundamental and central. Nor does it mean a social tourism operator cannot have economic concerns or pressures to stay competitive – still, the social aims should be the primary concern for a 'social tourism' denomination to stay valid. Not only would this have the benefit of defining the nature and the value of the sector more clearly, it would allow a greater exchange between countries of good practices – something that is now often difficult because of conflicting terminologies. Only if social tourism can be clearly and fundamentally 'social' will it be capable of justifying its distinction as a separate form of tourism and academic field of study. The following chapter goes on to explore some of these current practices and tensions in more detail.

References

Aguilar, M. (2001) Historical evolution of the Spanish social tourism policy. *Estudios Turísticos*, 147: 141–156.

Almeida, M. (2011) Case study: the development of social tourism in Brazil. *Current Issues in Tourism*, 14(5): 483–489.

Barkin, D. (2000) Social tourism in rural communities: an instrument for promoting sustainable resource management. Paper prepared for the 2000 meeting of the Latin American Studies Association, Hyatt Regency, Miami, 16–18 March.

Bélanger, C. and Jolin, L. (2011) The International Social Tourism Organisation – working towards a right to tourism and holidays for all. *Current Issues in Tourism*, 14(5): 475–482.

CESR (1999) *Le tourisme social et associatif dans la région de Nord-Pas-de-Calais.* Nord-Pas-de-Calais: Conseil Economique et Social Regional.

Chauvin, J. (2002) *Le tourisme social et associatif en France.* Paris: Harmattan.

Deakin, N., Davis, A. and Thomas, N. (1995) *Public Welfare Services and Social Exclusion: The Development of Consumer-Oriented Initiatives in the European Union.* Dublin: European Foundation for the Improvement of Living and Working Conditions.

Diekmann, A. and McCabe, S. (2011) Systems of social tourism in the European Union, a comparative study. *Current Issues in Tourism*, 14(5): 417–430.

English Tourist Board (1989) *Tourism for All: A Report of the Working Party Chaired by Mary Baker*. London: English Tourist Board.

European Economic and Social Committee (2006) Opinion of the Economic and Social Committee on Social Tourism in Europe. *Official Journal of the European Union*, C 318:12 (2006).

Eurostat (2008) *Tourism Statistics Pocketbook*. Luxembourg: Office for Official Publications of the European Communities.

Hardy, D. (1990) Sociocultural dimensions of tourism history. *Annals of Tourism Research*, 17: 541–555.

Haukeland, J. (1990) Non-travellers. The flip side of motivation. *Annals of Tourism Research*, 17: 172–184.

Hunzicker, W. (1951) *Social Tourism: Its Nature and Problems*. Geneva: International Tourists Alliance Scientific Commission.

Hunzicker, W. (1957) Cio che rimarrebe ancora da dire sul turismo sociale. *Revue de Tourisme*, 2: 52–57.

ISTO (2003) *Statutes*. Brussels: ISTO.

Jolin, L. (2003) Le tourisme social, un concept riche de ses evolutions. *Le tourisme social dans le monde*, edition spéciale 40ème anniversaire: 141.

Lanquar, R. and Raynouard, Y. (1986), *Le Tourisme Social*. Paris: Presses Universitaires de France.

McCabe, S. (2009) Who needs a holiday? Evaluating social tourism. *Annals of Tourism Research*, 36(4): 667–688.

Mignon J. (2002) *Introductory Conference to the Mexico BITS*, 13 May. Tourism for All World Congress, Mexico.

Minnaert, L., Maitland, R. and Miller, G. (2007) Social tourism and its ethical foundations. *Tourism Culture and Communication*, 7, 7–17.

Minnaert, L., Maitland, R. and Miller, G. (2009) Tourism and social policy – the value of social tourism. *Annals of Tourism Research*, 36(2): 316–334.

Minnaert, L., Maitland, R. and Miller, G. (2011) What is social tourism? *Current Issues in Tourism*, 5 (special issue on social tourism), 403–415.

Minnaert, L. and Schapmans, M. (2009) Tourism as a form of social intervention: the Holiday Participation Centre in Flanders. *Journal of Social Intervention: Theory and Practice*, 18(3): 42–61.

Seabrook, J. (1995) Far horizons. *New Statesman and Society*, 8(365): 22–23.

Sharpley, R. (1999) *Tourism, Tourists and Society*. Huntingdon: Elm Publications.

Tourism Flanders (2008) *Holidays Are for Everyone. Research into the Effects and the Importance of Holidays for People living in Poverty*. Brussels: Tourism Flanders.

Walvin, J. (1978) *Leisure and Society (1830–1950)*. London: Longman.

Case Study 2:
Holiday Participation Centre (Steunpunt Vakantieparticipatie), Flanders, Belgium

Marianne Schapmans *Coordinator*

Steunpunt Vakantieparticipatie / Holiday Participation Centre
Tourism Flanders
Grasmarkt 61
1000 Brussels
Belgium
Telephone: 0032 2 5040405
Email: vakantieparticipatie@toerismevlaanderen.be
http://www.vakantieparticipatie.be
http://www.holidayparticipation.be

toerisme
vlaanderen

Aims/Mission

The Holiday Participation Centre is a service established by Tourism Flanders, a department of the Flemish government. The Centre makes holidays accessible to all, including people on a low income. The underlying rationale for this work is that we believe that everyone is entitled to a breathing space from everyday life and access to experiences that can create a positive outlook for them. It targets persons and families in poverty who, for a variety of reasons, are unable to take a holiday. This target group is reached via social membership organisations.

There are seven main goals of the Holiday Participation Centre:

* to contribute to social tourism policy;
* *vakantiebemiddeling op maat,* which means to provide holiday mediation between target groups and the tourism industry;
* to search for tourism partners with a social vision;
* to engage in targeted promotion to persons on a low income;
* to organise training for social and tourism partners;

- to organise evaluation, consultation and exchange, to optimise effectiveness;
- to investigate the international context and make contact with similar organisations.

The Holiday Participation Centre is located at the intersection between supply and demand for social tourism in Flanders. On the supply side, there is the tourism sector, which offers special rates for persons who would otherwise not be able to make use of these facilities. The demand side is embodied by the many social organisations in Flanders. Some of these belong to the public sector (social services departments, welfare offices), whereas others belong to the voluntary sector (charities, not-for-profit organisations). They ensure that these rates are available to those who need them. Only close cooperation on the part of all concerned can make growth in access and provision possible, and ensure a fair distribution of the reduced tariffs.

The Holiday Participation Centre also participates by developing the research and evidence on the impacts of social tourism activities. It has already published different studies which deal with the positive role that holidays play for people on a low income. The Centre also produces more practical information for the organisations and holidaymakers we work with. Each year, the Centre publishes two holiday guides. One lists the prices of a variety of day trips; the other deals with individual holidays, group holidays and organised holidays. In 2010, we also published a 'fan of questions and answers' that gives answers to frequently asked questions.

The table below shows how the organisation has grown over the last 10 years.

Growth in social tourism activity of the Holiday Participation Centre

	Day trips	Group stays	Organised holidays	Individual holidays	Total
2001	0	0	752	0	752
2002	170	107	1,570	412	2,259
2003	6,500	718	2,216	526	9,960
2004	12,629	503	2,433	774	16,339
2005	14,865	1,238	3,183	1,567	20,853
2006	13,906	1,341	3,478	1,887	20,612
2007	44,523	1,693	2,854	1,910	50,980
2008	65,014	1,426	3,994	2,478	72,912
2009	77,715	2,661	4,207	2,702	87,285
2010	84,906	5,680	4,339	3,055	97,980

History

The Holiday Participation Centre, a service provided by Tourism Flanders and the Brussels city authority, was founded in May 2001, and quickly grew. In the space of just a few years, many organisations have joined forces with the Centre. The number of members, the numbers of holidaymakers and the offerings themselves have increased each year. Past evaluations also confirm our concern for quality – holidaymakers, tourism suppliers and social organisations are positive about their collaboration with the Centre. As a growing organisation, it is very important to keep our finger on the pulse of all the partners that contribute to making these social holidays possible.

Location

All tourism providers and all beneficiaries of this service are based in Flanders, the northern, Dutch-speaking region of Belgium. The head office of the Holiday Participation Centre is in Brussels.

Current Activities/Programmes

The Holiday Participation Centre's main activity is making bookings/reservations of holidays for people on a low income. It supports four pillars:

- *Day trips*. Day trips represent a low barrier. It is often easier to save for a day trip than for a holiday of several days. For some people, one day is a good start to overcoming the holiday barrier.
- *Group holidays and group stays*. Those who have never been on a holiday can take a first step in a group. Not being alone and having a safe group to fall back on often makes it easier to relax. More than 200 establishments offer group accommodation for people on a low income. The social organisations themselves organise the group holidays.
- *Organised holidays*. It is also possible to register for a fully organised holiday. More than 100 different holidays are offered by 40 organisations at a social rate, through intermediary organisations (social tourism associations), youth work, sports and other leisure organisations. The reactions to these holidays have been unanimously positive.
- *Individual holidays*. The individual holiday offerings are very diverse. Requests for holiday accommodation are handled by the staff of the Holiday Participation Centre. It is an intensive and personal approach that is highly appreciated.

Beneficiaries

'Tourism for all' as a general policy area concerns different target groups. The Holiday Participation Centre focuses on the financial barriers that people face and, in its aim to make holiday participation accessible for all, it targets its activities towards people on low incomes.

Often, persons living in poverty do not have access to the commercial holiday market. This target group is directly supported by the organisations that arrange holidays for and with this target group. Poverty is more than having no money. It concerns work, income, health, housing, culture and social exclusion.

Funding Sources

As the Holiday Participation Centre is part of Tourism Flanders, which in its turn belongs to the Flemish government, it is wholly dependent on the annual budget of the Flemish government.

Role in Social Tourism Provision

The target groups of the Holiday Participation Centre are those people living in poverty. In order to prevent the abuse of social rates, it decided to work with membership organisations in the social sector. Thus it protects the suppliers and makes sure the special rates are provided to those for whom they were intended. Organisations that are a member of the Holiday Participation Centre can sign in on the website. They receive a username and password from the Centre. Once they are signed in, they have access to the complete offer. This means they have access to the social rates. When you are not signed in, you can see our offer without the rates.

The discount on holiday centres that the Holiday Participation Centre provides is given to the holidaymakers themselves.

Each year, Tourism Flanders brings all partners together at the Holiday Participation Forum. Tourism providers, social organisations and holidaymakers exchange thoughts and get to know each other's world.

Areas and Examples of Best Practice

Each year, the Holiday Participation Centre makes it possible for people on a low income to enjoy a holiday or day trip. The number of holiday applications rises each year, proportional to the number of reservations we make.

The Centre is also proud of the research it has carried out and the publications it has produced (see, for example, http://www.holidayparticipation.be/downloads/tourism_research_notebook.pdf).

In 2011, the Centre founded a 'learning network'. This is a network meant for organisations that arrange social group holidays. They come together to share experiences and to learn from each other in order to improve their working and the holidays they organise.

The annual Holiday Participation Forum is a huge success. In 2011, 500 participants across the spectrum of stakeholders came together to discuss and contribute to the work of the Holiday Participation Centre.

3 Social Tourism Today: Stakeholders, and Supply and Demand Factors

Anya Diekmann, Scott McCabe and Lynn Minnaert

As highlighted in the previous chapter, the definitions and consequently the expression of social tourism have developed and changed since its inception in the 19th century. In post-modern times there has been a significant evolution of the needs, the expectations and the possibilities (or opportunities) for holidaymaking and travel in general for the majority of people in Europe. Socio-political, economic and technological developments have forged a new context for tourism and created new travel opportunities (see Chapter 6). While the numbers of tourism trips have grown steadily over time, tourism participation levels in Europe have largely stabilised: there are still a number of groups in contemporary society who are excluded from tourism. Social tourism has adapted to societal changes and has changed its focus from factory workers and manual labourers towards the current main four target groups:

- senior citizens;
- young people;
- families;
- people with disabilities.

Social tourism also had to adapt and respond to the needs of these groups, in many cases without neglecting the wishes of the original beneficiaries, but aiming to cater to a much broader clientele.

While the target groups of social tourism programmes are more or less consistent in all European countries (either focusing broadly on under-represented groups or specialising on disadvantaged people in a particular category, notably one of the above four), the supply side is extremely diverse in terms of both structure and organisation. Closely linked to the original and political (ideological) conception of social tourism, each country has developed a specific system, depending mainly on the historical funding programme and an emphasis on particular aspects of supply (holiday centres, accommodation, attractions or transport/tour operations and services). In consequence, the main stakeholders in social tourism across Europe vary widely. However, some common features and similar orientations can be observed. Similarities exist between stakeholders and, to some extent, the management systems. Another is the reorientation towards or closer collaboration between the social tourism and the commercial tourism sectors, driven by the need to stay competitive and sustainable in the tourism economy (see also Chapter 4). This chapter introduces current management systems within social tourism and the variety of organisational structures that are apparent in different European countries today.

The chapter highlights the similarities and differences by proposing an explanatory framework for the common organisational features linking demand and supply factors. It goes on to review demand in social tourism before examining the different systems. It then highlights the role of intermediary organisations (third-sector organisations often figure as intermediaries between beneficiary groups and social tourism providers). It also examines the increasing links between social and commercial tourism sectors and shows how the two sectors are intertwined, to the benefit of them both.

An Explanatory Framework for the Common Organisational Structure of Social Tourism in Europe

Despite the diversity of definitions and historical approaches to social tourism, a range of elements are similar across the variety of approaches. Many of these similar elements can be found in the types of beneficiaries and in the supply chains for the delivery of holidays, despite the diversity of organisational structures described in the previous chapter.

In Figure 3.1, supply and demand elements that are similar in social tourism structures across Europe are outlined. Although funding mechanisms and intermediary organisations are central to all European countries' social tourism systems, they can vary greatly from country to country, in contrast to the demand and supply features, which remain the same across different systems.

The common aspects of the *demand side* are that social tourism goals are generally directed towards groups in society that are excluded from travel and tourism. As indicated above, the four principal target groups across the European context are young people, persons with disabilities, senior citizens and families. These groups have also been recognised as key target groups by the EU in the Calypso project (see below), as they are perceived to be under-represented in tourism participation. However, the selection of these target groups can be assessed in two ways. Firstly, their definition is insufficiently

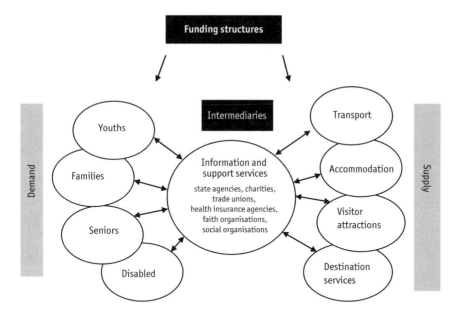

Figure 3.1 The common organisational structure for European social tourism

precise: not all young people, senior citizens, families and persons with disabilities are excluded from tourism and should therefore be beneficiaries of
social tourism. Secondly, these target groups do not cover all social groups
that are excluded from tourism. For example, one socio-demographic group
that can immediately be identified as excluded from these categories are
single people between 30 and 65, as they do not fit in the 'family' or in the
'seniors' category.

   There are ideological differences between countries regarding the treatment of these groups: in some countries they are specifically targeted for
funding, whereas in others they are included in more universal initiatives.
The Family Holiday Association in the UK, for example, directs funding
specifically at families on low incomes (see Case Study 3), and checks are
carried out to ensure the family does indeed lack the financial means to
pay for a holiday themselves. Other schemes, such as the French 'Cheques
Vacances' system (holiday vouchers), aim to increase holiday participation
across the whole population, so there are no specific demographic or income
criteria. Furthermore, the main aim of social tourism programmes in some
countries is to foster social change by promoting social accessibility. Social
accessibility can be defined as overcoming barriers for people who lack the
travel experience and/or skills, knowledge and confidence to organise travel.

The common aspects in terms of the *supply side* include transport, accommodation and destination services. In some countries, these can be part of the mainstream commercial tourism supply systems. In the UK, for example, the Family Holiday Association provides holiday grants for beneficiaries that can be spent with accommodation and transport operators in the commercial sector. As noted in Case Study 2, the Holiday Participation Centre in Flanders has built partnerships with private sector operators who offer voluntary discounts to target groups for social tourism. However, in others there are specific facilities for social tourism, for instance in Germany the holiday centres for families. Chapter 6 discusses the position of the social tourism sector in France, which is often in direct competition with the commercial tourism sector. Sometimes, transport and accommodation can be provided specifically for a social tourism market. Special provisions are rare, though, in terms of visitor attractions and destination services; it is unlikely that discrete facilities will be provided for specifically social tourism clients. One exception, however, is the Labour Market Holiday Fund in Denmark (see Case Study 4).

A third aspect is the presence of *funding structures* to support social tourism. According to the interpretation of social tourism in each country, funding structures can address specific groups. Funding mechanisms are complex and multilayered, consisting of:

- direct state funding at diverse political levels (local, regional, national and supranational) and, at national level, depending on different ministerial portfolios as well as, for example, the degree of integration of tourism within state welfare policies (see Chapter 7);
- indirect state funding, through health insurances or charities;
- trade unions or social tourism organisations;
- self-financed charities and faith organisations.

These funding mechanisms are directed towards the support of one or more target groups and often to achieve specific outcomes for those groups, such as short breaks for carers. In most countries there is a fairly segmented approach of target groups and a lack of holistic approaches. In practice, this means that many social tourism providers and intermediary organisations (see below) focus on one specific target group. For instance, trade unions and health insurance organisations focus on their affiliated members, while other associations and organisations specialise in providing for people with disabilities, children or families and so on.

Moreover, there are two major distinctions: funding may be directed towards supporting the individual (the demand side) or towards the provision of facilities and or other aspects of the supply side (such as accommodation). In France, for example, they distinguish between *aide à la pierre* (*pierre* is 'stone', so this is the support directed towards buildings and infrastructure) and *aide à la personne* (funding directed to the demand side, to address disadvantaged people).

A fourth recurring element defining the provision of social tourism is the presence of *intermediary organisations*. These are discussed under their own separate heading below.

Unpacking the Demand for Social Tourism

When considering supply and demand factors in social tourism there are a number of fundamental and conceptual issues to consider, chief of which is the lack of information on the demand for social tourism. Although there are some generally accepted figures on participation rates in tourism for Europe (Eurostat, 2008) of about 58–60%, we have little comparable evidence on the reasons for non-participation or participation rates across different sections of society. Even fewer data are available on the actual facilitators and barriers to holiday participation among the different target groups. It is known that 42% of all Europeans did not go on a holiday in 2008. Of these non-travellers, 41% did not participate for financial reasons and only 4% stated that they are not motivated to travel (Eurostat, 2008). For the remaining non-travellers, social demographic and health factors presented most of the barriers to participation. These barriers exist in all four target groups and are largely dependent on the characteristics of persons in the different categories.

Income seems to be the key factor in holiday participation. In the UK, according to the report *Households Below Average Income*, 55% of children living in the lowest income quintile do not have access to a week's holiday each year, compared with 3% in the top quintile (Department of Work and Pensions, 2007: 14). This may affect the 'families' category, but categories of target groups are also often combined. We know for example that families with a disabled member are more likely to be poorer than average, since it is three times more expensive to bring up a child who is disabled and 27% of disabled children are living in poverty in the UK (Dobson *et al.*, 2001).

If social tourism aims to open up access for the disadvantaged, there are many groups in society who can be defined as socially excluded: not only those suffering from material deprivation, but also those suffering from the social and relational aspects of poverty (Hills *et al.*, 2002). Different countries have different approaches to defining and measuring poverty and so comparative data are difficult to find (Bradshaw & Mayhew, 2010). Excluded groups include: families on low incomes; families with a member who has a disability or long-term illness; single-parent families; older people; children living in low-income households; socially isolated people; people with reduced mobility; and single people (CASE, 2002).

Another important factor for non-participation appears to be a lack of access to information. McGuire *et al.* (1986) considered this an external decisive factor for non-participation. For instance, many people with disabilities prefer to stay in their home country for they feel not well enough informed about facilities in other countries (EU, 2010). The lack of information about destinations or not being familiar with holiday booking procedures can be an important barrier. Fear of a foreign language and culture keeps people from travelling. However, statistics and research on non-participation are rare and social tourism providers mostly choose to focus on the four target groups without paying particular attention to the non-travellers.

So while there is merit in trying to identify the major beneficiaries or target groups for social tourism, there is a lack of good statistics to demonstrate that these four groups comprise the main sections of society that are excluded from participation in tourism. The four groups are also likely to consist of sub-groups with very different characteristics, such as income and health status, to name but two criteria. There is a need to identify the social characteristics of non-participating groups and to develop more inclusive categories of target social tourism consumer groups.

Along with the four declared target groups, social tourism in many countries attracts a broader public, often due to the historical development of its structures. In Chapter 2 it was highlighted for example how trade unions were originally often important providers of social tourism, as they owned accommodation facilities that were used by their members at preferential rates. In a number of countries these facilities are still owned by the unions, and union members still receive discounts, even though they are not always unable to participate in commercial tourism for financial reasons. In most cases, the accommodation facilities are now also open to non-members, so that they have become very similar to accommodation facilities in the private sector. In 2003, a study in Wallonia (Belgium) showed that, independent of economic considerations, users learned about the social tourism supply through brochures, the internet or other media or through other people or their employer (Observatoire du Tourisme Wallon, 2003). The same study provided evidence that social tourism clients are a mixture of employees, teachers, seniors as well as senior-management and middle-management employees – not traditionally seen as groups who are excluded from tourism for financial reasons. The prevailing reasons for choosing social tourism were that they did not want to spend too much money for holidays and not travel too far (average 300 km). This variety of users and beneficiaries of social tourism is linked to the national social tourism system and depends largely on the type of stakeholders and intermediaries involved.

Social Tourism Systems

As highlighted above, systems of national or regional social tourism are manifold, depending on funding structures and conditions within the country. However, even with the multitude of funding mechanisms, three

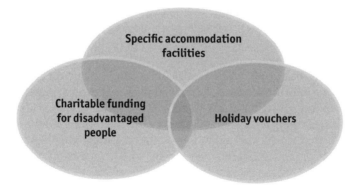

Figure 3.2 Social tourism provision structures

main delivery systems can be distinguished (Figure 3.2), although many countries combine more than one system.

The category entitled 'specific accommodation facilities' refers to organisations or trade unions that own holiday villages, hotels or camping grounds which are available for use by members. An example is the German Bundesarbeitsgemeinschaft Familienerholung (BAGFE), comprising three different organisations (Catholic, Protestant and secular), which provides about 130 family centres throughout Germany. The organisations distinguish themselves from commercial suppliers because their main aim is not profit, but family-oriented welfare, which is a core element of all policies and activities. Yet, in many countries, for instance Belgium or France, these social tourism accommodation facilities are open to a broader public, promoting 'tourism for all', as also seen in the aforementioned Belgian research (Observatoire du Tourisme Wallon, 2003). The underlying aim is indeed to attract more people and stay competitive on aspects such as sustainability and local tourism. The consequence of this policy is that the distinction between social and commercial tourism is becoming blurred and in some cases almost non-existent.

Sometimes specific accommodation facilities are combined with the use of holiday vouchers. For example, in France some workers receive holiday vouchers from their employer giving access to holiday centres owned by the trade unions or other public services. However, in most countries holiday vouchers allow the consumer to use commercial tourism infrastructures and are available to employees as a sort of tax-free bonus. In Romania, holiday vouchers were introduced only in 2009, while in other countries, like Austria, the system has been abandoned. Austrian trade unions now can negotiate advantageous prices for their members (around 30% of the official price) in commercial accommodation, which can be very upmarket (Diekmann *et al.*, 2009). Another example of specific accommodation facilities are the youth hostels, which concentrate (though not exclusively) on young people as their specific target group. Although youth hostels are aimed at young people, being below a certain age is not a requirement for the use of the accommodation. Youth hostels can be booked over the internet by anybody and, depending on the location, the prices per stay can vary widely.

This raises the question of the aims of such operations: do the social aims take priority, or are these organisations increasingly run like commercial enterprises? To benefit from an employee scheme, for example, such as the French Cheques Vacances system, the beneficiary needs to be in work – but in fact many of the persons excluded from holidays for financial reasons may be unemployed. This leads to the question of how 'social' some forms of social tourism really are, as many systems exclude to some extent the unemployed and disabled (Diekmann & McCabe, 2011). The two schemes mentioned above, specific accommodation facilities and holiday vouchers, can have exclusionary aspects, as they are often dependent on the beneficiary being in work.

The third system refers to charities providing holidays for disadvantaged people. This delivery system, often in use in Anglo-Saxon countries such as the UK, relies on charities, which may be directly or indirectly subsidised by the government and which may use commercial tourism supply for holiday provision. The Family Holiday Association in the UK and Sunshine Holidays in Ireland (see Case Study 6) are examples of social tourism charities. Most charitable organisations provide holidays for one particular target group and either select the beneficiaries themselves or work with social organisations in the public and voluntary sector for the selection of and communication with the beneficiaries.

All three categories overlap in the sense that they are state-backed systems; however, the level of state intervention varies greatly from one country to another. In reality, there are often two systems used, either in combination or individually, depending on the provider. In some countries the use of holiday vouchers leaves the consumer with a possibility of choosing between social and commercial tourism accommodation (e.g. France, Hungary, Romania). Although in most countries social tourism is state-backed, there are still charities in many countries acting at a more local level and taking specific target groups for a break. Another shared feature of all three categories is that they are benefiting or using commercial tourism supply; at the same time, there is a tendency for the social tourism providers to distinguish themselves from commercial tourism through aspects such as sustainability. Before discussing the connections between social and commercial tourism in more depth, it is important to examine the role of one of the main stakeholders within the organisational structure of social tourism in Europe, the intermediaries (Figure 3.1).

Intermediary Organisations

The provision of social tourism is generally facilitated by intermediary organisations. These range from charities to state agencies and welfare or faith organisations. In essence they play the same role as tour operators in the tourism system, in that they help to match components of the supply side to demand. However, unlike tour operators, the role of the intermediary organisations is also to stimulate demand where it is latent or weak, to reduce barriers and increase participation. They can create the conditions for easier access, for example through the provision of information (e.g. about funding, or to inform specific groups about specialist accommodation or service providers). Very often there is a link between the originating or funding organisations and the intermediaries.

For instance, in the case of the German Bundesarbeitsgemeinschaft Familienerholung, the main policy focus is to provide opportunities for social exchange and in particular to help families with psychological and/or educational issues and to enhance leisure and help manage daily life issues (BAGFE, 2009). In Belgium, the unions play an important role in the social tourism sector for they are the owners of many social tourism facilities. The purpose of their involvement in the provision of accommodation is comparable to the German case: to provide an opportunity for social exchange between people from different socio-economic backgrounds. There are also very different points of view on the services provided by social tourism. In Romania, for instance, social tourism focuses on three basic services: accommodation, meals and medical care in spas. In Belgium, where state programmes allow employment opportunities for non-profit services, social tourism, in particular for youth tourism, provides additional services and activities (guided tours, parties etc.). In the UK, funding for activity/adventure holidays for young people by central government via the Youth Hostels Association is comparable (although these programmes were cut from 2010). The common issues in terms of the supply of facilities seems to be the constant quest for quality improvement in social tourism facilities in order to meet the needs of more demanding clients and to sustain competition with commercial services (Diekmann *et al.*, 2009: 29).

Commercial and Social Tourism: An Ambivalent Relationship

In the wake of the financial crisis of 2007 and the consequent austerity measures many European governments have implemented, there is currently a tendency to reduce public funding for social welfare schemes and a growing need for social tourism operators to be self-financing. In a time of mass tourism, low-cost airlines and cheap package holidays, however, many of the original social tourism establishments find it hard to compete with the commercial sector. Public authorities consider that if social tourism providers go beyond their mission, by notably increasing prices, they should not benefit from state aid. The counter-argument by the sector is based on the fact that they are fighting for financial survival as a result of progressive funding cuts. The social tourism sector thus faces a dilemma. Because of the reduction in public funding, the charges for social tourism have to increase, while, at the same time, due to economies of scale and an increasingly integrated tourism sector, the prices of commercial tourism often decrease. This has led to some interesting anomalies, whereby it is sometimes cheaper to fly for a week all inclusive to an international destination than to spend a week in domestic social tourism accommodation.

Although the two sectors can be seen as in competition with each other, they are also mutually linked and to some extent interdependent. From the social tourism perspective, with the absence of specific social tourism accommodation in some countries at least, the intermediary organisations have to rely on the commercial sector to provide for social tourism customers. If specific accommodation is available, in order to keep an economic balance, the accommodation generally must attract commercial clients using commercial procedures such as marketing and promotional offers. On the other hand, from the perspective of the commercial sector, social tourism intermediaries bring customers. Some of the target groups, such as seniors, are more likely than other groups to travel during the low season, thus helping preserve employment at periods of the year characterised by redundancies.

Competing with and yet depending on and linked to commercial tourism, the social tourism sector is in transition and must adapt to a new landscape in the tourism industry. In many countries, an in-depth reflection is going on, on how to position social tourism within society and define a new role and a new image (see Chapter 11). One of the key issues of the debate concerns the quality of the social tourism supply, which has considerably increased over the last decade. There is also a tendency to change the image of the sector, emphasising sustainability and the fostering of social exchange, in a move which seeks to reconnect social tourism to its origins. Reflection on the role of social tourism and how it can be integrated into European policy is similarly taking place at European level.

Developing Unified Social Tourism Implementation Schemes

Social tourism has been of interest to the EU since the 1990s, but only since 2009 has the focus been on social tourism as a means of lowering seasonality within the accommodation sector. That year, the Tourism Unit of the DG Enterprise and Industry of the European Commission launched a preparatory action on social tourism, by the name of Calypso. The aim was to put into action some of the outcomes of the Lisbon Treaty and the objectives of the Tourism Sustainability Group of the EU. The preparatory action consisted initially of a call for tenders for the implementation of a social tourism scheme lowering seasonality in the accommodation sector by fostering at the same time intra-European mobility for specific target groups.

The final report from the Calypso consortium, however, highlights the difficulty of implementing such a scheme within Europe (European Commission, 2010). The reasons are manifold and in part can be understood in the context of the discussions in Chapters 1 and 2 in this volume, for these challenges are grounded in the different definitions and concepts of social tourism, accompanied by different systems and stakeholders and finally a broad range of target groups. As such, the project failed to deliver an implementation scheme. The development of best practices to implement exchanges between different countries throughout Europe is therefore the objective of the latest call for tenders from the Commission. Stakeholders and intermediary organisations were invited to test such an implementation. Critics argue, on one hand, that the target groups declared in Calypso are not inclusive enough. On the other hand, they explain that the aim of social tourism is not simply to fill tourist accommodation at low season, but to improve mobility and accessibility for all. This tension between the economic imperative for sustainable tourism advocated in the Lisbon Treaty and a larger, humanistic, socially oriented rationale for involvement in social tourism, placing the human need and rights for a vacation at the centre of the debate, is indeed the defining issue at the heart of current policy and practice across the EU. Another recurrent issue in the debate is the perception of sustainability. While social tourism considers sustainability an essential element of its definition, Calypso's approach to sustainability refers mainly to the economic pillar and excludes to a certain extent the two others, namely the environmental and socio-cultural pillars.

Yet, one achievement of Calypso is the opening of the aforementioned segregation between the different social tourism providers and stakeholders. Through the numerous conferences and interactions, stakeholders found themselves for the first time around one table and not at a national level but at the European level. The Calypso programme is likely to bear fruit since, at the time of going to press, the first projects were about to start. The outcomes of this programme should be able to show just how far the social tourism debate can take effect successfully at a European level or whether the differences between systems, intermediaries and so on, as highlighted in this chapter, are simply too great for unified social tourism policies to be developed.

Conclusions

The chapter has explored the issues surrounding the diversity of systems, intermediaries and stakeholders of the social tourism structures throughout

Europe. They are the logical consequence of a varying understanding of what social tourism is, whom it should provide for and how it should best be operated. One common feature is that in almost all countries of the EU, social tourism operations are confronted by numerous socio-economic changes and find themselves in a period of transition. First of all, funding structures have been reviewed in many countries, leaving the providers of social tourism with the need to find other sources of revenue. In that context, these providers have become very similar to commercial tourism operators. Another important shift has been in customer demand. Indeed, the former clientele, workers and member organisations tend to benefit more from commercial tourism as this has become more accessible during the last 30 years. At the same time, for other reasons, in some countries social tourism's infrastructure is still in use but for new target groups; nevertheless, in some systems there are groups in need who are excluded from social tourism. There is an urgent need to redefine social tourism and its place within EU society, however difficult and distant a prospect this may appear to be.

There may be value in defining a number of target groups to direct limited funding, although there is a need to ensure that target groups are not treated as homogeneous; within each there are diverse needs, and there has to be suitable provision in order to meet them. There is a need for recognition on the side of the intermediary organisations that they could have more success by identifying specific groups and outcomes and also, in some countries, a better understanding of social tourism needs to be promoted among intermediaries, including its potential outcomes and benefits to client groups. Yet, social tourism is an umbrella term that, at its heart, has the goals of reducing social inequalities, establishing norms about the right to participate in a holiday for all people in society, and encouraging a diverse and competitive tourism system. In these terms, finding common ground between stakeholders and policy makers across nations in the EU may not be an unrealistic dream.

References

BAGFE (Bundesarbeitsgemeinschaft Familienerholung) (2009) Retrieved from http://www.urlaub-mit-der-familie.de.

Bradshaw, J. and Mayhew, E. (2010) Understanding extreme poverty in the EU. *European Journal of Homelessness*, 4: 171–186.

CASE (2002) *Case Brief 23: Understanding Social Exclusion*. London: Centre for Analysis of Social Exclusion.

Department for Work and Pensions (2008) *Households Below Average Income: An analysis of the Income Distribution 1994/5–2006/07*. London: DWP.

Diekmann, A., Duquesne, A.-M., Maulet, G. and De Nicolo, B. (2009) *Employment in the European Social Tourism Sector*. Brussels: EFFAT and BITS, LIToTeS (ULB).

Diekmann, A. and McCabe, S. (2011) Systems of social tourism in the European Union: a critical review. *Current Issues in Tourism*, 14(5): 417–430.

Dobson, B., Middleton, S. and Braithwaite, I. (2001) *The Impact of Childhood Disability on Family Life*. York: Joseph Rowntree Foundation.

EU (2010) Workshop 1, 'Streamlining stakeholder initiatives towards Calypso', EC Calypso Conference, 10–11 June, Palma de Mallorca.

European Commission (2010) *Calypso Study: Final Report.* Brussels: DG Enterprise and Industry.

Eurostat (2008) *Tourism Statistics Pocketbook.* Luxembourg: Office for Official Publications of the European Communities.

Hills, J., Le Grand, J. and Piachaud, D. (2002) *Understanding Social Exclusion.* Oxford: Oxford University Press.

McGuire, F., Dottavio, D. and O'Leary, J. (1986) Constraints to participation in outdoor recreation across the life span: a nationwide study of limitors and prohibitors. *The Gerontologist*, 26(5): 538–544.

Observatoire du Tourisme Wallon (2003) *Le profil de la clientèle dans les centres de tourisme social de la région Wallonne.* Namur: Région Wallonne.

Case Study 3:
Family Holiday Association, UK

Thea Joldesma *Programme and Policy Manager*

The charity that gives families a break

The Family Holiday Association
3 Gainsford Street
London SE1 2NE
UK
Telephone: 02074363304
Email: info@familyholidayassociation.org.uk
http://www.familyholidayassociation.org.uk
http://www.breaksforall.org.uk

Aims/Mission

The Family Holiday Association works in partnership with others to promote the quality of family life for those parents and children in the UK who experience disadvantage as a result of poverty through the provision of, and by promoting access to, holidays and other recreational activities.

Its main objectives are:

- to increase the number of families who can gain access to holidays;
- to research and promote the value of holidays for families experiencing disadvantage;
- to increase awareness of the scale and scope of the problem of lack of access to holidays.

History

The Family Holiday Association was set up in 1975 and is the only national charity in the UK dedicated to promoting social tourism services through the provision of breaks to hundreds of disadvantaged families each year. Its working definition for social tourism is the inclusion of people living on a low income in holiday and leisure activities. In its early days the charity assisted a handful of families; in 2010 it provided breaks to over 2000 families.

Location

The Family Holiday Association provides a UK-wide service and is based in London.

Current Activities/Programmes

The families are referred by a range of professionals, such as healthcare staff, social workers, teachers and charities such as Barnardos, NSPCC and Gingerbread. All the families have not had a break for at least four years and many have never had the chance to get away as a family.

- The majority of the breaks are at UK holiday parks, such as those run by Haven or Butlins. They take the form of self-catering caravan holidays for three, four or seven nights. The break includes accommodation, entertainment passes, linen (when available) and holiday insurance (subject to medical conditions). The charity may also offer a small contribution towards the family's travel and treats when funding is available.
- Direct grants are one-off contributions towards any type of holiday offered to families in exceptional circumstances. Families choose their own destination and book dates convenient to them.
- Group breaks are one-off contributions towards an organised break for a group of four or more families organised by their welfare agent.

Beneficiaries

The Family Holiday Association provides financial support to families in need of a break away from home who:

- are referred by a welfare agent (a welfare agent is someone who knows the family in a professional capacity who is aware of the family circumstances, for instance a social worker, doctor, teacher or support worker);
- have at least one child in the family aged between 3 and 18 years at the time of the holiday;
- are on a low income;
- have not had a holiday in the last four years.

The Association considers a 'family' to consist of dependent children and those who care for them. Carers can be parents, grandparents, guardians and others with caring responsibilities, such as an older child.

Funding Sources

The Family Holiday Association relies on donations from individuals, companies, trusts and local groups to carry out its work. Every year the charity raises funds in a variety of ways through a range of events both in the UK and abroad with the help of travel industry partners, such as the Virgin London Marathon.

Role in Social Tourism Provision

In order that the Family Holiday Association can promote social tourism across the UK the charity continues to work and develop successful relationships with the travel industry, individual donors and the corporate world, policy makers, referring agents and like-minded organisations both in the UK and abroad. Following the economic downturn, the Association's work is becoming even more important.

- In 2008 the charity became the designated charity of the travel organisation TUI UK & Ireland. Since 2009, incoming Thomson Airways flights have shown the charity's fundraising DVD and carried out coin collections.
- A range of individuals and other corporate donors support the charity on a regular basis, both with cash and gifts in kind, including City Bond Insurance, First Great Western (the train operator), Haven Holidays and Malta Tourism.
- Three local groups in north London, Rotherham and Sheffield continue to raise money to fund breaks for families in need from those areas.
- Under the banner of 'Breaks for All', a group of like-minded organisations, including the Youth Hostel Association for England and Wales, Family Fund and UNISON Welfare, have joined with the Family Holiday Association to promote the benefits of social tourism. Anyone involved in social tourism is invited to sign the 2007 Social Tourism Declaration.
- On 15 December 2010 an All Party Parliamentary Group for Social Tourism was established. Paul Maynard, MP for Blackpool North & Cleveleys, was elected chairman. Among those present was the well known author and Labour peer Ruth Rendell. The work of the Group is to generate a wider understanding of social tourism as a means of improving the lives of people and families in the UK and its potential role as a significant economic driver for domestic tourism.
- As part of our European Holiday Experience project, we work together with like-minded organisations abroad such as Tourism Flanders and Pasar in Belgium and Vacances Ouvertes in France in supporting families on a low income to travel abroad. We are an active member of the International Social Tourism Organisation (ISTO) and the EU Calypso Working Party, which helps us raise the profile and understanding of social tourism across the UK and Europe.

Areas and Examples of Best Practice

- The diagram below of the UK social tourism holiday provision model shows how families can access a break thanks to the help of their welfare agent, the Family Holiday Association and a holiday provider. For example, in the case of a break with Haven Holidays, the Association has negotiated and paid for an accommodation voucher. The voucher is then distributed to the family via their referring agent. The voucher entitles the family to a free break for a specified number of nights (three, four, or seven nights) in self-catering accommodation at certain dates during the year. This voucher enables the family to book their break directly with the holiday provider, thereby empowering families and keeping administration costs down.
- Since 1975 over 130,000 people in the UK have been able to enjoy a break through the Association. The welfare agents working with the families assist with a grant application to the Association which assesses the application against published criteria for funding. Once a break has been awarded, the offer and payments are made to the family via their referring agent, who will assist the family with the preparation and planning as well as with the completion of the required feedback forms. In 2010 more than 2000 families (over 8000 people) enjoyed a break in this way.
- Over the years the referral processes have been improved where possible and online applications were introduced in 2009.
- The evidence gathered from both families and referring agents is collated and analysed annually. The data inform the charity's programme consolidation and expansion, research, promotion and fundraising.

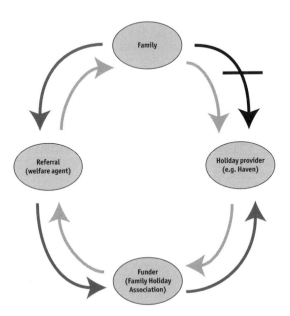

The UK model of social tourism

Areas of Best Practice

- *Caravan project.* This began with two caravans in 2004 and expanded to 12 caravans in 2010 for those families that cannot take a break during the low season: three at Butlins Skegness, three at Haven Devon Cliffs in Exmouth, two at Butlins Minehead, two at Hafan Y Môr in Gwent, one at Haven near Prestatyn in North Wales and one at Combe Haven in Kent. This type of provision enables the charity to speak with authority to practitioners and policy makers on what makes for a good, cost-effective holiday.
- *School projects.* These started with the first school in north London in 2006 but have subsequently been expanded to a range of schools in Glasgow, Reading and Rochester. The aim of this project is to measure the impact of breaks on the pupils, their families and the wider school community as a whole. Funding and support for the various school projects are aimed at embedding breaks and trips into family learning. The projects help inform the Association of the scope for statutory support for family breaks. Schools report that family breaks in this project help to build trust, resulting in better relationships with parents/carers, increased attendance and improved academic performance.
- *Healthy breaks: 'eat well, be active, feel good' project.* This was started with a development grant from the Big Lottery Fund in 2007, and in 2011 was provided at three locations and taken up by range of organisations across the UK. These breaks aim to improve the quality of life for children and their families struggling with depression and other health issues. Families are introduced to a range of activities that involve gentle exercise, such as exploring the countryside and orienteering, (new) healthy foods and relaxation exercises to encourage a positive mind-set. Families have felt less isolated as a result, their self-esteem has increased and many have taken the first steps in taking on training and finding better employment.
- *European Holiday Experience Partnership.* This project began with Tourism Flanders (Belgium) and Vacances Ouvertes (France) in 2006 and has continued with annual trips for UK families subsequently. It is a practical programme comparing experiences of families holidaying in Belgium, France and the UK, and demonstrates that families from one country can travel during their school holidays in another country's low season (termed 'asymmetric seasonality'). A shared publication and audio CD *Give Europe a Break*, which present evidence on children and their families, was produced in 2007. Annual meetings between the partners help share and improve expertise and continue to inform the development of a wider range of products and support mechanisms, such as the Holiday Pilot for Young Parents in 2009.
- *Credit Union holiday saving scheme.* This was developed with Reading and Berkshire Credit Union in 2008 and publicised to other Credit Union schemes across the UK. In this scheme a free short break is offered that is intended to serve as an incentive to start saving as a family on a regular basis towards a realistic goal.

4 Resisting the Hegemony of the Market: Reclaiming the Social Capacities of Tourism

Freya Higgins-Desbiolles

Tourism is touted as the world's largest industry. The standard reason given for the respect and support given to tourism as an industry is its economic value in providing foreign exchange, income, investment, employment and economic development opportunities to communities around the globe. This focus on the economic contributions of tourism should not be allowed to overshadow the significant contributions tourism makes to social wellbeing (Higgins-Desbiolles, 2006), but the hegemony of neoliberalism, or market fundamentalism as it is also known, has meant that little attention is given to the less commercial and socially focused niches of tourism, such as social tourism. It is important that we do not forget this equity pillar of tourism, because travel, rest and relaxation are in fact human rights enshrined in the Universal Declaration of Human Rights (1948) and they make important contributions to the social fabric within societies and between societies. This chapter overviews the effects of the hegemony of neoliberalism, examines its impact on tourism, explores the social capacities of tourism and mounts a human rights argument for resisting the hegemony of commercialised tourism and reclaiming the social capacities of tourism.

Hegemonic Neoliberalism and its Impacts

The current era could be characterised as one of hegemonic neoliberalism. Following the demise of the 'socialist alternative' with the breakup of the Soviet Union, fall of the Berlin Wall and China's 'socialist market economy' joining the World Trade Organization (WTO), neoliberalism has made an extraordinary advance in breadth and depth. According to David Harvey:

> Neoliberalism is in the first instance a theory of political economic practices that proposes human well-being can best be advanced by liberating individual entrepreneurial freedoms and skills within an institutional

53

framework characterized by strong private property rights, free markets, and free trade. (Harvey, 2005: 2)

Frank Stilwell claims that neoliberals advocate 'free market' policies in order to unfetter capitalist economies from excessive interventions by governments in economic matters, the latter being a product of the policies of the 'welfare state', supported since the 1950s and which neoliberals view as stifling economic efficiency. Stilwell claims that the outcomes of neoliberalism have 'reoriented governments':

> The economic activities of government are not reduced, only reoriented towards directly serving the interests of business; they become less concerned with progressive income redistribution and the amelioration of social problems arising from the operations of the market economy. The policies certainly create winners and losers whatever their effectiveness in relation to the dynamism of the economy as a whole: the removal of regulations protecting employment conditions predictably leads to more unevenness of employment practices and greater wage disparities; the relaxation of environmental controls leads to environmentally degrading activities; and the withdrawal of redistributive policies leads to growing problems of economic inequality and poverty. (Stilwell, 2002: 22)

Harvey reinforces this fact that neoliberalism has considerable social impacts as the ideology requires that states withdraw from all activities beyond creating an enabling environment for the market. Harvey (2005: 3) asserts that 'deregulation, privatisation, and withdrawal of the state from many areas of social provision have been all too common'.

Stephen Gill suggests:

> The present world order involves a more 'liberalized' and commodified set of historical structures, driven by the restructuring of capital and a political shift to the right. This process involves a spatial expansion and social deepening of economic liberal definitions of social purpose and possessively individualist patterns of action and politics. (Gill, 1995: 399)

With the rise of the 'Washington consensus', a term used to describe the free market policies promulgated by the Washington-based international financial institutions such the World Bank, the International Monetary Fund (IMF) as well as the United States Treasury Department, these neoliberal policies now have global reach. Countries around the world are urged to adopt such policies as 'structural adjustment' by these international financial institutions. Philip McMichael has claimed that the WTO offers the promise of development as the reward for joining the market so that a 'market rule' is installed whereby the markets and resources of the entire world are accessible (McMichael, 1998: 302–303). The result is an entrenched hegemony by the capitalist class that works to deliver greater profits to the beneficiaries of the system and which achieves the compliance of others through the promise that 'a rising tide floats all boats'.

Clive Hamilton has described the key tenets of neoliberalism as beliefs that 'the central objective of government must be the promotion of economic growth and that markets must prevail' (Hamilton, 2003: ix); the former he calls 'growth fetishism'. He states:

> In practice, growth fetishism has been responsible for a historic transfer of political authority from the state to the private market. If growth is the path to greater national and personal wellbeing, should not those responsible for growth be encouraged at every opportunity? Growth fetishism therefore cedes enormous political power to business, and corporations are never reluctant to argue that, since they are creators of wealth, it is their interests that should be paramount to government. (Hamilton, 2003: 17–18)

But the hegemony of neoliberalism is contested and its reign is undermined by recent economic, social and environmental crises, most recently by the global financial crisis (GFC) begun in 2007. While this has undermined support for the excesses of neoliberalism and resulted in minor changes to financial institutions and financial processes, the dynamics of neoliberalism remain largely unchanged. In fact, Harvey's analysis of neoliberalism suggests that these crises can be manipulated by the capitalist classes to extract further wealth and value from those on the periphery of the system. Harvey calls this 'accumulation by dispossession' (Harvey, 2005: 162) and states that it is most obviously operative in the 'debt trap' that many countries and individuals are caught in.

Neoliberalism and Tourism

It is not the purpose of this chapter to analyse the economic dynamics of neoliberalism, but rather to explore the social implications that the paradigm holds for our societies, specifically on the capacities for tourism to fulfil its potential as a social force. Tourism has been radically changed by the hegemony of the market. There has been much valuable analysis in the tourism literature about such developments and their impacts on developing countries (including Brohman, 1996; Mowforth & Munt, 2003; Reid, 2003; Scheyvens, 2002). In his discussion of volunteer tourism, Stephen Wearing (2001, 2002) is highly critical of tourism operations within the neoliberalism context. He states:

> Tourism in a free market economy can exploit natural resources as a means of profit accumulation, and consequently has been described

as the commercialization of the human need to travel. The notion of unlimited gain has led to the exploitation of host communities, their cultures and environments.

Tourism perpetuates inequality, with the multinational companies of the advanced capitalist countries retaining the economic power and resources to invest in and ultimately control nations of the developing world. In many cases, a developing country's engagement with tourism serves simply to confirm its dependent, subordinate position in relation to the advanced capitalist societies – itself a form of neo-colonialism. (Wearing, 2002: 238)

John Brohman (1996) has critiqued the use of tourism as part of the outward-oriented development strategies promoted by the neoliberally driven international financial institutions (IFIs) such as the International Monetary Fund and the World Bank. Reviewing Brohman's work, Regina Scheyvens has claimed that 'rather than encouraging domestic tourism or promoting tourism as a means of developing cross-cultural awareness, for example, for most Third World countries tourism is explicitly pursued as a means of earning foreign exchange' (Scheyvens, 2002: 24). However, in the wake of the GFC, it is clear that such dynamics are not limited to developing countries. As one journalist has put it:

Greece and Iceland now know what Indonesia, Malaysia and Thailand knew in 1999. Savage public spending cuts used to be the medicine the International Monetary Fund doled out to sickly developing countries; now we have to self-medicate. (Bunting, 2009)

Greece has been urged to sell off uninhabited islands and heritage assets to reduce its debt and get back into the sound fiscal fold of neoliberal orthodoxy. In such a context, integration into the international tourism system serves to assist in the process of disciplining societies to the neoliberal agenda.

Contemporaneous with the rise of neoliberalism, the mantra that tourism is an 'industry' which is subject only to the rules of the marketplace has been repeated so frequently that to think otherwise is viewed almost as nonsensical. The discourse of tourism as industry has been developed for particular political purposes and has important effects, which are vital to recognise.

Tourism as an Industry: The Marketisation of Tourism

Tourism is characterised as an industry in many academic and non-academic publications. While people more readily accept the notion of tourism as an industry today, following years of hearing the term repeatedly, the academic debate remains unresolved. Thea Sinclair and Mike Stabler state:

It is a composite product involving transport, accommodation, catering, natural resources, entertainments and other facilities and services, such as shops and banks, travel agents and tour operators. Many businesses also serve other sectors and consumer demands, thus raising the question of the extent to which suppliers can be considered as primarily suppliers of tourism. The many components of the product, supplied by a variety of businesses operating in a number of markets, create problems in analysing tourism supply. (Sinclair & Stabler, 1997: 58)

The drive to characterise tourism as an industry has resulted in a deleterious narrowing of the vision of tourism's role in societies. Neil Leiper traces the development of the term 'tourism industry' to the 1960s, when modernising forces looked to industries as engines of economic growth (Leiper, 1995: 97). He has shown that interested parties made a concerted effort to gain widespread acceptance of the notion of tourism as an industry and contends that this is partly the result of a simile (tourism is like an industry) going too far when extended to a metaphor (tourism is an industry) (Leiper, 1995: 99). Thomas Davidson, moreover, suggests that tourism businesses reacted against the common notion of tourism as 'fun and games, recreation, leisure, unproductive', which resulted in a failure of economists, economic developers and governments to take tourism seriously (Davidson, 1994: 20–21). He argues that the struggle to get tourism accepted as an industry was waged for the following purposes: to win respect, to enable data collection and to create an identity and secure self-esteem for those working in tourism (Davidson, 1994: 21–22). Leiper argues that the 'tourist industry' image was created to secure broad public relations goals for organisations such as the Pacific Asia Travel Association (PATA), the United Nations World Tourism Organization (UNWTO) and the World Travel and Tourism Council (WTTC). It also aimed to create pride and professionalism among employees and establish clout wieldable in politics (Leiper, 1995: 103–105). Davidson (1994) and Leiper (1995) convincingly argue that the effort to gain widespread acceptance of tourism as 'industry' was in part an attempt to gain considerable political advantage pursued for economic benefit.

Another academic proponent of the notion of tourism as an industry is Stephen Smith. He laments the gap that exists between the researchers and the practitioners of tourism, which results from lack of awareness of tourism as a business on the part of the former (Smith, 1988: 182). He offers an industrial definition of tourism, which he argues will rectify the poor regard that industry leaders, government officials and economists have for tourism, by allowing comparability with other industries. This he calls a 'supply-side' definition, in that it shifts focus away from tourists to the businesses which service them: 'Tourism is the aggregate of all businesses that directly provide goods or services to facilitate business, pleasure, and leisure activities away from the home environment' (Smith, 1988: 183).

The notion of tourism as an industry has generated extensive debate and disagreement. Davidson argues that tourism is *not* an industry, because an industry is composed of individual businesses grouped together, the revenue received by these businesses and the common product that they create and sell. Tourism, he claims, does not meet these criteria, as it is 'a social phenomenon, not a production activity'; it comprises the total of expenditures of all travellers or visitors for all purposes, and not just the receipts of a particular set of businesses, and it is 'an experience or process, not a product' (Davidson, 1994: 22–25). Davidson claims that by arguing for support for tourism as an industry, the tourism sector looks narrowly self-interested in achieving outcomes for its individual businesses while it could be achieving greater support for itself by highlighting its contributions to society in general. He states:

> When tourism – an industry composed of individual business firms seeking their own benefit – comes up against education, public health, crime prevention, infrastructure repair or development, etc. (all seen as serving society as a whole), the problem before the appropriations committee is clear. Why should government use limited funds to support one industry – and a 'frivolous' one at that – when there are so many social ills that demand attention? As an industry, tourism is often seen as self-serving when, in fact, it is a key ingredient in the economic health of a community. Thriving tourism can be key to attending to these other issues. (Davidson, 1994: 26)

In an increasingly competitive world, the notion of tourism as an 'industry' is used to obtain support and access to resources that would otherwise be unobtainable. As Davidson indicates above, these resources could be used for other purposes, such as education, health or other areas of economic development. The economic justifications for such support are debatable on the grounds of the jobs, foreign exchange, infrastructure and other outcomes that tourism does or does not deliver. While criticism has been levelled at tourism on such grounds as the low-skill, seasonal and fragile nature of its employment, or the economic leakages that it suffers, or the vulnerability and volatility of its markets (Mathieson & Wall, 1982: 86–89; Weaver & Oppermann, 2000: 266–272), this is not crucial to this discussion. What this chapter is focused upon is how the 'tourism as industry' discourse limits analysis of the tourism phenomenon to its 'marketised' or 'corporatised' attributes, and privileges the interests and demands of the tourism business sector while marginalising other important facets of tourism, addressed below.

Despite the criticism levelled at the notion of tourism as an industry, the designation is most probably here to stay. Particularly in the context of the current economic downturn, the economic and industrial discourse of tourism as industry allows it to argue for financial investment, favourable political climates, expensive infrastructural support and subsidies and other support mechanisms, even when public spending is under increased scrutiny. However, there are rival depictions of tourism that are worthy of attention.

Tourism as a Social Force: The Transformative Capacity of Tourism

The ability of tourism to contribute to important social aims was recognised at the birth of the modern tourism phenomenon. As Louis Turner and John Ash noted, the father of modern, mass tourism, Thomas Cook, viewed the railway and the journeys it enabled as 'a great and beneficial social force'; Cook described travel as 'appertaining to the great class of agencies for the advancement of Human Progress' (cited in Turner & Ash, 1976: 52, 53). Turner and Ash argue further:

> He saw 'excursionism' as an agent of democratisation, and in 1861 he demonstrated the sincerity of his democratic principles by organising an excursion of 1,500 to 1,600 people to support a working men's demonstration in Paris. Cook made a loss of 120 pounds and described the venture as a 'labour of love minus profit'. Nevertheless, a similar excursion was organised in the following year. (Turner & Ash, 1976: 53)

Since the 1980s there has been a growing acknowledgement of the power of tourism as a social force. Jost Krippendorf envisioned a 'new tourism' that 'may well become again a true discovery, a place of experiences and learning, a means of human enrichment, a stimulus for a better reality and a better society' (Krippendorf, 1987: 530). Philip McKean boldly claims:

> Underlying tourism is a quest or an odyssey to see, and perhaps to understand, the whole inhabited earth, the *oikumene*. Tourism can be viewed as not an entirely banal pleasure-seeking escapism ... but as a profound, widely shared human desire to know 'others,' with the reciprocal possibility that we may come to know ourselves. (McKean, 1989: 133)

In a critical discussion on peace through tourism, Dann argues that 'tourism has strong interpersonal and cultural components [including spirituality] which cannot be captured by economic analysis alone' and this is what gives it its ultimate potential as a vital force for peace (Dann, 1988: 28).

From these brief quotations, it is evident that tourism is an important social force with transformative capacities and deserves considered analysis in this regard. The words of the 1980 Manila Declaration on World Tourism (UNWTO, 1980) highlight the strongest vision for tourism:

In the practice of tourism, spiritual elements must take precedence over technical and material elements. The spiritual elements are essentially as follows:

- The total fulfilment of the human being.
- A constantly increasing contribution to education.
- Equality of destiny of nations.
- The liberation of man [sic] in a spirit of respect for his identity and dignity.
- The affirmation of the originality of cultures and respect for the moral heritage of peoples.

This document also notes that:

Modern tourism was born out of the application of social policies which led to workers obtaining annual paid holidays, this in turn reflecting an acknowledgement of the human being's fundamental right to rest and leisure. It has become a factor of social stability, mutual knowledge and understanding of man [sic] and peoples, and the betterment of the individual. Apart from its well-known quantitative dimension, it has gained a cultural and moral dimension which it is important to encourage and to protect from negative distortions due to economic factors. (UNWTO, 1980)

Tourism and Travel as a Human Right

The right to travel, rest and relaxation is mentioned in the Universal Declaration of Human Rights of 1948, and travel and tourism are specifically referred to in the International Covenant on Economic, Social and Cultural Rights (ICESCR) of 1966, the UNWTO's Tourism Bill of Rights and Tourist Code of 1985 and the Global Code of Ethics for Tourism of 1999. The Universal Declaration of Human Rights has two passages that underpin the right to travel: articles 13(2) and 24. Article 13(2) states that 'Everyone has the right to leave any country, including his own, and to return to his country' (United Nations, 1948), which Darren O'Byrne (2001: 411–413) describes as underpinning the human right to travel. Combined with article 24, which states that 'everyone has the right to rest and leisure, including reasonable limitation of working hours and periodic holidays with pay' (United Nations, 1948), this fundamental document of international law is credited with situating travel and tourism as part of human rights. The justification for asserting such new rights can be gleaned from the words of the UNWTO, which declare tourism's potential value in 'contributing to economic development, international understanding, peace, prosperity and universal respect for, and observance of, human rights and fundamental freedoms for all' (UNWTO, 1999). Making such important and varied contributions to the human good, tourism and travel are uniquely worthy among 'industries' to be elevated to a human rights status. The Manila Declaration on World Tourism states:

> Tourism is an activity essential to the life of nations because of its direct effects on the social, cultural, educational and economic sectors of national societies and their international relations. Its development is linked to the social and economic development of nations and can only be possible if man [sic] has access to creative rest and holidays and enjoys freedom to travel within the framework of free time and leisure whose profoundly human character it underlines. Its very existence and development depend entirely on the existence of a state of lasting peace, to which tourism is required to contribute. (UNWTO, 1980)

The 1985 Tourism Bill of Rights and Tourist Code reinforces the 'human dimension of tourism' and reiterates the claims that tourism contributes to the social, economic, cultural and educational sectors of national societies and improves the international community (UNWTO, 1985).

The more recent Global Code of Ethics for Tourism (UNWTO, 1999) enunciates the roles and responsibilities of the various stakeholders in tourism. Although the preamble states that 'The world tourism industry as a whole has much to gain by operating in an environment that favours the market economy, private enterprise and free trade and that serves to optimize its beneficial effects on the creation of wealth and employment' (UNWTO, 1999), the Code also reflects concerns contemporaneous with its development. For example, it acknowledges the need to balance economic development with environmental protection and the alleviation of poverty, informed by the sustainability discourse of the 1990s. The Code's passage on the right to travel, found in article 7, proves interesting: it not only reiterates the right to travel and tourism already stated in other key documents, such as the Universal Declaration of Human Rights, but it also advocates government support of initiatives such as 'social tourism' and other processes to promote access to tourism for disadvantaged groups, including the disabled, youth, seniors and families.

Social Tourism: A Forgotten Commitment to Humanity

The discussion of tourism and travel as a human right raises the topic of 'social tourism'. Some Eastern and Western European countries have fostered the phenomenon of social tourism as an important aspect of the obligations a state owes its citizenry and society in order to fulfil the right to tourism. While social tourism has different meanings in different contexts (Murphy, 1985: 23), the basic principle of social tourism is 'access to travel and leisure opportunities for all' (International Social Tourism Organisation, 1996). In particular, social tourism advocates the provision of tourism opportunities for the 'economically weak or otherwise disadvantaged elements of society' (Hunzinger, cited in Murphy, 1985: 23).

> The International Social Tourism Organisation (ISTO) has formulated a strong argument for the right *of all* to tourism, travel and leisure. In particular it exhorts governments to move beyond 'recognition of the right' to tourism to actual pragmatic programs to enable all to enjoy the exercise of their right. (International Social Tourism Organisation, 1996)

The first Secretary-General of the ISTO (or Bureau International du Tourisme Social, BITS, as it then was), Arthur Haulot, described social tourism as 'a type of tourism that concentrates essentially on man and his [*sic*] destiny, and not on the profits to be made from his status as a consumer' (Haulot, 1985: 220). In the era of neoliberalism, the idea that tourism's purpose may be to serve human needs and not only to deliver profits to the business sector or economic growth for governmental accounts is often disregarded. Nevertheless, from the arguments presented in this chapter, it could be suggested that tourism should not be about economic development for its own sake, as seems to be the ideology of a tourism sector subject to the 'growth fetish' under contemporary neoliberalism.

There were few references to social tourism initiatives in the tourism literature until very recently (see, though, for example, McCabe, 2009; Minnaert *et al.*, 2009; and see Chapter 1 of the present volume). Historical notable exceptions to the blinkers concerning social tourism include: Barkin (2000), Connell (2000), Hall (1998), Haulot (1985), Murphy (1985); Ryan (2002) and Teuscher (1983). A look through several dozen major tourism textbooks in search of references to social tourism yields surprisingly few results. This perhaps indicates just how dominant the neoliberal paradigm has become in the tourism context, for one would expect that at least anthropological and sociological tourism literature would find some interest in the social tourism phenomenon. Presumably it is not helpful to have such a title as 'social tourism' at a time when the socialist alternative is largely viewed with contempt. One suspects that the debate held by the ISTO to consider a change of title from 'social tourism' to 'tourism for all' was a reaction to this unfortunate situation (see ISTO, 2002: 3).

In the current context of neoliberalism, it seems unlikely that social tourism will make much headway and the promise of 'tourism for all' will remain unrealisable for the vast majority of people. At the moment, the obligation to fulfil the precepts of social tourism is given to governments and this greatly reduces the likelihood that such rights (which are still very much contested) will be truly universally provided, as many countries fail to meet their citizens' most basic needs, let alone fulfil a right to travel. As David Barkin pointed out in his examination of Mexico, even the wealthier countries which could provide resources for social tourism's facilitation will not choose to support its capacities as 'an instrument for environmental management and social well-being' because the neoliberal agenda sees 'public policy ... driven by the service providers organized to respond to the demands of the tour operators who focus their efforts on the most profitable segments of the globalized market' (Barkin, 2000: 52). It is perhaps because of the unlikelihood of a fully social tourism eventuating in the short to medium term that Chris Ryan connects his discussion of social tourism to recent developments in stakeholder theory and sustainability. Ryan states, 'it thus seems that if "Social Tourism" is to become a meaningful and practical policy, attention must be paid to the concept of stakeholders and mutual responsibilities, as is recognised by the [UN]WTO Code' (Ryan, 2002: 20). This in particular will require the support of the government, taxpayers and the tourism industry, who will all have to be persuaded of the merits of such a public policy.

That the industry should support widened access to its benefits through the phenomenon of social tourism is well argued by Haulot. He claims that 'tourism in the broad sense owes much of its enormous scope and potential to those who have fought so hard for social tourism over the years' (Haulot, 1985: 220). He argues it was the struggle of the 1930s for workers' rights to paid annual holidays and the later efforts to develop facilities and amenities for social tourism that led to widespread increase in the numbers of people interested in touring. This in turn fed the expansion and development of the tourism industry. Much like sustainability, supporting the expansion of social tourism to all segments of the community in communities throughout the world makes sound 'business' sense for some in the tourism sector.

In order to secure the backing of governments and taxpayers, it will be necessary for the supporters of social tourism to document and substantiate the full benefits of specific initiatives in economic, social, environmental and human wellbeing terms. It may be necessary to communicate these in the language of economics, as this is the current hegemonic discourse. This is perhaps well exemplified in Minnaert et al.'s (2009) study of social tourism and the work of the Family Holiday Association of the UK, in which the authors argue that social tourism is a cost-effective way to implement government social policy.

Ryan argues in his analysis of the Global Code of Ethics for Tourism that 'the point has been to show that "Social Tourism" and "Social Equity" is [sic] not a mere will of the wisp of idealists and marginalised pressure groups, but an aspiration shared at the highest levels of industry and governments' (Ryan, 2002: 19). Current practice under neoliberal governments challenges Ryan's assertion that segments of industry and governments are alive to the need for social equity, though there is no doubt that pressure for it will not go away, as other stakeholders in tourism, including non-governmental organisations and communities, will continue to agitate for it.

Tensions are clear. While, currently, the neoliberal era demands that the benefits of tourism be allocated according to the 'invisible hand' of the market, the discourse of tourism as a 'human right' demands a social tourism agenda, which requires continued intervention by governments and communities to ensure that tourism contributes to a better quality of life and an equitable sharing of tourism's bounties. However, vigilance is required to uncover the hypocrisies of the current era. For example, although the Global Code of Ethics for Tourism may idealistically make a commitment to social tourism, it also states: 'the world tourism industry as a whole has much to gain by operating in an environment that favours the market economy, private enterprise and free trade and that serves to optimize its beneficial effects on the creation of wealth and employment' (UNWTO, 1999). As a result, social tourism is left to the purview of those governments that are wealthy enough and willing to create social tourism programmes for their citizenry. Several institutions, including the European Economic and Social Committee, apparently now accept the rhetoric of a universal right to travel and tourism but they demonstrate no eagerness to make it a reality for the majority of the world's inhabitants, who are hemmed in by their poverty and life circumstances. Could the UNWTO and the stakeholders who assisted in the drafting of the much-supported Global Code of Ethics for Tourism be accused of hypocrisy for formulating a provision on social tourism and espousing the right to travel when they know such rhetoric is unrealistic within the current market reality? An investigation of the industry's rhetoric on poverty alleviation, peace through tourism and sustainability suggests that such hypocrisy is not limited to the social tourism sector.

We cannot ignore the current reality which sees a privileged elite within the global community with high disposable incomes serving as the drivers of current tourism and travel. A press release entitled 'Rich minority "fuelling air travel boom"' reported the results of a Civil Aviation Authority (United Kingdom) survey which indicated that, despite 'the huge array of cheap flights on offer', the lowest-income groups took just 6% of UK flights while representing 27% of the population, whereas the wealthiest income groups took 40% of UK flights while representing 24% of the population (Gillett, 2004). This press release quoted John Stewart, of the activist group Clear-Skies, which opposes airport expansion, as saying, 'The absence of any tax on aviation fuel or VAT on air tickets amount to a £9 billion subsidy for the better-off to enjoy their jet-setting lifestyle' (Gillett, 2004). Instead of relying on the high consumption rates of a set of elite travellers and tourists, the tourism industry should fulfil its commitments as espoused in the Global Code of Ethics for Tourism to share the tourism opportunity equitably, by fostering social tourism initiatives.

Our best hope for equitable tourism through initiatives such as social tourism may lie in the demise of neoliberalism itself. Although this ideology has entrenched itself so successfully that many have succumbed to the presupposition that there is no alternative, the hegemony of neoliberalism is contested and its reign has been undermined by, for example, the GFC. In response to the GFC, former Prime Minister of Australia, Kevin Rudd, wrote:

> The time has come, off the back of the current crisis, to proclaim that the great neo-liberal experiment of the past 30 years has failed, that the emperor has no clothes. Neoliberalism, and the free-market fundamentalism it has produced, has been revealed as little more than personal greed dressed up as an economic philosophy. And, ironically, it now falls to social democracy to prevent liberal capitalism from cannibalizing itself. (Rudd, 2009: 25)

While the recent crisis has undermined support for the excesses of neoliberalism, the underlying dynamics remain largely unchanged. Yet its foundations have been weakened and victims of its excesses are beginning to mobilise. Like all ideologies, its time will pass. What will remain will be the need to create social systems which create balance, fairness and relationships which will lead us through the more difficult, resource-constrained futures we face, with ever-larger populations seeking quality of life and wellbeing in the context of finite and fragile environments.

Economist Frank Stilwell (2002: 14–16) offers a model of a balanced relationship between economy, society and ecology wherein lie the possibilities of distributional equity, ecological sustainability and the quality of life (see Figure 4.1). We need to harness the social capacities of tourism through programmes such as social tourism in order to ensure that tourism plays its part in establishing this more balanced relationship rather than serving the neoliberal market model, where economic priorities are allowed to ride roughshod over social values and ecological understandings.

Tourism geared to wellbeing, self-esteem, education, cross-cultural interaction, spiritual growth, conservation, solidarity, development assistance and other eco-humanistic values should be encouraged and fostered. These options are available when we challenge the narrow paradigm set by neoliberalism and marketised tourism by recognising that social values have an importance no less valuable than economic ones in our utilisation of and support for tourism. Perhaps we should turn to Inayatullah's checklist for tourism for a final perspective on the ends to which tourism could be directed:

> How does tourism affect the distribution of wealth? Does tourism create conditions where economic growth is sustaining? Does tourism reduce structural violence (poverty, ill-health and racism caused by the system) or does it contribute to the further impoverishment of the periphery? Does tourism reduce personal direct violence? Can we create types of tourism that enhance individual and social peace? Does tourism create

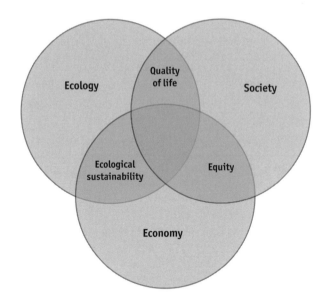

Figure 4.1 A model of interdependent systems: Ecology, society and economy
(source: Stilwell, 2002: 14)

the possibilities for cultural pluralism, that is, conditions where one culture understands the categories of the other culture...? Can knowledge
of the Other reduce intolerance, creating the possibility of a multicultural
peaceful world? Does tourism help create economic democracy? Is tourism progressive? Is there a progressive use of resources, from physical to
mental to cultural-spiritual? (Inayatullah, 1995: 413)

Conclusions

It is worth noting that, more than 50 years ago, renowned historical
economist Karl Polanyi (1944) envisioned the danger posed by the market
fundamentalism that accompanies neoliberalism:

> To allow the market mechanism to be the sole director of the fate of
> human beings and their natural environment ... would result in the
> demolition of society. (Cited in Harvey, 2005: 167)

This is certainly a key challenge of our era, as we must overturn the narrow,
myopic lens of economism through which all human relationships and
values are now seemingly measured. Social tourism offers us one tool to

mount this challenge. Tourism is indeed a powerful social force which contributes vital benefits to society when not limited by the narrow measures of economic returns demanded by neoliberalism and its associated market fundamentalism.

References

Barkin, D. (2000) Strengthening domestic tourism in Mexico: challenges and opportunities. In K.B. Ghimire (ed.), *The Native Tourist: Mass Tourism Within Developing Countries* (pp. 30–54). London: Earthscan.

Brohman, J. (1996) New directions in tourism for third world development. *Annals of Tourism Research*, 23(1): 48–70.

Bunting, M. (2009) Seattle: a warning ignored. *The Age Online*, 17 December. Online at http://www.theage.com.au/opinion/politics/seattle-a-warning-ignored-20091216-kxdu.html.

Connell, J. (2000) The role of tourism in the socially responsible university. *Current Issues in Tourism*, 3(1): 1–19.

Dann, G.M.S. (1988) Tourism, peace and classical disputation. Paper presented at Tourism: A Vital Force for Peace, 1st Global Conference, 23–27 October, Montreal, pp. 25–33.

Davidson, T.L. (1994) What are travel and tourism: are they really an industry? In W. Theobold (ed.), *Global Tourism: The Next Decade* (pp. 20–26). Oxford: Butterworth-Heinemann.

Gill, S. (1995) Globalisation, market civilisation and disciplinary neoliberalism. *Millennium: Journal of International Studies*, 24(3): 399–423.

Gillett, T. (2004) Rich minority 'fuelling air travel boom'. Travelmole.com, 2 November. Online at http://www.travelmole.com/stories/102052.php.

Hall, C.M. (1998) *Introduction to Tourism* (3rd edn). Melbourne: Longman.

Hamilton, C. (2003) Growth fetish. Crows Nest, NSW: Allen and Unwin.

Harvey, D. (2005) *A Brief History of Neoliberalism*. Oxford: Oxford University Press.

Haulot, A. (1985) The environment and the social value of tourism. *International Journal of Environmental Studies*, 25(4): 219–223.

Higgins-Desbiolles, F. (2006) More than an industry: tourism as a social force. *Tourism Management*, 27(6): 1192–1208.

Inayatullah, S. (1995) Rethinking tourism: unfamiliar histories and alternative futures. *Tourism Management*, 16(6): 411–415.

International Social Tourism Organisation (1996) Montreal Declaration. Online at http://www.bits-int.org/en/index.php?menu=45.

International Social Tourism Organisation (2002) Editorial. *Le Tourisme Social dans le Monde*, 139: 3.

Krippendorf, J. (1987) *The Holiday Makers: Understanding the Impact of Leisure and Travel*. Oxford: Butterworth-Heinemann.

Leiper, N. (1995) *Tourism Management*. Melbourne: RMIT Press.

Mathieson, A. and Wall, G. (1982) *Tourism: Economic, Physical and Social Impacts*. New York: Longman.

McCabe, S. (2009) Who needs a holiday? Evaluating social tourism. *Annals of Tourism Research*, 36(4): 667–688.

McKean, P.F. (1989) Towards a theoretical analysis of tourism: economic dualism and cultural involution in Bali. In V.L. Smith (ed.), Hosts and Guests: The Anthropology of Tourism (pp. 119–138). Philadelphia, PA: University of Pennsylvania Press.

McMichael, P. (1998) Demystifying globalisation, briefly. In M. Alexander, M. Alexander, S. Harding, P. Harrison, G. Kendall, Z. Skrbis and G. Western (eds), *Refashioning*

Sociology: Responses to a New World Order (pp. 299–304). TASA Conference Proceedings. Brisbane: QUT Publications.

Minnaert, L., Maitland, R. and Miller, G. (2009) Tourism and social policy: the value of social tourism. *Annals of Tourism Research*, 36(2): 316–334.

Mowforth, M. and Munt, I. (2003) *Tourism and Sustainability: Development and New Tourism in the Third World* (2nd edn). London: Routledge.

Murphy, P.E. (1985) *Tourism: A Community Approach*. New York: Methuen.

O'Byrne, D. (2001) On passports and border controls. *Annals of Tourism Research*, 28(2): 399–416.

Polanyi, K. (1944) *The Great Transformation*. Boston, MA: Beacon Press.

Reid, D.G. (2003) *Tourism, Globalization and Development*. London: Pluto Press.

Rudd, K. (2009) The global financial crisis. *The Monthly*, February, 42: 20–29.

Ryan, C. (2002) Equity, management, power-sharing and sustainability issues of the 'new tourism'. *Tourism Management*, 23(1): 17–26.

Scheyvens, R. (2002) *Tourism for Development: Empowering Communities*. Harlow: Prentice-Hall.

Sinclair, M.T. and Stabler, M. (1997) *The Economics of Tourism*. London: Routledge.

Smith, S.L.J. (1988) Defining tourism: a supply-side view. *Annals of Tourism Research*, 15(2): 179–190.

Smith, S.L.J. (1997) Challenges to tourism in industrialized nations. In S. Wahab and J.J. Pigram (eds), *Tourism, Development and Growth* (pp. 147–163). London: Routledge.

Stilwell, F. (2002) *Political Economy: The Contest of Economic Ideas*. Melbourne: Oxford University Press.

Teuscher, H. (1983) Social tourism for all – the Swiss Travel Saving Fund. *Tourism Management*, 4(3): 216–219.

Turner, L. and Ash, J. (1976) *The Golden Hordes: International Tourism and the Pleasure Periphery*. London: Constable.

United Nations (1948) Universal Declaration of Human Rights. Online at http://www.un.org/en/documents/udhr.

UNWTO (United Nations World Tourism Organization) (1980) Manila Declaration on World Tourism. Online at http://www.unwto.org/sustainable/doc/1980%20Manila-eng.pdf.

UNWTO (1985) *Tourism Bill of Rights and Tourist Code*. Madrid: UNWTO.

UNWTO (1999) Global Code of Ethics for Tourism. Online at http://www.unep.org/bpsp/Tourism/WTO%20Code%20of%20Conduct.pdf.

Wearing, S. (2001) *Volunteer Tourism: Experiences That Make a Difference*. Oxon: CABI.

Wearing, S. (2002) Re-centering the self in volunteer tourism. In G.S. Dann (ed.), *The Tourist as a Metaphor of the Social World* (pp. 237–262). Oxon: CABI.

Weaver, D. and Oppermann, M. (2000) Tourism Management. Milton: John Wiley.

Case Study 4: Labour Market Holiday Fund (Arbejdsmarkedets Feriefond), Denmark

Anne-Mette Hjalager *Managing Director,*

Advance/1 Research Consultancy, Aarhus, Denmark

ARBEJDSMARKEDETS FERIEFOND

Arbejdsmarkedets Feriefond
Postbox 1192 – 1011
Copenhagen
Denmark
Telephone: +3348 7000
Telefax + 3348 7001
Email: feriefonden@aff.dk
https://www.aff.dk/

Aims/Mission

The Labour Market Holiday Fund is a national non-governmental organisation set up to administer funds to support holiday opportunities mainly through the provision of activities, attractions and accommodation. The Fund supports institutions or organisations through co-financing schemes, loans or subsidies to other non-profit organisations – public or private – that provide relevant facilities within the statutes of the Fund. It has a capital of €110 million, and spent €7.5 million to support holiday activities in 2009.

History

The history of the Fund stems back to the Holiday Act of 1938. As part of the labour settlement, the government wished to ensure not only that were employees entitled to time off work but also that they had the means to afford a holiday, thus institutionalising the financing of holiday benefits. For every week of work, employees who are entitled to holiday pay receive 'holiday stamps'. The stamps are an equivalent to a holiday savings scheme (of 12.5% of salary) and are paid instead of the main salary paid when an employee is on leave. The stamps represent a postponement of the wage until the holiday is actually taken. Every year, there are always some holiday stamps that are not cashed in. In the period between purchase of the stamps to their payment, interest is paid on the accumulating capital. These funds, which belonged to no one, grew significantly, and they were placed in a foundation – the Labour Market Holiday Fund, under the control of the Ministry of Labour and Social Affairs. With further institutionalisation, this became of major importance to the tourism system in Denmark from the 1950s. In 1974, the Fund became completely independent, although members of the board are still appointed by the Minister of Labour. The board represents the governmental institutions, labour unions and employers' organisations.

Initially, the activities supported by the Labour Market Holiday Fund centred on facilities in modern and well equipped holiday centres available for rent at very competitive prices. The centres had a prominent location and were of high quality. They were mostly located in coastal rural districts. However, towards the end of the 20th century, a majority of families now lived in suburban areas. A competition for new uses of the Holiday Fund resulted in the idea of providing better family holiday facilities in attractive urban areas. One of the contributions suggested that a former Copenhagen slum district be restored and used for 'working class retro' holidays. That idea was never realised, however, possibly because it was politically and socially 'painful' at the time, because it exposed previous social deprivation. Soon after the competition, urban holiday centres were established in provincial towns, but their designs were advanced and modern.

The financial situation of the holiday centres worsened during the 1980s. Occupancy rates were lower than expected, due both to recessions and to fierce competition from foreign destinations and substantial numbers of holiday homes available for rent in the private sector. Interest rates for supplementary financing were high at that time, even in the heavily subsidised facilities. In addition, the private providers, now better organised and networked in the hotel and restaurant association, claimed that the facilities supported by the Labour Market Holiday Fund distorted competition. The Fund responded by stopping support for new accommodation and, in 2002 by further restricting the terms of support for the renovation and updating of existing holiday centres, except for schemes to improve access for the disabled.

The gradual withdrawal from the accommodation market increased the need to find other investment possibilities in the 1990s. New political and ideological coalitions were established with other actors in the tourism sector than just the labour unions, the employers' associations and the Ministry of Labour. A committee, which also included the National Tourist Board, the trade association Horesta and the Ministry for Cultural Affairs, identified the need to support an extension of the holiday season, an increase in services and quality, and – most importantly – to devise new, preferably innovative, attractions. The committee succeeded in wresting some of the power away from the traditional (centralised) labour market actors by determining that projects supported by the Fund should involve local initiatives and co-financing. Since the 1990s the Fund has been involved a number of projects, mainly in the attractions sector, where support has been given for the building of new facilities.

Location

The Fund's head office is in Copenhagen. The holiday centres are distributed all over Denmark. One holiday centre was established in Malta.

Current Activities/Programmes

The Fund's activities are at 'arm's length', in that it is not specifically concerned with the direct provision of activities or with the specific methods used by the organisations it supports. In this sense, the Fund has no direct influence on whether organisations involved in the delivery of social tourism initiatives apply for support. The responsibility for pursuing a moral purpose is 'outsourced' to these specialist organisations by the Fund. Denmark's social system is such that unemployed people, students and people with disabilities or in a caring role within the family generally also have access to holiday facilities and activities.

Beneficiaries

The Fund has a very wide understanding of beneficiaries, such that they include formerly employed people who are now retired or on social benefits. There is a strong emphasis on children.

The Fund does not own facilities, but co-finances other organisations' activities and facilities. Many public facilities, such as museums and attractions, are beneficiaries. The non-profit tour operator and accommodation provider Dansk Folkeferie (Danish Folk Holidays) is the owner of a number of holiday resorts which have been co-financed by the Fund. In addition, the Fund supports non-governmental organisations which provide holidays for the most disadvantaged groups – children and single mothers living in (relative) poverty, drug addicts, alcoholics, the disabled and so on. These organisations are in charge of organising the holidays for their target groups without much further interference from the Fund. One example of a co-financing project was the construction of a holiday centre together with the Muscular Dystrophy Association. The centre caters for many different kinds of disabilities, with specialist technical equipment available. The building (finished in 1998, and an extension planned for 2012) contains separate apartments, and is striking in its innovative use of architectural design and decoration; environmental concepts are integrated throughout into the design and operations of the holiday centre, which has received a 'Green Key' environmental label.

Funding Sources

The Fund relies on its original sum, but still receives income from annual 'uncashed' holiday stamps.

Role in Social Tourism Provision

The Fund has a high profile in terms of quality and innovation. It is inundated by a large number of competitive project proposals, which allows it to be extremely selective. The Fund chooses to involve itself quite heavily in projects, which include professional advice and assistance – in exchange for substantial grants. The involvement of staff from the Fund is supposed to enhance quality far beyond what was normally seen in tourism attractions.

Areas and Examples of Best Practice

Over the years, there has been a switch to supporting finance for attractions, including extensive investments to accommodate the needs of people with disabilities. Funds are also provided for interpretations, which are often aimed at the needs of schoolchildren. Recent examples of best practice include:

2009   Royal Copenhagen Theatre, open-air facilities in Ulvedalene for action drama;
2009   nature trails on the Island Funen;
2009   Cold War Museum – Recycling of the Langelands Fort;
2009   labelling and certification organisation for access for the disabled to holiday activities;
2009   Voliere for the Copenhagen Zoo;
2008   Geological Centre, Møn;
2008   new interpretation the open-air museums in Århus;
2008   the Rock Museum Roskilde;
2088   the experience centre, The Prison, Horsens;
2008   development of access to a number of national parks.

References

Hjalager, A.-M. (2005) Innovation in tourism in a welfare state perspective. *Scandinavian Journal of Hospitality and Tourism*, 5(1): 46–54.

Hjalager, A.-M. (2006) The marriage between welfare services and tourism – a driving force for innovation. *Journal of Quality Assurance in Hospitality and Tourism*, 6(3–4): 7–30.

5 Social Tourism and the Social Economy

Gilles Caire

The third sector, not-for-profit organisations, social enterprises, the voluntary sector, popular associations, the community economy, social cooperatives, the social and solidarity economy: all of these are different terms used in Europe to refer to productive structures that are neither state nor private companies and which primarily focus on individual and social goals rather than on profit generation (Draperi & Frémeaux, 2006). These different approaches are specifically mentioned in the 1996 Montreal Declaration of the International Social Tourism Organization, updated in 2006, as important actors in the social tourism sector. Indeed, article 13 affirms this importance when it addresses the identification criteria of social tourism and stipulates that:

> Any tourist organization (association, cooperative, mutual society, foundation, federation, not-for-profit organization, company etc) which, by its articles of association or statement of aims clearly identifies with social objectives and the aim of making travel and tourism accessible to the greatest number, – thereby differentiating itself from the sole aim of profit maximization – may claim membership of the social tourism movement. The word 'social' may evoke an increased sense of solidarity and fraternity, and be a source of hope for those many people in the world today who still have no leisure time.

In France as well as in Belgium, Portugal and Spain, the term most commonly used for these types of enterprises is the 'social and solidarity economy' (*économie sociale et solidaire*). This category includes cooperatives, mutual societies and associations, and is generally characterised by five principles: free membership, limited profitability, democratic and participative management, a collective or social purpose and financing by public and private funds (CNLAMCA, 1995). Enterprises in the social economy focus

73

on social goals that are not perceived to be appropriately addressed by the public sector; within the tourism sector, the provision of social tourism is one of those goals. An example of such an enterprise is the National Union of Tourism Associations (Union Nationale des Associations de Tourisme, UNAT) in France. This organisation represents a wide range of tourism associations and not-for-profit businesses that aim to widen access to tourism. Its charter of 2002 stipulates the four following ambitions:

- to guarantee that a large number of people from various social backgrounds will have access to holidays, and to encourage social exchange via holidays;
- to emphasise the humanist and collectivist values of tourism to society, and the role of tourism in the increase of personal wellbeing and social cohesion;
- to support the sustainable development of tourism accommodation, with respect the environmental and socio-cultural features of the destination;
- to achieve economic benefits via the support of social organisations and youth and family associations working in the social and solidarity economy.

To understand how these principles affect French social tourism in practice, the chapter briefly introduces the history of social tourism in France. The discussion highlights how most associations became involved in tourism through the creation of summer camps, youth hostels and holiday homes, before developing their tourism product further with the advent of holiday villages in the 1960s, because of contracts with the government, the Child and Family Allowance Fund (CAF, *Caisses d'Allocations Familiales*, created in 1945 within the social security budget, and which manages all social aid granted to families) and trade unions. The evolution from a small-scale tourism product to larger, publicly funded tourism provision is typical for many social tourism organisations in the social economy. Yet, since the early 1980s, the distinctions between social and commercial tourism have become less clear, despite the resistance of many associations. The adoption of commercial approaches of the market economy by some sectors in the social economy is also apparent in other fields, such as cooperative banks and mutual health insurance companies.

Social Tourism in France: A Considerable Economic Player

The French tourism associations operate in five sectors:

(1) holiday villages accommodating families and groups – for example Villages Vacances Familles (VVF), Ternelia, Cap France, Association Nationale de Coordination des Activités de Vacances des Comités d'Entreprise – Tourisme et Travail (ANCAV-TT) and Vacances Tourisme Familles (VTF);

(2) centres welcoming young people and/or sportsmen – for example Fédération Unie des Auberges de Jeunesse (FUAJ) and Ligue Française pour les Auberges de la Jeunesse (LFAJ), the two youth hostelling federations, the Ethic Etapes network, the Union nationale des Centres sportifs de Plein Air (UCPA) and the French Alpine Club;

(3) holiday camps for children and teenagers, discovery classes, school trips and linguistic stays – for example Ligue de l'Enseignement, Union Française des Centres de Vacances et de loisirs (UFCV) and Pupilles de l'Enseignement Public (PEP);

(4) international holidays for adults – for example Association de Rencontres, de Voyages, d'Etudes et de Loisirs (ARVEL), and Vacances Bleues – and solidarity tourism associations – such as Tourisme et Développement Solidaires (TDS), Croq' Nature and Route des Sens;

(5) associations with an intermediary role, providing neither accommodation nor trips but supporting popular education, social assistance or travellers' groups, and providing human, material and information support to enable travel – for example JPA, Vacances Ouvertes, APF évasion (further details are available in French at http://www.unat.asso.fr).

UNAT provides an umbrella organisation for the sector, and so it is useful to outline its background. UNAT was created in 1920 and includes 54 national organisations and 470 regional organisations operating in tourism. It represents about 1500 accommodation centres totalling 227,000 beds, which accounts for 4.6% of the total beds sold in tourism in France. In 2008, its national members accommodated 4.7 million people, for a total of 30 million nights (statistics from http://www.unat.fr). The revenue from these operations totalled €1.5 billion, 7% of the total tourist accommodation revenue in France; the sector also accounts for 20,000 full-time jobs. It is important to mention that these data do not take into account the centres and beds managed by workers' councils and their likes. These organisations were created after 1945, when companies with over 50 employees had to set up a council to represent the workers. They are funded via a contribution of 0.2% from the total wage bill, and finance social and cultural activities for the workers. If the accommodation capacity of these organisations were to be added, it is estimated that the total amount of non-profit tourism beds would amount to over 500,000, and this would equal 10% of the total commercial accommodation provision.

The Origins of Social Tourism in France

Originally, social tourism in France was developed as a cost-saving and non-monetary form of tourism with a social and educational aim targeting children, youngsters and workers' families. The following section outlines the key developments in this movement.

Summer Camps: A Philanthropist and Hygienic Innovation

Summer camps for children and adolescents were introduced at the end of the 19th century through the intervention of parochial patronage (Rauch, 2001). In 1881, Pastor Loriaux and his wife founded the Œuvre des Trois Semaines, which sought to improve the health of working-class children and teach them good manners. The aim was to provide 'both school age boys and girls (from 7 to 13) with holidays of at least three weeks in the country or at the seaside; they were accommodated in buildings renovated for that purpose or at individuals' homes.... This makes it possible for everybody to enjoy a break from noise and dust' (cited by Rauch, 2001: 65). Holiday camps were part of the paternalist social policy initiated at the end of the 19th century and pursued hygienic, patriotic and moral goals (Caire, 2002). Their formation was part of a more general concern among the elite about growing urbanisation and moral and intellectual decay. In a report presented to the National Congress of Holiday Camps in 1910, Grancher, a professor of medicine, made it clear that 'to save the race decimated by infectious disease, it was necessary to preserve the grain by transplanting it in a sane and vivifying environment' (Rauch, 2001: 70). The non-religious organisations for public education, the Ligue de l'enseignement and the Sou des écoles, established as early as 1883, also included the promotion of democratic equality, an educational purpose and a discovery of the world through observation of nature.

In 1906, the first National Congress of Holiday Camps was held but the religious affiliations created divisions among the participants. Despite that, the number of holiday camps rose significantly (from 100,000 children catered for in 1913 to 400,000 in 1936), boosted in by municipalities, mainly socialist or communist, which created their own camps. Following the demographic boom after 1945, the camps reached a peak in the early 1960s, with more than 1.3 million children and adolescents benefiting (Houssaye, 1977: 5). The view that clean country air was necessary for children's health was prevalent until the late 1970s.

Youth Hostels: An Innovation with a Pacifist Goal

Marc Sangnier (1873–1950) was one of the founders of the Sillon Movement. The Movement aimed to promote exchanges and develop a spirit of self-organisation among young people, but it also sought to reconcile

Catholicism with the Republic and aimed at 'developing the social forces of Catholicism within contemporary society'. After a meeting with Richard Schirrmann (founder of the first German youth hostel, in 1907), Sangnier founded the first French youth hostel, in Bierville, in August 1930: the Home of Peace. He then founded the French Youth Hostel League (LFAJ, Ligue Française des Auberges de Jeunesse), which had an allegiance to the Catholic Church.

In 1933, the Non-Religious Centre for Youth Hostels (CLAJ, Centre Laïque des Auberges de Jeunesse) was created; it was supported by the communist trade union (the CGT), the national schoolmasters' trade union and the General Federation for Education. Similar to the split that existed in the development of holiday camps, its aim was to promote the provision of non-denomination youth hostels. Again, the number of youth hostels grew very fast, to 900 hostels and 40,000 members by 1939. The tensions between the two approaches lasted until 1956, when today's United Federation for Youth Hostels (FUAJ, Fédération Unie des Auberges de Jeunesse) was created.

Léo Lagrange: An Innovative Creation of Mass Leisure Activities without Military Influence

In June 1936, the Popular Front government initiated the office of Under-Secretary of State for the Organisation of Leisure and Sports, held by Léo Lagrange. Lagrange (1900–1940) had been a scout in his youth, a lawyer and member of the Socialist Party, and became the Deputy of the North in 1932 and served in the French government from 1936 to 1938. He became President of the Non-Religious Centre for Youth Hostels in 1939 and died in the war in 1940. (Pierre Mauroy, French socialist Prime Minister from 1981 to 1984, was one of the main founders of the Léo Lagrange Federation in 1950.)

As Under-Secretary of State, Lagrange initially reported to the Ministry of Health, as the contemporary vision of leisure and holidays was driven from a 'hygiene' perspective (as noted above), with a purpose of regenerating the labour force. However, he later reported to the Ministry of National Education, with a broader perspective of popular education (Ory, 1994). Lagrange argued that, beyond the enforcement of the right to paid holiday, the government had a duty to provide 'mass leisure' but it had to firmly reject any military organisation of leisure chosen by the state and other centralised structures of authoritarian governments of the time, especially the Italian Fascist Opera Nazionale Dopolavoro (National Recreational Club) established in 1925 and the Nazi Kraft durch Freude ('Strength Through Joy'), created in 1933.

Lagrange said, 'Sports, tourism and cultural activities are the three complementary aspects of the same social need: the conquest of dignity, the search for happiness ... I rely on the active collaboration from all the existing organizations and especially from working class organizations' (cited by Raude & Prouteau, 1950: 119). In 1936, he prompted the development of independent 'associative' popular tourism with the support of trade unions, popular education associations (especially the Education League) and the two (Catholic and non-denominational) networks of youth hostels (Mauroy, 1997).

This laid the foundations for the main principles of democratic solidarity of social tourism:

- holiday accommodation for everybody, whatever their social class;
- sports and cultural collective activities with a humanist vision;
- the active participation of users in some tasks and in defining the programme of activities;
- a non-profit associative management with logistic support from the government.

Family Holiday Homes: A 'Makeshift' Innovation

After the 1936 law on paid holidays and despite Léo Lagrange's efforts, there was still no general structure for social holiday provision for families. Hotels were not adapted to low-income families with regard to their rooms, activities or pricing structure. After the Second World War, the government no longer regarded going on holiday as a policy priority.

It was in this context that 'family holiday homes' were created by activists' and volunteer organisations. These homes often originated with three different types of family associations: Christian; non-religious and trade unionist. The homes accommodated between 5 and 20 families, who often came from the same area. The holiday-makers themselves were in charge of the management of activities and chores, and this arrangement allowed for very inexpensive holidays. In 1956, there were more than 300 of these holiday homes, generally comprising old hotels, mansions or castles, with an average of 100 beds per home. They were soon financially supported by the CAF (Family Allowance Fund) through the allocation of holiday vouchers or investment aid; hence they became part of the government's family social policy.

The Implementation of a Fordist Form of Social Tourism

Until the end of the 1950s, the numbers of people being assisted through these programmes remained low, mainly due to the reliance on volunteering, the lack of financial means and the limited professionalism of the organising associations. In 1958, only 31% of French people went on holiday. Access

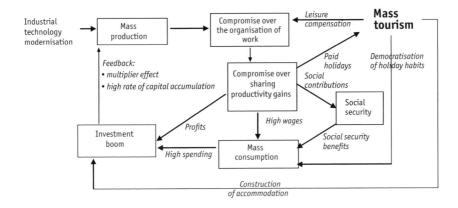

Figure 5.1 Mass tourism and wage relations

to holiday opportunities (Guerrand, 1963) for the majority was achieved through the industrialisation of non-profit and commercial tourism supply in the context of the French welfare state.

Mass tourism and especially the 'leisure society' (Dumazedier, 1962) is a consequence of Fordist wage relations, defined as 'all the juridical and institutional conditions that rule the use of salaried work as well as the reproduction of workers' existence' (Boyer, 1986: 18). Tourism was perceived to provide positive interactions between economic growth and social progress on three levels (see Figure 5.1):

- *By strengthening the institutionalised role of leisure in the organisation of work.* The creation of 'significant blocks of free time', as articulated by Pascal Cuvelier (1998), allowed workers to accept a trade-off for increased working hours and contributed to sustaining their motivation and productivity.
- *By playing a role in the division of shared productivity gains,* via profits, direct and indirect salaries (through social security) and paid holidays which could be complemented by holiday bonuses and aid from workers' councils.
- *By becoming one of the norms of Fordist consumption practice.* Tourism then contributed towards balance in the equation between mass production and mass consumption through the multiplier effect generated by tourism spending and consequently the development of the tourism industry sector, with increased construction of accommodation (including secondary homes). It also contributed to the processes of imitation

and differentiation considered to be the socio-economic driving forces of consumer society.

This Fordist approach, combined with government support for the sector, allowed tourism to acquire an economic, social and political legitimacy that ultimately benefited social tourism.

Holiday Villages: Professionalisation and Standardisation

Another critical stage in the process of social tourism's integration into the social economy was the emergent collaboration between the various organisations and social movements involved. In 1958, the association Villages Vacances Familles (VVF) built the first two holiday villages for the general public, in Obernai and Albé in Alsace. The association was founded by the French Federation for Popular Tourism, the Bas Rhin department and the Caisse des Dépots et Consignations (this last organisation is a publicly funded institution in charge of carrying out projects of general interest to society). The National Social Security Fund, the National Union of Family Allowance Funds, the social services of higher administrations and workers' councils of companies contributed funds. The association aimed to 'allow families to spend healthy, enjoyable and relaxing holidays in relation with their needs as well as with their means thanks to material and educational collective services' (Guignand & Singer, 1980: 15). In 1959, in Albé and Obernai, the price of the stay on a daily basis (in July and August) represented six hours of work at an adult's minimum wage and 3.5 hours for a child aged between five and nine years. This marked the beginning of the successful implementation of holiday villages, which was sustained thanks to the support of the non-religious organisations, workers' and trade union movements as well as family and Christian movements that already existed.

Partnership and Collaborative Development of Supply and Demand

The gradual institutionalisation of associative (social) tourism is put into perspective in Figure 5.2, which characterises the social economy. Adapting Figure 5.2, the boom of social tourism between 1960 and 1980 can be considered the result of a convergence between volunteer efforts together with a whole range of public, social and joint aid, as shown in Figure 5.3.

The Fourth Government Plan (1962–65) aimed to support the construction of holiday homes for the first time, with the aims of reducing social and regional inequalities, and of responding to growing demand. Subsidies stemmed from five sources (Froidure, 1997): (1) government subsidies (from the tourism and agriculture ministry, territory planning and regional

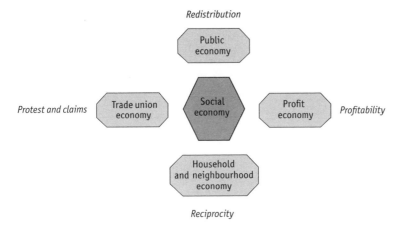

Figure 5.2 The social economy within the wider economy (adapted from Demoustier, 2003)

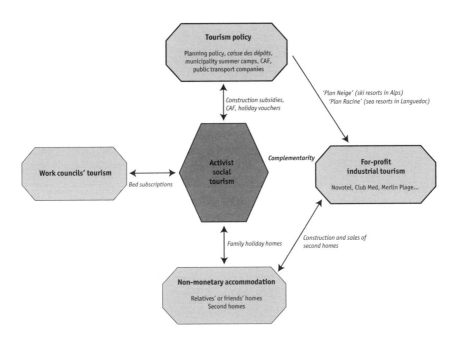

Figure 5.3 Social tourism within plural Fordist tourism

action commissions); (2) financial aid from the national and regional family allowance funds; (3) bed subscriptions from workers' councils, retirement allowance funds or friendly societies; (4) contributions from local collectives hosting the holiday homes (through free land, concession agreements or loan securities); and (5) advantageous loans within the Caisse des Dépôts. In the meantime, the family allowance funds adopted a policy of supporting low-income families' access to holiday homes (and children's access to holiday camps) with holiday vouchers. Public transport companies – SNCF (the national rail operator), Air France – proposed a subsidised fare tariff for low-income families.

France became the only European country with state-owned accommodation aimed specifically at extending access to all sections of society. The number of facilities belonging either to associations or local collectives grew from 85 holiday villages in 1965 (with a total of 32,000 beds), to 168 in 1970 (66,000 beds) and 318 in 1974 (112,000 beds), to 533 in 1980 (185,000 beds). As a result, social tourism gradually became industrialised and standardised. Employees and qualified professionals were recruited and an increasing number of contracts were signed with the authorities. Robert Lanquar and Yves Raynouard noted that, during this period:

> both associations and organisations evolved, adopting more professional, sometimes even bureaucratic practices. Holiday programmes were modified: new constructions and bed and board programmes replaced villages of tents and old constructions that had been renovated as family homes. (Lanquar & Raynouard, 1994: 45)

This process would ultimately lead to competition between social tourism structures and the mainstream (profit-driven) tourism industry. Yet until the early 1980s, social tourism and the mainstream tourist industry were not in competition. They did not target the same segments and during the high season (February and summer holidays) there still was a shortage of

Table 5.1 Growth in number of customers: Villages Vacances Familles (VVF) versus Club Méditerranée

	VVF	Club Méditerranée
1960	6,500	45,000
1965	52,000	90,000
1970	149,000	250,000
1975	330,000	432,000
1979	450,000	615,000

Source: Réau (2005).

accommodation. The two sectors operated side by side (sometimes even in the same resorts on the Côte d'Azur and in the Alps): they were complementary and experienced strong growth, as shown in Table 5.1, which illustrates the situation through the parallel evolution of VVF and Club Méditerranée:

The Beginning of Competition, Resistance and Innovation

From 1980, the changes in the French economy and cultural attitudes towards greater individualism were in line with the trends across Europe and the US brought about through Reaganism/Thatcherism. Public aid and contributions from workers' councils declined. Going on holiday was no longer considered a priority in the context of high levels of long-term unemployment, social exclusion and an overall reduction in social spending. Bouyer (1992) estimates that the total contribution of public subsidies granted to social tourism were cut by a quarter between 1979 and 1986. The situation worsened with the stagnation of salaried workers' buying power, increasing costs (especially construction costs), higher expectations and norms, as well as regulations regarding comfort and safety, a significant change in demand (more demanding and individualistic) and, increasingly, direct competition with the commercial tourism industry.

This evolutionary process has contributed to growing similarities between social tourism and the commercial sector, which can be seen as 'a constraining process that forces one unit in a population to resemble other units that face the same set of environmental conditions' (Di Maggio & Powell, 1983: 149). The services provided kept some of their initial specificity; nonetheless, as in other social economy sectors, the market, products, funding means and management methods have become standardised.

A More Affluent Target Market

The profile of the target market for holiday homes has changed significantly over time (AFIT, 2000). The lower middle class had long been the core market for holiday homes but nowadays people from the upper middle class make up the bulk of the demand for this product. Working-class families are significantly under-represented today (Caire, 2007a) and prefer less costly programmes (for example tourism products that exclude catering, children's and teens' clubs, and in fact entertainment and activities in general), such as accommodation at relatives' or friends' homes, campsites or renting apartments (either tourist residences or individuals' homes).

Though retired people were marginally represented in the 1960s and 1970s, they have now become the main consumers of associative holiday villages. This may be the result of a twofold effect on demand: the income effect (retired people's income being today higher than the average income of salaried people); and the generation effect (retired people today are used to going on holiday, which was not the case in the 1960s and 1970s). There is also a supply effect – for a better amortisation of their investment costs, the holiday villages have strongly expanded their focus on this target market group, as this allows them to stimulate demand in the low season.

Therefore it seems that the ambition of encouraging 'social integration' among holidaymakers in associative holiday villages may have been better achieved than in the past but at the expense of participation among the lower-income groups.

A Standardised Product

As for the product represented by holiday homes, it seems that differences have started to vanish. The commercial holiday clubs have followed the example of social tourism centres regarding the organisation of collective activities for adults and children. As for social tourism, the range of sports activities proposed are more and more comparable to those provided by the mainstream tourist industry; social tourism now meets a demand for a wider choice of activities and comfort, as well as a demand for fewer constraints (e.g. regarding meal times and the length of stay).

However, it is worth mentioning that the costs involved in taking care of children and participating in some activities are not always included in holiday clubs in the same price range. Even if the activities proposed seem similar, their practices and the way they are experienced may remain significantly different, as social tourism initiatives explicitly aim for these to be more collective, participative and more concerned with sustainability (Réau, 2005).

Some associations, Renouveau among them, still encourage the development of cultural and artistic actions and practices in their holiday villages (Casagranda, 2002). The conveyance of 'militant' messages during holidays, however, has largely disappeared, even in social tourism. As a result, most tourists who stay at a holiday village do not feel they have chosen 'another form of tourism'; they often freely choose between social and commercial forms of tourism.

Social tourism still retains an essential advantage, which is its affordability. UNAT (2006) quantified the price spreads between associative tourism and commercial tourism on renting and full board programmes in 2005. (It is important to note here that only prices were compared, and differences in service and product quality were not taken into account.) In almost all cases social tourism was on average 20–30% cheaper than commercial tourism. Moreover, the price differences between high season and low season and between destinations are smaller and the prices for children are substantially lower.

Financial Aid

Another factor explaining the growing similarities between the commercial and the social tourism sectors results from the substantial decrease in subsidies granted to social tourism and the move from financial aid for construction to financial aid to individuals. Rather than subsidising the construction of social tourism facilities, the public sector lends financial support to the holiday-maker directly – the beneficiary can then choose to spend the money in the social tourism or the commercial tourism sector. An example is the holiday voucher scheme, implemented in 1982 and managed by a public agency (ANCV, Agence Nationale pour les Chèques-Vacances). This scheme does not differentiate between the non-profit sector and the commercial sector in where the cheques can be spent. The holiday voucher is worth €10 or €20, partly or wholly financed by the employer. They can be used with registered transport, accommodation or leisure companies.

Implemented by the socialist government under the impulse of trade unions and tourism associations, the holiday voucher was conceived as an element of social democracy which would increase equity and holiday accessibility. Yet its functioning seems paradoxically more in line with neoliberal principles: responsibility, an employer's contribution, free choice of service provider, budget surplus allocated to social action measures and no spending from the government budget (excluding tax exemption measures).

Furthermore, European Union Directive 2006/123/CE, concerning unfair competition in the internal market for services, implies that the government cannot link state allocations to a non-profit status. This threat led the actors of social tourism to try to have their activity recognised as 'services of general interest' but, at the European level, this strategy encountered two main difficulties: the absence of a right to holidays and the predominant position of commercial tourism (Caire, 2006). This has threatened the ability of the French government to support social tourism infrastructure through direct state aid.

A More Commercial Approach to Management

The increasing industrialisation and professionalisation of social tourism has led to a new management profile. Social tourism organisations now recruit managers who have had training and/or qualifications in hotel business or management, unlike their predecessors, who were usually association activists and received only 'on the job' training. The management skills required for managers are now similar to those in the commercial sector.

However, in most cases, the new managers of social tourism organisations still appreciate the history of their facilities being founded on social activism, and work in partnership with volunteer managers of associations. In the pricing structures that are operated in social tourism facilities (which often vary prices according to the income or family structure of the tourist) a 'social management yield' still prevails, as argued by Chauvin (2002: 122), where 'economic relevance and management are compatible with accessibility to a majority of people'.

A collective agreement specific to family and social tourism means that associations generally provide their employees with better working conditions than their counterparts in the commercial sector; the agreement concerns not only remuneration, social provision and training but also working hours and accommodation of seasonal workers (Daniel, 2005).

Current Challenges

Today, tourism associations are facing new challenges, such as: the encouragement of social integration via tourism without appearing to be too directive in the offer in terms of the range of activities (Hilaire, 2005); the objective to combine social goals with environmental sustainability; the development of eco- and solidarity tourism; and the fair distribution of the resources generated (Caire, 2007b).

These challenges show that social tourism organisations still have a social and societal role to play. They are 'socially useful' (Caire, 2005), in that they contribute to reducing economic, territorial and social inequalities, to developing solidarity and sociability, and to improving the collective conditions favourable to sustainable human development. These 'goals' are essential for public allocations for projects, for the maintenance of a differentiation from the commercial sector, for the renewal of social economy values and for a renewed emphasis on the human and social aspects of holidays.

Conclusions: Social Tourism and the French Model: A Cultural Exception

The French social tourism organisations share the same goal as their European counterparts: to promote 'a humanist and social vision of tourism' that contributes to 'development and solidarity', to paraphrase the terms of the Montreal Declaration of 1996 (International Social Tourism Organisation, 1996). However, French organisations present three distinctive characteristics of a French-style social economy: its activism; economic production; and the refusal of a 'second rate' economy.

Historically, they are strongly linked to left-wing or Christian democratic parties, workers' trade unions and movements of popular education. Their status as associations, federations and the networks that were built up as a result of this process have always allowed them to benefit from a democratic autonomy in management and decision making, even when they were financially supported by the state.

From the very beginning, they made the choice of directly managing tourist accommodation. If we make an exception for youth hostels, the third sector in other European countries (apart from socialist countries and to a lesser extent Belgium, Italy and Portugal) rarely got involved in providing accommodation and limited its role to providing organisational services (e.g. information provision, negotiation of prices, making bookings) and financing (financial aid to the poorest) for social tourism groups.

Finally, they have consistently refused to target the most underprivileged sections of the population *only*, those who could not go on holidays (MEDEF, 2002) and have instead aimed for the integration of different social groups. Tourism associations have always kept the same ambition: making sure that a majority of people get access to holidays, especially low-income workers, the unemployed, large or single-parent families, people with disabilities, but in the context of a social melting-pot (*mixeté sociale*) as far as possible. It is this stance, and the historical antecedents deriving from the ideological linkages between holidaymaking and worker's rights which has led to both the widespread success of the social tourism system in France but also the challenges and current issues highlighted in this chapter. The refusal of a form of tourism only for the poor undeniably remains the most distinctive feature of French social tourism.

References

AFIT (2000) *Tourisme associatif: étude sur les clientèles familiales*. Paris: Cahiers de l'AFIT.

Bouyer, C. (1992) *Le tourisme associatif familial en France de 1945 à 1990* (Mémoire de recherche de DESES). Paris: Université de Paris I.

Boyer, R. (1986) *Théorie de la régulation: une analyse critique*. Paris: La Découverte.

Caire, G. (2002) *Economie de la protection sociale*. Paris: Bréal.

Caire, G. (2005) *Critères opérationnels d'évaluation de l'utilité économique et sociale: l'exemple du tourisme associatif* (Rapport pour la DIES). Poitiers: Université de Poitiers.

Caire, G. (2006) Les associations françaises de tourisme social face aux politiques européennes. *RECMA*, 300 (May): 30–44.

Caire, G. (2007a) Les associations françaises de tourisme: de l'impulsion d'un marché de masse aux difficultés d'un 'autre' tourisme. In A. Dussuet and J.M. Lauzanas (eds), *L'économie sociale entre informel et formel: paradoxes et innovations* (pp. 129–150). Rennes: Presses Universitaires de Rennes.

Caire, G. (2007b) Le tourisme solidaire et équitable: 'niche de solidarité' ou champ d'expérimentations d'un tourisme 'socialement durable'? *Économie et Solidarités*, 37(2): 186–202.

Casagranda, M. (2002) *Le village de vacances, lieu privilégié pour l'action artistique* (Mémoire de DESS). Lyon: Université de Lyon II.

Chauvin, J. (2002) *Le tourisme social et associatif en France*. Paris: L'Harmattan.

CNLAMCA (1995) *Charte de l'économie sociale*. Paris: Comité National de Liaison des Activités Mutualistes, Coopératives et Associatives.

Cuvelier, P. (1998) *Anciennes et nouvelles formes de tourisme: une approche socio-économique*. Paris: L'Harmattan.

Daniel, Y. (2005) *Des histoires, des valeurs et des points de vue*. Paris: USGERES.

Demoustier, D. (2003) *L'économie sociale et solidaire*. Paris: La Découverte.

Di Maggio, P. and Powell, W. (1983) The iron cage revisited: institutional isomorphism and collective rationality in organizational fields. *American Sociological Review*, 48(103): 147–160.

Draperi, J.-F. and Frémaux, P. (2006) *L'économie sociale de A à Z* (Hors-série pratique no. 22). Paris: Alternatives Économiques.

Dumazedier, J. (1962) *Vers une civilisation des. Loisirs?* Paris: Éditions du Seuil.

Froidure, J. (1997) *Du tourisme social au tourisme associative: crises et mutations françaises du tourisme*. Paris: L'Harmattan.

Guerrand, R.-H. (1963) *La conquête des vacances*. Paris: Editions Ouvrières.

Guignand, A. and Singer, Y. (1980) *Villages vacances familles* (QSJ no. 1825). Paris: PUF.

Hilaire, M.-M. (2005) *Coordonner et optimiser les aides au départ en vacances des Familles*. Paris: Conseil National du Tourisme.

Houssaye, J. (1977) *Un avenir pour les colonies de vacances*. Paris: Éditions Ouvrières.

International Social Tourism Organisation (1996) Montreal Declaration. Online at http://www.bits-int.org/en/index.php?menu=45.

Lanquar, R. and Raynouard, Y. (1994) *Le tourisme social et associative* (QSJ no. 1725). Paris: PUF.

Mauroy, P. (1997) *Léo Lagrange*. Paris: Denoël.

MEDEF (2002) *Pour que la France reste en tête: les recommandations de l'industrie touristique*. Paris: Rapport du Groupe Tourisme.

Ory, P. (1994) *La belle illusion: culture et politique sous le signe du Front populaire*. Paris: Plon.

Rauch, A. (2001) *Vacances en France: de 1830 à nos jours*. Paris: Hachette.

Raude, E. and Prouteau, G. (1950) *Le message de Léo Lagrange*. Paris: La Compagnie du Livre.

Réau, B. (2005) *Clubs de vacances et usages sociaux du temps libre: une histoire sociale du Club Méditerranée*. Paris: Thèse EHESS.

UNAT (2002) *Charte de l'UNAT*. Paris: Union Nationale des Associations de Tourisme.

UNAT (2006) *Le tourisme associatif: une réalité économique et sociale*. Paris: Union Nationale des Associations de Tourisme.

Case Study 5:
Floreal (Joie et Vacances), Belgium

Kim Beuten *PA to the General Manager*

Floreal, Joie et Vacances
Rue Haute 42
1000 Brussels
Belgium
www.florealclub.be

Aims/Mission

Floreal offers coastal and rural holidays in campsites and holiday centres. Via a range programmes, packages and pricing strategies the organisation aims to make the benefits of holidays and recreation accessible to all people.

History

Floreal originated in the 1920s, when the socialist movement started to stimulate holidaymaking among the working classes. In Belgium, this resulted in legislation on paid holidays and the planning of a holiday centre in 1923. This holiday centre, Floreal Blankenberge, opened in 1925, offering cheap family holidays for members of the Socialist Workers' Union. After the Second World War, four further holiday centres were opened: Floreal Malmedy (1964), Floreal La Roche-en-Ardenne (1967), Floreal Nieuwpoort (1978) and Floreal Mont Saint-Aubert (1982). Floreal still operates these five holiday centres, as well as four campsites.

Location

The holiday centres are located both in Flanders (the northern, Dutch-speaking part of Belgium) and in Wallonia (the southern, French-speaking part of Belgium). In Flanders, the holiday centres in Nieuwpoort and Blankenberge are situated near the sea, whereas in Wallonia the centres (La Roche-en-Ardenne, Malmedy and Mont Saint-Aubert) are in rural locations. In Flanders, there are rural campsites (Het Veen and Kempen) in the region around Antwerp, and in Wallonia there are camping opportunities in La Roche-en-Ardenne and Rendeux. The headquarters of the organisation are in Brussels.

Current Activities/Programmes

Floreal offers a wide range of accommodation options, such as hotel rooms, flats with one or two bedrooms, studios, caravans, trekking huts and tents. Holidaymakers can opt for self-catering holidays or they can make use of the restaurants and cafes. The holiday centres and campsites offer a range of indoor and outdoor leisure activities.

Beneficiaries

The Floreal facilities attract clients from a wide range of social groups. Originally the accommodation was available only to members of the Socialist Workers' Union – the aim of the centres was to offer members the opportunity to take an affordable holiday. Over time, however, this restriction was lifted, and nowadays the centres are open to all. Members of the Socialist Union still represent a significant number of holidaymakers, and certain discounts are still available to them. Other groups that are specifically targeted are senior citizens, young (single-parent) families, persons on low incomes, persons with financial problems, young people from different social, cultural, financial backgrounds, and young people with disabilities.

Funding Sources

Floreal receives subsidies from three sources:

- *Flemish tourist authority (Tourism Flanders)*. Floreal meets the criteria to be classified as a centre for social tourism. The subsidies apply to campsites and holiday centres in the Flemish region, and can be used for the part-funding of improvements to infrastructure and the organisation of leisure activities. The employment costs of the coordinator for the holiday centres in Brussels are also partly subsidised by the Flemish tourist authority.
- *Wallonian regional government*. Subsidies from this funding body are awarded for the social tourism services of the campsites and holiday centres in the Wallonian region. The subsidies can be used for the part-funding of investments in infrastructure.
- *Socialist Union*. Those holiday centres and campsites that were originally solely accessible to members of the Socialist Union are managed and coordinated by the not-for-profit organisation Joie et Vacances ('Joy and Holidays'). The activities of this organisation are still partly funded by the Socialist Union.

Role in Social Tourism Provision

Floreal, and its managing organisation Joie et Vacances, was one of the key partners in the establishment of social tourism legislation in Flanders and in Wallonia. The organisation represents the social tourism sector in the media, and has a lobbying function at the level of national government.

Joie et Vacances still plays the role of social tourism lobbyists and advocates in the International Social Tourism Organisation. It aims to promote the principles of social tourism at the international level and to build cooperation with international organisations, for example to establish holiday exchanges.

Finally, Floreal is a responsible tourism employer. The holiday centres and campsites of the Floreal group are open throughout the year, and offer secure, permanent employment to 300 employees.

Areas and Examples of Best Practice

Floreal voluntarily offers reductions to low-income groups in Flanders via the Holiday Participation Centre (Case Study 2). Around 40% of the Belgian population does not have the opportunity to participate in tourism – this non-participation is mostly for financial reasons. It is expected that the economic climate after the global financial crisis of 2007 will cause this figure to rise. Floreal therefore strives to offer accommodation for these groups during certain times of the year at the lowest possible cost.

6 Mobilities and Social Exclusion: Towards a Research Agenda

Kevin Hannam

As noted in other chapters in this volume, the idea of social tourism has been conceptualised in terms that promote the social benefits of tourism for those who have been marginalised or in other ways excluded from participation in tourism. Despite the long history of social tourism development and provision in Europe, the tourism academy has generally had an ambivalent relationship with understanding the social value of tourism and thus relatively little research has been done in this area – particularly by UK researchers – until recently, with scholars having to draw upon evidence from Continental Europe and the Americas (often not translated into the English language). Hence, in countries like the UK, where the prevailing ideology has led to holidays being largely viewed as luxuries, there is a greater emphasis within the social sciences on access to basic elements of leisure, which has been positioned as a right of citizenship. This is in contrast to the situation in France, Germany and other European countries which have placed access to holidaymaking in a more central role in social life. There is little material evidence (conceptual or empirical) in English on the benefits of these provisions. As a consequence, perhaps, there has been a great deal more mainstream social science research into aspects of leisure and social inequalities, as opposed to tourism and social inequalities. In contrast, research in leisure studies has had a much more positive relationship with discourses on quality of life and has therefore embedded issues surrounding social inclusion into its core research trajectory.

The aim of this chapter is to position the debate on social tourism within the wider context of social mobilities and, indeed, perhaps more importantly, immobilities. The central argument of this chapter is that an understanding of social tourism needs to be connected with more everyday issues of social exclusion and social mobility/immobility, since an understanding of the barriers/constraints and other personal and social issues affecting how people get around their everyday environments has consequences for both their everyday travel practices as well as for social tourism policies and services. Moreover, the new mobilities literature has, to date, tended to focus more on elite and middle-class tourism and to neglect the social value of tourism and travel, and so the chapter also seeks to make a call to researchers within the mobilities field to encompass wider issues of immobilities within their theorising, through an engagement with social tourism issues.

Hence, to begin with, I outline the new mobilities 'paradigm' and I argue that, to date, this has tended to focus rather more on the mobile elite than on issues of immobility – despite recognition that researching immobilities is equally important. I then go on to discuss contemporary issues of social exclusion, immobility and leisure before drawing some conclusions on the need for us to relate social tourism to the theoretical mobilities literature for a more nuanced analysis. In order to illustrate this, I draw upon work by a range of authors who have focused in particular on the analysis of children's mobilities. Thus, what I hope to foreground in this chapter is a range of issues concerning the politics of mobility in relation to social tourism discourses and practices. To begin with I outline what has been termed the new mobilities paradigm (Sheller & Urry, 2006) in terms of its relevance for social tourism.

The Mobilities Paradigm

John Urry (2006) has argued that the concept of mobility has become an evocative keyword for life in the 21st century. Peter Adey (2010: 1) has similarly argued that 'mobility is ubiquitous'. Moreover, the concept of mobility has recently become a term which has begun to replace 'tourism' in many academic discourses (Hall, 2005). However, it is not as simple as just replacing the concept of tourism with one of mobility. The contemporary conceptualisation of the term 'mobilities' is much more complex. At the core of the mobilities paradigm is recognition of the importance of movement in all social life, and hence tourism becomes just one aspect of mobility among a range of diverse travel/movement patterns. It has been argued that the concept of mobilities encompasses both the large-scale movements of people, objects, capital and information across the world, as well as the more local processes of daily transportation, movement through public space and the travel of material things within everyday life (Hannam et al., 2006). Thus Sheller and Urry (2004: 1) write in their book *Tourism Mobilities*:

> We refer to 'tourism mobilities', then, not simply to state the obvious (that tourism is a form of mobility), but to highlight that many different mobilities inform tourism, shape the places where tourism is performed, and drive the making and unmaking of tourist destinations. Mobilities of people and objects, airplanes and suitcases, plants and animals, images and brands, data systems and satellites, all go into 'doing' tourism....

Tourism mobilities involve complex combinations of movement and stillness, realities and fantasies, play and work.

Hannam and Knox (2010) have recently argued that the study of *tourism mobilities* involves many interconnections: between tourism and the wider movement of people in terms of migration; between tourism and the use of different modes of transport; between tourism and channels of communication (telecommunications, the internet and so on); and between tourism and the movement of material things such as food, souvenirs or even the spread of disease. However, such mobilities cannot be described without attention to the necessary spatial, infrastructural and institutional *moorings* or places that configure and enable mobilities (Hannam *et al.*, 2006).

A great deal of contemporary critical research into these forms of mobilities has focused on those privileged, mobile persons who have been able to live the dreams of 'hyper-mobility' and 'instantaneous communication', while those who have been left relatively immobile have tended to be overlooked (Hannam *et al.*, 2006). In this context, Tesfahuney (1998: 501) has noted that: 'Differential mobility empowerments reflect structures and hierarchies of power and position by race, gender, age and class, ranging from the local to the global.' Rights to travel, for example, are highly uneven and skewed, even between a single pair of countries (Timothy, 2001). Moreover, there are also new biometric technologies at work in mobility-enabling platforms such as airports that enhance the mobility of some people while restricting the mobility of others, especially as they try to cross borders (Timothy, 2001; Verstraete, 2004; Wood & Graham, 2006). Thus, different types of tourists may have different mobility empowerments: tourists from India, China or Jordan visiting England may have very different entitlements to tourists from England, Germany or France visiting, say, Jordan (Hannam & Knox, 2010). Similarly, a tourist with a restricted financial position will probably have very different mobility empowerments to a tourist with a much higher disposable income. Thus, as we shall see, I will argue that the concept of 'mobility empowerments' is important for our understanding of social tourism.

From the theoretical perspective of mobilities, the analysis of social tourism needs to be (re)positioned within a broader context of human mobility – both spatially and socially. Indeed, it could be argued, further, that much mainstream tourism social science needs to pay attention to the material differences in participation among groups in society. Political, technological, financial and transportation changes have greatly lowered the barriers to mobility for many, but not for all. Nevertheless:

> Those who first experience tourism and travel as children, are probably more likely to become independent youth travellers, and then to take their own children on holiday, and finally to become well-travelled

elderly people. Each round of tourism and travel, at different points in the life course, extends direct experience of particular places and general familiarity with tourism. This in turn establishes the knowledge base and the expectations that will sustain high levels of mobility in later stages of the life course. (Williams & Hall, 2002: 14–15)

The crucial point, as Williams and Hall (2002) argue here, is that the experience of tourism can lead to higher levels of mobility in later life. Hence, the ways in which physical movement pertains to upward and downward social mobility is also pertinent here. Moving between places physically or virtually can be a source of status and power for many travellers and tourists over their life course (see for example, Hannam & Ateljevic, 2008; Hannam & Diekmann, 2010; Richards & Wilson, 2004). Thus, the ability to negotiate and navigate places, technologies and 'gates' enhances the tourism mobilities of some people while reinforcing the immobilities (or demobilisation) of others through various categorisations such as gender, class, race, ethnicity or sexuality (Hannam *et al.*, 2006). However, tourism research, per se, has not as yet paid much attention to these diverse social immobilities. In contrast, much of the literature on leisure and social exclusion has examined issue of immobility and it is to this that I now turn.

Leisure, Social Inequalities and Mobilities

As I argued above, tourism studies have had an ambivalent relationship with the social value of tourism partly because it has been undecided as to whether tourism should be viewed as a universal 'good' or a more ethically situated product (see Butcher, 2003). In contrast, leisure studies have succeeded, particularly in the policy sphere, in having a much more positive engagement with debates on quality of life. For instance, Fred Coalter (1998) developed the analysis of the relationships between leisure and inequalities by examining leisure policy and the welfare state of the 1990s. He questioned the frequently taken for granted assumption that public leisure provision is about the extension of citizenship rights. He noted that Ravenscroft (1993: 39) had argued that 'the state has a social responsibility, regardless of its dominant economic ideology, to provide for the basic leisure needs of society' and, similarly, that Clarke (1992: 119) had argued for the 'universality of leisure rights'. Furthermore, he argued that 'Much theorizing and research [in leisure studies] is concerned to illustrate differential participation patterns (inequality) and identify, usually structural, "constraints" to participation among particular social groups' and that 'leisure is viewed as a site for the *reproduction* (or at least reflection) of wider economic, social and cultural inequalities' (Coalter, 1998: 23).

As a consequence much leisure studies research 'is characterized by *normative theorizing* about how the world *ought* to be in which public leisure provision plays a central role in securing social citizenship' (Coalter, 1998: 23). Indeed, we can see a similar ideology underpinning recent work on the need for social tourism (McCabe, 2009). Coalter suggested that leisure studies' defence of recreational welfare and leisure needs can be critically examined, as they risk proposing welfare without citizenship and overestimate the role of public leisure facilities as a component of citizenship. He concluded that what is needed is a better analysis of the changing relationships between public and commercial provision of leisure facilities. In her critique of Coalter's (1998) work, Rosemary Deem (1999) argued that: 'Social exclusion, although still a major political issue in many countries, is no longer a popular concern either for western politicians or for many social scientists.' She developed her argument based on three sets of separate but related reasons, namely: changes in the welfare state, the part or full privatisation of leisure services; and a shift of emphasis from an analysis of producers of services to consumers of services. Coalter (2000), meanwhile, extended his analysis further to examine the wider notions of social inclusion and exclusion within leisure studies.

In their paper in the *Sociological Review*, Cass *et al.* (2005: 539) argue that 'much of the literature on social exclusion ignores its "spatial" or "mobility" related aspects'. They examine the mobile processes and infrastructures of travel and transport that engender and reinforce social exclusion in contemporary societies through the notion of 'access' to activities, values and goods. They cite Kenyon *et al.* (2002: 200–201), who argue that there is a 'mobility dimension to exclusion', defined as:

> The process by which people are prevented from participating in the economic, political and social life of the community because of reduced accessibility to opportunities, services and social networks, due in whole or in part to insufficient mobility in a society and environment built around the assumption of high mobility.

Hence, they recognise that the low travel horizons of socially excluded people can work to reduce their chances of participating in other forms of everyday mobility, including leisure, tourism and education.

Cass *et al.* (2005: 539) further argue as follows:

> improving access is a complex matter because of the range of human activities that might need to be 'accessed' ... in order to know what is to be accessed the changing nature of travel and communications requires examination, and ... some dimensions of access are only revealed through changes in the infrastructure that 'uncover' previously hidden social exclusions. Claims about access and socio-spatial exclusion routinely make assumptions about what it is to participate effectively in society.

They turn this question around, by asking how different forms of mobilities constitute contemporary societal values and sets of relations, participation in which may become important for social inclusion. In this vein, they note that:

> What is necessary for full 'social' inclusion varies as the means and modes of mobility change and as the potential for 'access' develops with the emergence of new technologies such as charter flights, high speed trains, budget air travel, SUVs, mobile phones, networked computers and so on. These developments transform what is 'necessary' for full social inclusion. (Cass *et al.*, 2005: 542)

Their point is well made. In terms of our understanding of what is necessary for social inclusion in the 21st century, access to some form of vacation has been put forward as an indicator of social exclusion in the UK context. But, more broadly, such a position needs to be situated within a discussion of access to other forms of mobilities. I illustrate this below with reference to recent work on children's mobilities, in particular, because of the importance of children in terms of tourism and leisure motivations (Thornton *et al.*, 1997; Turley, 2001; Connell, 2005; Carr, 2006) as well as the centrality of the concept of the family in contemporary discourses of social tourism (Hazel, 2005; McCabe, 2009; Minnaert *et al.*, 2009). As McCabe (2009: 683) has noted: 'It is also clear that children's experience of new places, activities and "adventures" has the potential to link into education policies and also ... social mobility'.

Children's Mobilities

Over the past decade there has been much interest in researching what have been called 'children's geographies'. This research has emphasised that children and young people should be understood as social agents in their own right at a variety of spatial scales and places (see Holloway & Valentine, 2000; Hopkins & Alexander, 2010; Horschelmann & Schaefer, 2007; Katz, 2004; McKendrick, 2000; Skelton, 2007; Zeilig & Ansell, 2008). Barker *et al.* (2009) note that children's geographers have also explored ideas about where children should or should not spend their leisure time, whether in schools (Kraftl, 2006; Valentine, 2000), playgrounds (Woolley, 2008), urban spaces (Collins & Kearns, 2005; Valentine, 1997), rural spaces (Leyshon, 2008; Tranter & Pawson, 2001; Tucker, 2003), out-of-school care spaces (Smith & Barker, 2001) or other built environments (see Kraftl *et al.*, 2007) and how children's everyday spaces and their identities are co-constitutive (Ansell & van Blerk, 2007; Beazley, 2003; Dwyer, 1999; Holloway *et al.*, 2000; Hopkins, 2006; Horton & Kraftl, 2006). My argument is that studies of social tourism need to take into account the insights of these studies of children's geographies in order to produce a fuller account of the various issues surrounding social mobilities that children and families face.

For example, in their editorial to a special issue of the journal *Mobilities*, Barker *et al.* (2009) note that research in Western countries has shown that in terms of their leisure and tourism activities, children from lower social classes are less likely to have space to play at home, and are often more likely to spend time unsupervised outdoors (Matthews, 1992). In contrast, more affluent children often participate in more institutionalised and commodified leisure and tourism activities (Frønes *et al.*, 2000; Smith & Barker, 2001). Moreover, 'children from higher social class families often have less independent spatial mobility, with higher levels of adult escorted spatial mobility – although such children often succeed in subverting adult imposed rules' (Barker *et al.*, 2009: 4). Barker *et al.* (2009) elaborate a number of ways in which intersections of mobilities and (young) age ought to pose significant questions for future research regarding mobility, and, I would argue, studies of social tourism. Children experience contemporary everyday mobility spaces, such as cars, homes and public spaces, in three distinct ways: independent mobility; global mobility; and controlled mobility (Barker *et al.*, 2009).

In terms of independent mobility, there is a need to analyse, at a micro-level, the everyday multiple material, temporal movements that characterise children's and young people's use of urban and rural tourism and leisure spaces and that underlie particular dynamic life course stages in childhood (Barker, 2003). In this context, Sue Milne (2009) has argued that understanding children's affective and bodily perceptions as well as representations of their expanding public worlds is important for challenging assumptions about what it means to 'grow up'. In the Danish context, Mikkelsen and Christensen (2009) argue that both physical and social environments are complicit in 'patterning' children's mobilities in outdoor leisure and tourism environments. Traditionally, 'independent' mobility has assumed the absence of adults; however, Mikkelsen and Christensen pay attention to the multiple other actors (friends, animals) and knowledge that are incorporated in the conditions of children's movement around everyday outdoor spaces.

Secondly, as Ruddick (2003) suggests, discourses around youth have been increasingly globalised and are increasingly characteristic of Western consumer cultures and lifestyles for all ages. As the boundaries between young and old become increasingly blurred (Valentine, 2003), so the concept of 'youth' has gained ideological, aesthetic, economic and even political pre-eminence:

> There is, then, a key duality at play, wherein the self-reflexive and flexible society (and identity) is also a youthful one. Put simply: flexible, youthful identities privilege certain kinds of mobilities, encompassed by opportunities as diverse as international travel, global communication,

educational status and personal financial power (see Horschelmann and Schaefer, 2007). These identities and opportunities may reflect the global ideal of youth: yet the experience of (and beyond) this ideal is often very different. (Barker *et al.*, 2009: 6)

Hence, any discussion of social tourism needs to pay attention to the global discourses of mobility that have increasingly emphasised the status of travel for young people. A good example of research in this context is Dan Knox's (2009) analysis of youth tourism to the resorts of Ayia Napa in Cyprus and Faliraki in Greece, where he notes the relationships between global music trends and the iconographies of youth tourism. While the hedonistic nature of much of this mass tourism has been heavily criticised, it is important to note its importance for much youth culture and hence youth tourism. There are links to be explored here between global mobilities and social inclusion agendas through social tourism initiatives aimed at young travellers (or indeed at other target groups).

Thirdly, there is a need to attend to the multiple modalities of control that surround children's mobilities. Social theorists have become increasingly concerned with analysing the development of the society of control (Deleuze, 1990) and the manipulation of mobilities, performances and emotions by what have been termed 'affective technologies' and architectures (Adey, 2007, 2008; Kraftl & Adey, 2008; Thrift, 2004). For example, recently some researchers have paid attention to the way in which migrant minors and children who become trapped in asylum systems attempt to develop their mobilities in the face of government controls (see Crawley, 2010; Mai, 2010). Indeed, there is a need to examine further the controlled tourism mobilities (or the lack of them) of particularly excluded groups such as child migrants as part of a broader social tourism research agenda.

Conclusions

We have seen how the idea of social tourism has been conceptualised in terms of the broad movement, particularly in Europe, to highlight the social benefits of tourism for those who have been marginalised in society (McCabe, 2009; Minnaert *et al.*, 2009). Research in leisure studies, meanwhile, has had a much more engaged relationship with quality of life and has foregrounded issues of social inequalities and social exclusion. The aim of this chapter has been to position the debate on social tourism within the wider context of social mobilities and immobilities. The central argument of this chapter, then, has been that an understanding of social tourism cannot be divorced from more mainstream social science debates on social exclusion and social mobility/immobility. To begin with, this chapter outlined the new mobilities 'paradigm' and I argued that this has tended to overlook issues of immobility, as much research had focused on the mobile elite. It then went on to discuss contemporary issues of leisure and social inequalities and social exclusion, before developing the argument for the need for researchers to relate social tourism to the theoretical mobilities literature for a more nuanced analysis of the former. In order to illustrate this, I have discussed recent work that has focused on the analysis of children's mobilities. In particular, notions of independent mobility, global mobility and controlled mobility are important for a fuller understanding of children's life-worlds and as a consequence social tourism policies and practices. On the one hand, research in social tourism can contribute to the wider discourse on mobilities and can further develop understanding of particular contexts and consequences of immobility and tourism's relationship to social inclusion. On the other hand, social tourism researchers can benefit greatly from drawing upon mobilities theory in shaping new research agendas as outlined in the example of children's mobilities above. Thus, what I hope to have emphasised in this chapter is the importance of wider issues concerning the politics of mobility in relation to social tourism discourses and practices.

References

Adey, P. (2007) 'May I have your attention': airport geographies of spectatorship, position and (im)mobility. *Environment and Planning D: Society and Space*, 25(3): 515–536.

Adey, P. (2008) Airports, mobility, and the calculative architecture of affective control. *Geoforum*, 39(1): 438–451.

Adey, P. (2010) *Mobility*. London: Routledge.

Ansell, N. and van Blerk, L. (2007) Doing and belonging: toward a more-than-representational account of young migrant identities in Lesotho and Malawi. In R. Panelli, S. Punch and E. Robson (eds), *Global Perspectives on Rural Childhood and Youth: Young Rural Lives* (pp. 17–28). London: Routledge.

Barker, J. (2003) Passengers or political actors? Children's participation in transport policy and the micropolitical geographies of the family, *Space and Polity*, 7(2): 135–152.

Barker, J., Kraftl, P., Horton, J. and Tucker, F. (2009) Editorial. The road less travelled – new directions in children's and young people's mobility. *Mobilities*, 4(1): 1–10.

Beazley, H. (2003) The construction and protection of individual and collective identities by street children and youth in Indonesia. *Children, Youth and Environments*, 13(1): unpaginated. Online at http://www.colorado.edu/journals/cye/13_1/Vol13_1Articles/CYE_CurrentIssue_Article_ChildrenYouthIndonesia_Beazley.htm.

Butcher, J. (2003) *The Moralisation of Tourism: Sun, Sand ... and Saving the World?* London: Routledge.

Carr, N. (2006) A comparison of adolescents' and parents' holiday motivations and desires. *Tourism and Hospitality Research*, 6(2): 129–142.

Cass, N., Shove, E. and Urry, J. (2005) Social exclusion, mobility and access. *Sociological Review*, 53: 539–555.

Clarke, A. (1992) Citizens and consumers. In J. Sugden and C. Knox (eds), *Leisure in the 1990s: Rolling Back the Welfare State* (pp. 109–120). Leisure Studies Association Publication no. 46, Eastbourne: Leisure Studies Association.

Coalter, F. (1998) Leisure studies, leisure policy and social citizenship: the failure of welfare or the limits of welfare? *Leisure Studies*, 17(1): 21–36.

Coalter, F. (2000) Public and commercial leisure provision: active citizens and passive consumers? *Leisure Studies*, 19(3): 163–181.

Collins, D. and Kearns, R. (2005) Geographies of inequality: child pedestrian injury and walking school buses in Auckland, New Zealand. *Social Science and Medicine*, 60(1): 61–69.

Connell, J. (2005) Toddlers, tourism and Tobermory: destination marketing issues and television-induced tourism. *Tourism Management*, 26(5): 763–776.

Crawley, H. (2010) 'No one gives you a chance to say what you are thinking': finding spaces for children's agency in the UK asylum system. *Area*, 42(2): 162–169.

Deem, R. (1999) How do we get out of the ghetto? Strategies for research on gender and leisure for the twenty-first century. *Leisure Studies*, 18(3): 161–177.

Deleuze, G. (1990) Postscript on the societies of control. *L'Autre Journal* (1). Online at http://www.abdn.ac.uk/modern/node/109.

Dwyer, C. (1999) Contradictions of community: questions of identity for young British Muslim women. *Environment and Planning A*, 31(1): 53–68.

Frønes, I., Jenks, C., Qvortrup, J., Rizzini, I. and Thorne, B. (2000) Editorial. Children's places and spaces in the world. *Childhood*, 7(1): 5–9.

Hall, C.M. (2005) *Tourism: Rethinking the Social Science of Mobility*. Harlow: Pearson.

Hannam, K. and Ateljevic, I. (eds) (2008) *Backpacker Tourism*. Clevedon: Channel View Publications.

Hannam, K. and Diekmann, A. (2010) *Beyond Backpacker Tourism*. Bristol: Channel View Publications.

Hannam, K. and Knox, D. (2010) *Understanding Tourism*. London: Sage.

Hannam, K., Sheller, M. and Urry, J. (2006) Editorial. Mobilities, immobilities and moorings. *Mobilities*, 1(1): 1–22.

Hazel, N. (2005) Holidays for children and families in need: an exploration of the research and policy context for social tourism in the UK. *Children and Society*, 19(3): 225–236.

Holloway, S. and Valentine, G. (eds) (2000) *Children's Geographies: Playing, Living, Learning*. London: Routledge.

Holloway, S., Valentine, G. and Bingham, N. (2000) Institutionalising technologies: masculinities, femininities and the heterosexual economy of the IT classroom. *Environment and Planning A*, 32(3): 617–633.

Hopkins, P. (2006) Youthful Muslim masculinities: gender and generational relations. *Transactions of the Institute of British Geographers*, 31(3): 337–352.

Hopkins, P. and Alexander, C. (2010) Politics, mobility and nationhood: upscaling young people's geographies. *Area* 42(2): 142–144.

Horschelmann, K. and Schaefer, N. (2007) 'Berlin is not a foreign country, stupid!' – Growing up 'global' in Eastern Germany. *Environment and Planning A*, 39(8): 1855–1872.

Horton, J. and Kraftl, P. (2006) Not just growing up, but going on: children's geographies as becomings; materials, spacings, bodies, situations. *Children's Geographies*, 4(3): 259–276.

Katz, C. (2004) *Growing Up Global: Economic Restructuring and Children's Everyday Lives*. Minneapolis, MN: University of Minnesota Press.

Kenyon, S., Lyons, G. and Rafferty, J. (2002) Transport and social exclusion: investigating the possibility of promoting inclusion through virtual mobility. *Journal of Transport Geography*, 10(3): 207–219.

Knox, D. (2009) Mobile practice and youth tourism. In P. Obrador, M. Crang and P. Travlou (eds), *Cultures of Mass Tourism* (pp. 143–156). Farnham: Ashgate.

Kraftl, P. (2006) Building an idea: the material construction of an ideal childhood, *Transactions of the Institute of British Geographers*, 31(4): 488–504.

Kraftl, P. and Adey, P. (2008) Architecture/affect/inhabitation: geographies of being in buildings. *Annals of the Association of American Geographers*, 98(1): 213–231.

Kraftl, P., Horton, J. and Tucker, F. (2007) Special issue of *Built Environment – Children, Young People and Built Environments*, 33(4).

Leyshon, M. (2008) The betweeness of being a rural youth: inclusive and exclusive lifestyles. *Social and Cultural Geography*, 9(1): 1–26.

Mai, N. (2010) The politicisation of migrant minors: Italo-Romanian geopolitics and EU integration. *Area*, 42(2): 181–189.

Matthews, H. (1992) *Making Sense of Place: Children's Understandings of Large-Scale Environments*. Hemel Hempstead: Harvester Wheatsheaf.

McCabe, S. (2009) Who needs a holiday? Evaluating social tourism. *Annals of Tourism Research*, 36(4): 667–688.

McKendrick, J. (2000) The geography of children: an annotated bibliography. *Childhood*, 7(3): 359–387.

Mikkelsen, M. and Christensen, P. (2009) Is children's independent mobility really independent? A study of children's mobility combining ethnography and GPS/mobile phone technologies. *Mobilities*, 4(1): 37–58.

Milne, S. (2009) Moving into and through the public world: children's perspectives on their encounters with adults. *Mobilities*, 4(1): 103–118.

Minnaert, L., Maitland, R. and Miller, G. (2009) Tourism and social policy: the value of social tourism. *Annals of Tourism Research*, 36(2): 316–334.

Ravenscroft, N. (1993) Public leisure provision and the good citizen. *Leisure Studies*, 12(1): 33–44.

Richards, G. and Wilson, J. (eds) (2004) *The Global Nomad*. Clevedon: Channel View Publications.

Ruddick, S. (2003) The politics of aging: globalization and the restructuring of youth and childhood. *Antipode*, 35(2): 334–362.

Sheller, M. and Urry, J. (eds) (2004) *Tourism Mobilities: Places to Play, Places in Play*. London: Routledge.

Sheller, M. and Urry, J. (2006) The new mobilities paradigm. *Environment and Planning A*, 38(2): 207–226.

Skelton, T. (2007) Children, young people, UNICEF and participation. *Children's Geographies*, 5(1): 165–181.

Smith, F. and Barker, J. (2001) Commodifying the countryside: the impact of out-of-school care on rural landscapes of children's play. *Area*, 33(2): 169–179.

Tesfahuney, M. (1998) Mobility, racism and geopolitics. *Political Geography*, 17(5): 499–515.

Thornton, P., Shaw, G. and Williams, A. (1997) Tourist group holiday decision-making and behaviour: the influence of children. *Tourism Management*, 18(5): 287–297.

Thrift, N. (2004) Intensities of feeling: towards a spatial politics of affect. *Geografiska Annaler Series B*, 86(1): 57–78.

Timothy, D.J. (2001) *Tourism and Political Boundaries*. London: Routledge.

Tranter, P. and Pawson, E. (2001) Children's access to local environments: a case study of Christchurch, New Zealand. *Local Environment*, 6(1): 27–48.

Tucker, F. (2003) Sameness or difference? Exploring girls' use of recreational spaces. *Children's Geographies*, 1(1): 111–124.

Turley, S. (2001) Children and the demand for recreational experiences: the case of zoos. *Leisure Studies*, 20(1): 1–18.

Urry, J. (2006) *Mobilities*. Cambridge: Polity.

Valentine, G. (1997) 'Oh yes I can' 'Oh no you can't': children and parents' understandings of kids' competence to negotiate public space safely. *Antipode*, 29(1): 65–89.

Valentine, G. (2000) Exploring children and young people's narratives of identity. *Geoforum*, 31(2): 257–267.

Valentine, G. (2003) Boundary crossings: transitions from childhood to adulthood. *Children's Geographies*, 1(1): 37–52.

Verstraete, G. (2004) Technological frontiers and the politics of mobility in the European Union. In S. Ahmed, C. Castaneda, A.M. Fortier and M. Sheller (eds), *Uprootings/Regroundings: Questions of Home and Migration* (pp. 225–250). London: Berg.

Williams, A. and Hall, C.M. (2002) Tourism, migration, circulation and mobility. In C.M. Hall and A. Williams (eds), *Tourism and Migration* (pp. 1–52). Dordrecht: Kluwer.

Wood, D. and Graham, S. (2006) Permeable boundaries in the software-sorted society: surveillance and the differentiation of mobility. In M. Sheller and J. Urry (eds), *Mobile Technologies of the City* (pp. 177–191). London: Routledge.

Woolley, H. (2008) Watch this space! Designing for children's play in public open spaces. *Geography Compass*, 2(2): 495–512.

Zeilig, L. and Ansell, N. (2008) Spaces and scales of African student activism: Senegalese and Zimbabwean university students at the intersection of campus, nation and globe. *Antipode*, 40(1): 31–54.

Case Study 6: The Sunshine Fund, Ireland

Tom MacMahon *Vice-President and Head of the Children's Department*

The Sunshine Fund.
4th Floor SVP House,
91–92 Sean MacDermott Street
Dublin 1
Ireland
Sunshine@svpdublin.ie
http://www.sunshinefund.ie

Aims/Mission

The Sunshine Fund is a special works conference of the Society of St Vincent de Paul (SVP), the largest voluntary, charitable organisation in Ireland. The SVP nationally aims to tackle all forms of poverty, disadvantage or social exclusion and is involved in a diverse range of activities to help achieve this. The Sunshine Fund contributes to the SVP's overall mission by primarily organising week-long residential summer holidays for children living in areas of disadvantage throughout Dublin and surrounding counties.

Many families living in disadvantage cannot afford a holiday, a fact which is accepted by the UK Department for Work and Pensions as an indicator of both adult and child material deprivation. The benefits of holidays have been extensively examined, and include (Hazel, 2005):

- relief from routine or stressful situations;
- improvement in physical and psychological health;
- opportunities for social interactions with new people;
- broadening of experiences;
- developing independence in a safe environment;
- strengthening relationships with friends and siblings.

The Sunshine Fund believes that children living in areas of disadvantage should not miss out on these benefits and positive effects, which society often takes for granted. We aim to achieve all of these outcomes for each child we work with, improving their quality of life and providing a standard of care equalling or exceeding that offered by the child's own parents or guardians.

Specifically, we believe that the most beneficial aspect of a Sunshine holiday is the unique personal interest and positive attention that our volunteers show towards the children. Just as importantly for some, these holidays form a break from poor home environments, where bullying and corrosive anti-social behaviour are significant daily stressors. Finally, Sunshine gives all children a valuable opportunity to interact with peers from other areas of the city and country, and of differing ethnic origins, such as refugees or the travelling community, facilitating the breakdown of artificial barriers.

History

In the 1920s and 1930s, the inner-city slums of Dublin were regarded as among the worst in Europe. An official survey in 1914 conservatively estimated that 87,000 (20%) of the capital's inhabitants were living in tenements in the city centre, with over 80% of those families occupying a single room. The appalling conditions had a disproportionately large effect on children: infant mortality was high, tuberculosis and measles were rife and malnutrition common – so much so that Dublin's death rate rivalled that of Calcutta.

Against this bleak backdrop, concerned individuals recognised that children growing up in this environment were being denied their childhood. Determined to bring a little sunshine into the lives of young people living among the dark slums and narrow lanes, in 1928 they began by organising day trips to the seaside, where fresh air, good food and sandy beaches offered a chance to escape briefly the conditions at home only a few miles away: the Sunshine Fund was born.

To meet the obvious need, in 1935 the programme was significantly expanded through the purchase and conversion of a house in Balbriggan, a small seaside town about 25 miles north of Dublin city. Rochfort House was renamed Sunshine House, a name which would become familiar to generations of Irish children.

Through the 1940s, living conditions in Dublin remained poor, but the Sunshine Fund continued to serve the youngest members of the community. During the war years, children would bring their ration tickets to allow the Fund to buy the food that would be needed during the holiday; the Fund's name also cropped up at national level in a Dáil (parliamentary) debate on tuberculosis sanatoria in 1945. In the 1970s and 1980s, the spectre of drug addiction cast a long shadow over many neighbourhoods, but we maintained our tradition of care. Through the late 1990s and early 2000s, Ireland's much heralded economic boom left many behind; yet the Fund continued to support thousands of young people who had been forgotten in the rush towards economic prosperity.

Today, the need and demand for the service we offer is stronger than ever. Barnardos estimated in 2009 that over 90,000 Irish children (8.7%) lived in consistent poverty and current difficult economic circumstances are sure to see this figure rise. Over 75 years after we were founded, the Sunshine Fund still plays a uniquely valuable role.

Location

Our head office is in the heart of inner-city Dublin, in the headquarters building of the SVP, surrounded by the council flat complexes where many of our young guests live.

Our state-of-the-art holiday centre is in Balbriggan, north County Dublin. Situated conveniently close to beaches, playgrounds and shops, it is set in five acres of landscaped grounds. Indoors, we can accommodate over 120 children in single beds, looked after by a team of up to 20 volunteers and supported by kitchen and laundry staff. We have significantly upgraded our indoor and outdoor play areas to ensure that the holiday experience we offer is unrivalled.

Current Activities/Programmes

We primarily organise eight-day seaside breaks (Saturday to Saturday) for boys and girls who might otherwise never get a holiday. Groups of up to 100 children travel with us each week for the duration of the holiday season, which normally runs from mid-May to late August each year – over 1200 young people have the holiday of a lifetime with us annually. We estimate that we have hosted over 100,000 children since we were founded.

We also organise holiday weekends at other times of the year, and entertain children at specially organised Christmas parties each December.

The Fund is managed and the holiday programme delivered exclusively by volunteers, supported by a small number of paid household staff. That team of over 200 volunteers of all ages and walks of life give up a full week of their time to care for and play with our young guests, entertaining them from when they wake up until they go to bed, by organising football and basketball leagues, sand-castle competitions, marathons, arts and crafts, treasure hunts and a whole range of other activities.

Beneficiaries

We aim to provide high-quality social tourism activities for children aged 7–11 years living in areas of disadvantage. We focus primarily on children from Dublin and surrounding counties, although we have hosted children from as far away as Limerick, Tipperary and Louth. Children are invited on holidays with their siblings or cousins, if they are within the designated age range, and more generally with other children attending their school or living in their area. We mix several different areas together each week to facilitate integration. Parents do not accompany their children on holidays.

Funding Sources

Providing everything for the perfect holiday at Sunshine House requires approximately €400,000 annually, but we do not charge parents, to ensure that all children who would benefit are able to travel with us. We receive no government support. Instead, we rely entirely on the efforts of our team of volunteers and the generosity of the people of Dublin to generate the funds we need every year. Our major fundraising event is the annual

'Advocate' collection held on Palm Sunday outside every church in the Dublin archdiocese, supported by our national parent body, the SVP. This raises about €230,000; other fundraising initiatives, donations, legacies, subscriptions and bequests make up the remainder of our budget.

Role in Social Tourism Provision

We have extensive partnerships with organisations across the country that work with us by nominating children for holidays at Sunshine House. We are very active in a large number of schools across the Dublin area, and also work with social workers, refugee, homeless and traveller organisations, youth and community groups and other organisations such as Barnardos or the Irish Society for the Prevention of Cruelty to Children. Members of our parent organisation (SVP) also make referrals for families they work with. Lastly, parents can apply directly to us if they wish their children to be considered for the holiday programme.

Areas and Examples of Best Practice

The Sunshine Fund is committed to best practice in the delivery of social tourism. As part of that process, in 2006 we worked with a research team from the Tourism Research Centre at Dublin Institute of Technology, facilitating them in conducting qualitative research into the impact of holidays as part of social tourism (Quinn *et al.*, 2008). Their rigorous independent analysis of the benefits associated with the work we do vindicated our longheld belief of the importance of Sunshine holidays. To quote their research paper:

> structured, child-centred holidays ... broadened children's social horizons; created opportunities to learn and acquire new skills; offered exposure to positive role models and promoted positive behavioural change. In addition, further benefits were generated for guardians and the wider family unit.

As leaders in social tourism for children in Ireland, the Sunshine Fund will continue to define, develop and follow best practice in this area.

References

Hazel, N. (2005) Holidays for children and families in need: an exploration of the research and policy context for social tourism in the UK. *Children and Society*, 19(3): 225–236.

Quinn, B., Griffin, K.A. and Stacey, J. (2008) *Poverty, Social Exclusion and Holidaying: Towards Developing Policy in Ireland* (Research Working Paper 08/01). Dublin: Combat Poverty Agency.

7 The Welfare Society and Tourism: European Perspectives

Derek Hall and Frances Brown

This chapter attempts to provide the context for the right to travel, recognised by a number of welfare state regimes in Europe, and its recent erosion. It addresses the links between welfare, inequalities and access to leisure time. Different European models are discussed, with an emphasis on the experience of Central and Eastern Europe. It is concluded that recent international financial crises are likely to place increasing short- to medium-term pressures on European welfare provision, suggesting a further convergence of (European Union) welfare systems and the marginalisation of access to holiday provision as a subsidised welfare good.

Access to Leisure Travel as Welfare

The consumption of tourism in different regions and between different social groups can be shaped significantly by welfare state structures and policies, either directly through the recognition of holidays as a social right, or indirectly through redistributive mechanisms (Hamnett, 1996). Following the piecemeal dismantling of welfare state regimes, the promotion of holidays as an element of the quality of life has become more problematic (Hall & Brown, 2006). In the last decades of the 20th century, tourism was promoted more for its beneficial economic externalities than for the health and social benefits that had justified an extension of vacation rights in the past. The productivist approach to tourism and leisure viewed holidays not only as a necessary support for work, but as a source of employment and income generation in themselves (Richards, 1999). This productivist role has been further emphasised in the redistributive assumptions of such concepts as pro-poor and volunteer tourism. Yet the health and welfare paradigm can be identified in a refocus on the 'self' (in contradistinction to 'the Other') through a growth in health, medical, wellness, spiritual and related areas of tourism product and experience (e.g. Seaton, 2002; Sharpley & Sundaram, 2005; Singh, 2009; Smith, 2003).

That opportunities to go on holiday should be treated as an important indicator of social wellbeing was emphasised more than two decades ago by Haukeland (1990), who interviewed non-travellers in Norway to investigate a causal relationship between social welfare and holiday opportunities. He argued that if one's personal or household living conditions are 'unsatisfactory', these will, in most cases, restrict the quantity and quality of opportunities available to that individual. Similarly, the boundaries surrounding opportunities open to any individual often extend into the field of holiday travel. Within the perspective of 'social right', there is a fundamental difference between those persons who are obliged to stay at home and those who actually have the opportunity to take a vacation but prefer to remain at home. In the latter case, the main question is whether or not a person's decision to forego travel can be described as an effect of an unsatisfactory social situation (Haukeland, 1990).

Haukeland's conceptualisation viewed the two dichotomies combined in a four-quadrant model. A simple matrix yielded a typology of four different non-travelling characteristics:

1   Persons who are not confronted with any obstacles to going on holiday. Their general social situation is unproblematic and these individuals prefer to stay at home in order to maximise their wellbeing.
2   Social living conditions are satisfactory, but other constraints – either temporary or permanent – prevent individuals from taking holidays.
3   Constrained non-travellers who are placed in an unsatisfactory social situation, such as lack of economic means, health resources or personal freedom. Non-travel under such circumstances reflects social welfare problems, and the lack of opportunity to go on holiday can exacerbate (a sense of) social deprivation.
4   Unconstrained non-travel with unsatisfactory living conditions (an unlikely combination).

What kind of social values does holiday travel represent from the non-traveller's viewpoint? Among those in category 3, Haukeland found that a feeling of lack of change in everyday life seemed to be the most important deprivation. A characteristic shared by most of the members of this category was an expressed desire to have the opportunity to go on holiday. Restricted opportunities for rest and relaxation, both mental and physical, were much emphasised. Other values associated with holiday trips, such as social contacts with other people, getting closer to nature, and access to amusements and entertainment were not emphasised in the same way by the Norwegian group.

Smith and Hughes (1999) found that for families who are rarely able to go on holiday because of personal economic and social circumstances, the meaning and significance of the rare possibilities for holidaymaking emphasised notions of 'change' and of establishing relationships. Haukeland (1990: 182) concluded from his sample that push factors appeared to be more relevant than pull factors for the socially deprived in determining the need to take a holiday.

Overall, however, there has been a limited (English language) literature exploring the welfare consequences of being excluded from tourism and travel as part of 'everyday life'. Similarly constrained in the tourism literature is research on the effects of individuals being restricted to the vicarious experience of leisure travel, such as viewing websites and webcams, reading about other places and cultures, being told about overseas holidays, receiving postcards and holiday souvenir gifts, viewing others' holiday photographs or camcorder videos, watching television holiday programmes or receiving advertising for exotic holidays (Moore *et al.*, 1995: 81).

By contrast, much academic literature has endeavoured to identify, conceptualise and exemplify factors influencing people's motivation to travel for tourism purposes. But in addition to understanding why people choose to travel, it is equally important to know what factors may act as barriers and constraints to travelling, such as lack of time, poor health, disability, financial limitations, safety and security concerns, and a lack of information. In certain circumstances, if the motivation to travel is strong enough, these barriers may be negotiated (Gladwell & Bedini, 2004), so that individuals may perceive themselves as having the freedom to make choices and retain some degree of personal control over their own leisure experiences. Without such feelings of freedom and personal control, tourism cannot be considered to offer the potential for leisure (Iso-Ahola, 1980), and any welfare value is diminished (Cole & Morgan, 2010; Hall & Brown, 2006).

If 'subsidised facilities for the less advantaged can ... be considered as core welfare ideology of the 20th century' (Hjalager, 2005: 46), then the practice and conceptualisation of, and challenges to, such ideology should be an important element of tourism research, not least because of the assumed welfare benefits derived from leisure and tourism.

The individual and collective health and welfare benefits derived from citizens being able to take a holiday have been formally acknowledged in a number of ways. First, at national level, many governments, especially in the developed world, have given legal sanction to vacation rights. Second, at a supranational level, the United Nations has recognised access to rest and leisure as a basic human right since 1948. This was followed by the World Tourism Organization undertaking international declarations on vacation rights and freedom of movement in 1980 and 1982 (see Chapter 1). Further, the World Health Organization includes 'participation in and opportunity for recreation and pastimes' in its quality of life assessments (de Vries, 1996).

The exercising of such acknowledged rights is thus seen by many (in the privileged, developed world at least) as an essential element of their quality of life. But, of course, along with such rights there also come responsibilities. Most critically, while growing numbers of people are taking advantage of their 'right' to vacations and the 'freedom' to travel, they are also increasing fossil fuel consumption and greenhouse gas emissions, contributing to climate change (as well as imposing the oft-documented range of direct impacts on destination areas and cultures). Thus, increasing access to leisure travel for individual health and welfare reasons has wider and arguably paradoxical welfare consequences for the collective future.

Such 'democratisation' of travel in practice means that while the majority of the citizens of the developed world are able to participate in such leisure, those who are unable to do so, for whatever reasons, may be being denied an important element of their (potential) quality of life. And they are likely to experience that quality of life being further eroded by the environmental (and possibly cultural) degradation consequent upon developed world patterns of consumption (including tourism).

Thus, the concept of 'vacation rights' highlights massive global inequalities. For much of the world's population, and notably those citizens of the least developed countries of Africa, Asia and Latin America – global regions receiving increasing numbers of international tourists – the concept may be meaningless and irrelevant, because of their structural poverty, powerlessness and immobility. Indeed, such relative deprivation may be powerfully expressed when brought into contact with the affluence, power and mobility of international tourists, especially if dependency relationships are created through such contiguity.

In contrast, in the developed world, an inability to undertake leisure travel is an inability to participate in a commonly accepted lifestyle. Involuntary non-participation can highlight overall structural socio-economic constraints and may be an indicator of (relative) poverty and (perceived) deprivation (Hughes, 1991). Two decades ago Tony Seaton (1992: 110) argued that, in Britain, 'differential tourism opportunity' was a significant component of socio-economic inequality, and suggested that 'probably 20–30 per cent' of the population, notably the aged and unemployed, had 'little share' in the growth of tourism.

The importance of tourism as an element of consumption and wellbeing is reflected in the movement to gain the right to paid holidays. In Europe, this fell into three general periods (Richards, 1999). First, up to the First World War it was employers who decided whether to grant holidays to their workers. In practice this meant that many manual workers had none.

Second, during the inter-war period social and economic demands of most groups of workers were encouraged, especially after 1936, when the International Labour Organisation (ILO) adopted its first convention on paid holidays. In Switzerland, for example, while in 1910 only 8% of the country's factory workers were entitled to holidays, by 1937 this figure had risen dramatically, to 66% (Teuscher, 1983).

Third, after the Second World War, with prosperity increasing and the development or consolidation of welfare states in a number of countries, the holiday demands of workers met a more favourable response from employers. Legislation was enacted in a number of European states in the 1950s and 1960s guaranteeing minimum periods of paid holiday for workers. In the Netherlands, the average entitlement rose from 13 days a year in 1946 to 25 days in 1972. In France, the pre-war 12-day minimum vacation allowance was extended in 1956 to 18 days, and in 1969 to 24 days, or four weeks (Samuel, 1986, 1993).

The Welfare State in Europe

Two sets of macro-scale observations on the European welfare state are relevant to this discussion. First, several analysts (e.g. Ferrera & Hemerijck, 2003; Leibried, 2000) have recognised a four-fold typology of national welfare regimes within the (pre-2004) European Union (EU). Most significantly, the Scandinavian/Nordic model, developed after the First World War, stresses rights (access to work, health, education, mobility) and the subsidies to support these. By contrast, the German-Austrian-Swiss model, emanating from what Leibried (2000) refers to as the 'Bismarck countries', tends towards compensatory strategies to alleviate social problems and the social impacts of market failure. The 'Anglo-Saxon' and Southern European types – offering lower and lowest levels of social welfare support – complete the range of 'traditional' models. Within Europe, however, there is emerging an overlapping and to some extent cross-cutting converging continuum rather than a series of discrete model types.

The second observation, however, as noted by a number of authors (e.g. Ferrera & Hemerijck, 2003; Kautto & Kvist, 2002; Rhodes, 1995), points to a degree of convergence of welfare systems through restructuring. This has entailed a weakening of the Nordic model in particular, through what Rhodes (1995) refers to as 'subversive liberalism'. This is attributed to a range of factors: globalisation – especially greater international capital mobility; European integration and competitiveness; and domestic economic and political pressures. Sinn (1998), for example, warned that in pursuit of the realisation of the EU's 'four liberties' – the free movement of capital, labour, goods and services across its internal borders – increased mobility of production factors incurred the risk of dismantling the welfare state.

Nevertheless, Kautto and Kvist (2002) maintain that parallel trends in different welfare states have contributed to a persistent diversity of welfare regimes in Europe. While the EU's competence in tourism continues to be the source of some debate (e.g. see Anastasiadou, 2006), the translating of welfare policy into leisure opportunity remains a national domestic prerogative for central, regional and local governance.

International Differences in Access to Holidays

Within this European context, major structural differences continue to exist between countries in terms of holiday entitlement, such that access to holidays is not distributed equally between nations. European surveys undertaken in the mid-1980s within the then EEC (Faits et Opinions, 1987, cited in Haukeland, 1990: 173), suggested that 44% of the Community's population did not go on holiday in 1985. National extremes in such a figure ranged from 35% in the Netherlands to 69% in Portugal. About half were classified as 'permanent' non-travellers, that is, who did not intend taking a holiday the following year. They were characterised as being relatively old, manual workers, fishermen, farmers, those in the lowest income quartile and rural dwellers. Social class differences between countries were highlighted in that only 16% of the wealthiest quarter of the populations of Britain and France were non-travellers, while 91% of the poorest quarter of Portugal's population fell into this category. Nearly half (44%) of all non-travellers cited lack of financial ability as the reason for not taking a holiday. Richards (1999) reported levels of annual holidaymaking in Spain at 53% of the population, compared with 78% in the Netherlands.

Not all European nations have formalised holidays as a social right. In the UK, for example, they have been subject to collective or individual negotiation, with the result that entitlements have tended to be lower than in other West European countries (Rathkey, 1990). The trans-Atlantic ethic behind this discrepancy was articulated in 2005, when the UK government opposed the European Parliament's vote to phase out the UK's opt-out clause from the European Working Time Directive's ceiling of a 48-hour working week (Castle, 2005).

The UK aside, the pattern of holiday entitlement in much of Europe contrasts sharply with that of the economies in North America and Japan. Having achieved a 40-hour work week in 1940, well ahead of their European counterparts, US workers did not succeed in gaining significant subsequent holiday entitlements. Most US workers can expect two weeks of vacation a year – less than half the entitlement of workers in some Northern European countries (Sunoo, 1996). For example, by the early 21st century Americans were working an average of 25.1 hours per week, compared with a German average of 18.6 hours, and the average American worked 46.2 weeks per year compared with the French average of 40 (Alesina et al., 2005; see also Cushman et al., 2005). Schor (1991) attributed the post-war divergence between America and Europe to the tendency for Americans to invest increases in productivity in greater consumption rather than in an extension of their leisure time.

By contrast, a decade and a half ago research in Germany indicated that leisure and vacations had become more important life spheres for most people than work or politics (Tokarski & Michels, 1996). In the Netherlands workers have had an advantage in that the system actively encourages saving money for holidays. The *vakantietoeslag*, or vacation money 'saved' for most workers by their employers, had increased to 8% of annual salaries by the mid-1990s (Richards, 1999).

In spite of the increasing spread of tourism consumption, holidays are still a contested element of social rights in many parts of the world. Work is still the most important aspect of most people's lives. Although the holiday time available to many people has increased, Richards (1999) discerned that a ceiling appeared to have been reached in many countries in terms of the proportion of the population who can take holidays in any year. In the UK and France this proportion seems to be around 60%, whereas in the Netherlands participation seems to have levelled off at around 75%. Further extensions of tourism participation have been precluded by the dismantling of the welfare state in a number of social democratic and corporatist states.

For 2009, one Europe-wide survey (Gallup Organisation, Hungary, 2010) concluded that 33% of EU citizens did not travel for leisure purposes during the year. Such a proportion was highest in certain countries of Central, Eastern and Southern Europe – Romania (51%), Latvia (54%), Hungary (57%) and Malta (58%) – with Portugal (48%) and Italy (44%) somewhat better positioned. The largest proportion cited financial reasons for their position. Twenty-one per cent of the sample were certain they would not take a holiday in 2010, the countries with the highest rates in this category being Turkey (44%), Hungary (40%), Slovakia (36%), Malta and Italy (both 35%).

On the basis of time and money availability, Richards (1999) identified three broad groups of societies regarding constraints on holidaymaking:

- Less developed countries: 'time poor and money poor'. Most people have relatively little leisure time and lack the financial means to engage in tourism.
- Northern Europeans: 'time rich and money rich'. Large parts of the population have relatively few constraints on their ability to take vacations. Southern Europeans have similar vacation entitlements but generally have lower standards of living.
- America and Japan: 'time poor and money rich'. Many people have few financial constraints but relatively severe time constraints.

Differences Within Countries?

The time and money structures that produce significant differences in tourism consumption between nations are also evident to a lesser extent within nations. In fact, the convergence evident in vacation consumption between European countries in some cases has masked increasing inequalities in the distribution of leisure time and income within nations.

In Europe, at least, there is a dual trend towards increasing convergence of tourism consumption between nations, fed by rising incomes in some poorer nations, and increasing divergence of tourism consumption between social groups within nations as a result of income polarisation (Richards, 1999). How have successive EU enlargements to 2007 and the availability of relatively cheap air travel since the mid-1990s influenced these trends? Has the latter phenomenon broadened accessibility to tourism consumption, and/or has the continued 'hollowing out' of the state and erosion of welfare systems across Europe encouraged greater disparities in quality-of-life experiences?

Models of Social Tourism in Europe

As noted earlier in this book, social tourism can be defined as 'the relationships and phenomena in the field of tourism resulting from participation in travel by economically weak or otherwise disadvantaged elements of society' (C.M. Hall, 2000: 141).

Hans Teuscher (1983) identified three models of social tourism in Europe. First was the Northern European model. Here, institutions of social tourism were essentially holiday organisations for everybody: applying commercial principles, they catered on a practical basis for the holiday wishes of people with small budgets. 'Pleasure' was a principal objective, with educational aims and public influence not prominent. Indeed, in Scandinavian countries, the concept of 'social tourism' has meant that everybody, regardless of economic or social situation, should have the opportunity to take a holiday.

Subsequent research, by, for example Anne-Mette Hjalager (2004, 2005, 2006), has highlighted how far a Nordic model of social tourism has persisted in the face of the diminution of welfare states across Europe. She indicates, for example, how both internal and external driving forces are continuously challenging the Danish welfare model (Hjalager, 2006: 7). Hjalager (2005: 46) argues that, in the face of economic and political pressure to further diminish welfare statism, 'only an international approach to the idea of social tourism can re-establish the formerly so favourable innovative trajectories'.

Second, Teuscher (1983) noted that Mediterranean (and Alpine) Europe possessed a structure of social tourism that remained a distinct tourist activity even though the ways of life of different socio-economic classes were converging.

Third, in Central and Eastern Europe under state socialism, 'social' domestic tourism and recreation were employed as a means of improving the health and welfare of the labour force while inspiring them with a sense of local and national patriotic pride (Hall, 1991: 82–89).

The Evolution of Social Tourism under State Socialism

In socialist societies where both social and spatial mobility were inhibited to varying degrees – through such instruments as internal passport systems, exit visa requirements and employment exclusion threats – such opportunities were heavily subsidised from the workplace by enterprises or trade unions in terms of transport and accommodation, although fairly rigid methods of allocation were employed that favoured urban industrial families (Pearlman, 1990). Provision thereby excluded a substantial element of the rural population, who were viewed mechanically as low-cost producers of food for the urban-industrial proletariat, rendering them unsubsidised and relatively immobile.

Such a system of assured markets and limited funding for the upgrading of facilities often resulted in notoriously poor service quality. This phenomenon tended to overflow into the international tourism provision sector.

Despite the human rights clauses of the 1975 Helsinki Accords, strictly limited numbers of citizens were permitted to travel to the capitalist world. Currency inconvertibility, restricted access to hard currency and stringent vetting and exit visa policies proscribed most forms of extra-bloc tourism. Thus outbound tourism was socially and spatially distorted, being dominated by exchanges of 'friendship groups' between severely prescribed like-minded countries. Until 1989 it was easier, for example, for citizens of Bulgaria to travel several thousand kilometres to take a holiday in Vietnam or Cuba than to cross the Bulgarian border into capitalist Greece. Such international social tourism nonetheless provided opportunities for socialist youth to travel. For example, one of the present authors once encountered a number of brigades of FDJ East German Communist Youth engaged in solidarity voluntary work in Cuba.

Indeed, 'volunteer tourism' was an integral component of intra-bloc social tourism, and offers an interesting precedent for the current fashionability (at least in the West) of the activity (e.g. McGehee & Santos, 2005; Sin, 2009; Wearing, 2001). A distinctive form of domestic 'volunteer tourism' was also a characteristic of some of the more centralised regimes of Central and Eastern Europe. For example, in Albania 'volunteer' youth brigades were despatched to remoter regions of the country for the declared purposes of recreation and character building, to gain a better knowledge of their own country and fellow citizens (thereby encouraging the inter-regional marriage of young people to help overcome regional particularism) and, not least, to aid construction work (notably agricultural hillside terracing, or the laying of new railway lines, often alongside well supervised local convict labour) (Hall, 1975, 1984).

Members of the *nomenklatura* with access to convertible currency, however, were able to travel to the capitalist world and to profit from the patronage and privileges flowing from such access. There were clearly several layers of tourist and recreational underclass as a consequence of prevailing social, economic and political relations (Hall, 2001):

- those unable to afford or gain access to domestic tourism because of their structural and/or spatial positions within the economy (essentially the rural peasantry);
- those workers denied access to overseas vacations within the socialist bloc because of their structural position, lack of access to hard currency or record of non-compliance (or combinations of these factors);
- those denied access to non-bloc overseas visits because of their lack of ideological or bureaucratic status and connections, which comprised most of the population.

In the later stages of European state socialism, domestic tourism became more sophisticated, with rising levels of car and rural second-home ownership in the more advanced economies. Opportunities to organise individualised holidays grew considerably. Intra-bloc international flows also became more complex, relating not only to recognised tourist areas but also to increasing levels of diaspora tourism. This resulted from loosening constraints on minorities wishing to visit friends and relatives located on the other side of international boundaries, together with influences from emigrant communities in North America, Western Europe, Australasia and other diaspora regions.

Subsequent political change further reordered priorities. Although a residual of collective provision remained in the early years of post-communism to provide low-cost holidays (e.g. Bachvarov, 2006: 248; Williams & Baláz, 2001), with mass privatisation, ability to pay became the major criterion for access to domestic tourism. This was severely undermined by national and local inflation, unemployment, various forms of privatisation, subsidy withdrawal, and the imposition of sometimes high rates of value-added tax. New constraints modified pathways of outbound tourism. The 'Iron Curtain' was replaced by a 'dollar curtain' lowered by potential Western host countries out of fear of a flood of Eastern immigrants. The need to secure exit visas from home countries was largely removed, but, despite bilateral and EU-wide agreements, the requirement for hard-currency entry visas, often costing more than a month's income, was imposed by Western governments on the citizens of several post-communist and all remaining state socialist societies.

Complex and often interdependent patterns of mobility arose, whereby in the more developed countries urban to rural migration accelerated (e.g. Brown & Schafft, 2002). By contrast, in some of the less advanced economies of the region, the pent-up demand for rural to urban (and beyond) migration was released (e.g. King, 2005; Sandu, 2005; Turnock, 1999). In these latter conditions, remaining rural dwellers, especially the old, for whom such mobility had not been an option, faced the prospect of being packaged as 'exotic' and 'authentic' objects for the rural tourism gaze, for example in Romania (e.g. Light, 2006: 265–267).

For many citizens of Central and Eastern Europe, post-communist restructuring, privatisation and monetarist policies severely reduced their access to travel and holidays. In Estonia, for example, in 2004 only 54% of the population travelled for holiday purposes across an (Estonian) internal administrative boundary. Of these movements, 44% were day trips without accommodation. Only 6.4% of travellers took holiday trips of four days or more (Briksne, 2005).

Bulgaria witnessed a substantial reduction in the domestic tourism market as a result of the withdrawal of financial support from the state. Most trade union and spa facilities were privatised, some changing their function, and others abandoned. Better-positioned domestic tourists were already accustomed to using commercial accommodation in mountain resorts and seaside locations. By contrast, those less well positioned were adversely affected by short- to medium-term price increases and relatively lower incomes (Bachvarov, 2006).

As a corollary, with depressed incomes, large-scale unemployment and limits to mobility, the many low-spending visitors from former state socialist societies crossing adjacent borders has been a persisting problem for tourism destinations, particularly in East Central Europe. For example, by the end of the 1990s half of all international arrivals in Hungary were day trippers or hikers (Behringer & Kiss, 2004; Puczkó & Rátz, 2006). More than 60% of intending Polish visitors to Bulgaria surveyed in 2005 claimed to have a budget of less than €360 (http://www.bulgaricus.com, cited in Bachvarov, 2006: 247).

Following the preliminaries for, and formal accession to, the EU of 10 former socialist societies in 2004 and 2007 (Coles & Hall, 2005; Smith & Hall, 2006), a substantial flow of labour migration to Western Europe has been one expression of post-communist structural conditions. Indeed, 'freedom of movement' for new EU citizens has created wider potential opportunities (despite the cost differentials) for the citizens of those 10 states. These include educational, cultural and employment opportunities, as well as the possibilities for visiting distant friends and relatives more easily. However, visa requirements for non-EU countries created barriers to cross-border travel for ethnic groups straddling EU external borders. Such impositions have also adversely affected cross-border petty trading and shopping tourism.

Conclusions

The advocates of extending holiday participation have argued that it should not be seen simply as a charitable, altruistic exercise of inclusion, nor as just exploiting a hitherto untapped market, but as an investment in the wellbeing and fabric of society (Hughes, 1991: 195–196). The fact that better-positioned socio-economic groups can take advantage of widening tourism opportunities reinforces the notion that holidays are seen as a positive and necessary part of life. The chapter has drawn on a range of European examples to explore how tourism is linked to public welfare, rights and entitlements in the region. It has shown that the phenomenon has a wide variety of expressions in different European countries, which can be linked to their political history and public attitude to welfare. Considering the rich diversity of state support for tourism in Europe, it comes as no surprise that this is also the region where the question should be coined if tourism is a fundamental human right.

Yet, with heightened budgetary stringency, especially following the banking crisis of 2007 and the consequent global financial crisis, welfare regimes across Europe have been facing further critical constraints, which may act to encourage greater policy convergence while permitting the 'subversive liberalism' of global market forces to pervade ever more comprehensively. As personal discretionary spending – such as that for tourism and leisure – is often the first to be trimmed in financially difficult times, so 'subsidy' for improving access to tourism and leisure is equally vulnerable at a broader level under such circumstances. This suggests the likelihood of the further marginalisation of access to a holiday as a subsidised welfare good within Europe.

References

Alesina, A., Glaeser, E.L. and Sacerdote, B. (2005) *Work and Leisure in the U.S. and Europe: Why So Different?* Working Paper no. 11278. Cambridge, MA: National Bureau of Economic Research.

Anastasiadou, C. (2006) Tourism and the European Union. In D. Hall, M. Smith and B. Marciszewska (eds), *Tourism in the New Europe: The Challenges and Opportunities of EU Enlargement* (pp. 20–31). Wallingford: CABI Publishing.

Bachvarov, M. (2006) Tourism in Bulgaria. In D. Hall, M. Smith and B. Marciszewska (eds), *Tourism in the New Europe: The Challenges and Opportunities of EU Enlargement* (pp. 241–255). Wallingford: CABI Publishing.

Behringer, Z. and Kiss, K. (2004) The role of foreign direct investment in the development of tourism in post-communist Hungary. In D. Hall (ed.), *Tourism and Transition: Governance, Transformation and Development* (pp. 73–81). Wallingford: CABI Publishing.

Briksne, I. (2005) *Survey: Traveler in Latvia*, press release, 17 February. Riga: Central Statistical Bureau of Latvia.

Brown, L.D. and Schafft, K.A. (2002) Population deconcentration in Hungary during the post-socialist transformation. *Journal of Rural Studies*, 18(3): 233–244.

Castle, S. (2005) UK fury over MEP vote to end working time opt-out. *Independent*, 12 May, p. 67.

Cole, S. and Morgan, N. (eds) (2010) *Tourism and Inequality: Problems and Prospects.* Wallingford: CAB International.

Coles, T. and Hall, D. (2005) Tourism and European Union enlargement. Plus ça change? *International Journal of Tourism Research*, 7(2): 51–61.

Cushman, G., Veal, A.J. and Zuzanek, J. (eds) (2005) *Free Time and Leisure Participation: International Perspectives*. Wallingford: CAB International.

de Vries, J. (1996) *Beyond Health Status: Construction and Validation of the Dutch WHO Quality of Life Assessment Instrument*. Unpublished PhD thesis, Tilburg University.

Faits et Opinions (1987) *Europæenes Feriemønster*. Paris: Faits et Opinions.

Ferrera, M. and Hemerijck, A. (2003) Recalibrating Europe's welfare regimes. In J. Zeitling and D.M. Trubek (eds), *Governing Work and Welfare in a New Economy: European and American Experiments* (pp. 88–128). Oxford: Oxford University Press.

Gallup Organisation, Hungary (2010) *Survey of the Attitudes of Europeans Towards Tourism: Analytical Report Wave 2*. Brussels: European Commission Directorate General Enterprise and Industry.

Gladwell, N.J. and Bedini, L.A. (2004) In search of lost leisure: the impact of caregiving on leisure travel. *Tourism Management*, 25(6): 685–693.

Hall, C.M. (2000) *Tourism Planning – Policies, Processes and Relationships*. Harlow: Prentice-Hall.

Hall, D.R. (1975) Some developmental aspects of Albania's fifth five-year plan, 1971–5. *Geography*, 60(2): 129–132.

Hall, D.R. (1984) Albania's growing railway network. *Geography*, 69(4): 263–265.

Hall, D. (ed.) (1991) *Tourism and Economic Development in Eastern Europe and the Soviet Union*. London: Belhaven.

Hall, D.R. (2001) Tourism in communist and post-communist societies. In D. Harrison (ed.), *Tourism and the Less Developed World: Issues and Case Studies* (pp. 91–107). Wallingford: CABI Publishing.

Hall, D. and Brown, F. (2006) *Tourism and Welfare: Ethics, Responsibility and Sustained Well-being*. Wallingford: CAB International.

Hamnett, C. (1996) Social polarisation, economic restructuring and welfare state regimes. *Urban Studies*, 33(8): 1407–1430.

Haukeland, J.V. (1990) Non-travellers: the flip-side of motivation. *Annals of Tourism Research*, 17(2): 172–184.

Hjalager, A-M. (2004) Sustainable leisure and rural welfare economy. The case of the Randers Fjord area, Denmark. *International Journal of Tourism Research*, 6(3): 177–188.

Hjalager, A-M. (2005) Innovation in tourism from a welfare state perspective. *Scandinavian Journal of Hospitality and Tourism*, 5(1): 46–62.

Hjalager, A-M. (2006) The marriage between welfare services and tourism – a driving force for innovation? *Journal of Quality Assurance in Hospitality and Tourism*, 6(3–4): 7–29.

Hughes, H. (1991) Holidays and the economically disadvantaged. *Tourism Management* 12(3): 193–196.

Iso-Ahola, S.E. (1980) *The Social Psychology of Leisure and Recreation*. Dubuque, IA: Wm. C. Brown.

Kautto, M. and Kvist, J. (2002) Parallel trends, persistent diversity: Nordic welfare states in the European and global context. *Global Social Policy*, 2(2): 189–208.

King, R. (2005) Albania as a laboratory for the study of migration and development. *Journal of Balkan and Near Eastern Studies*, 7(2): 133–155.

Liebried, S. (2000) Towards a European welfare state? In C. Pierson and F.G. Castles (eds), *The Welfare State: A Reader* (pp. 190–206). Cambridge: Polity Press.

Light, D. (2006) Romania: national identity, tourism promotion and European integration. In D. Hall, M. Smith and B. Marciszewska (eds), *Tourism in the New Europe: The Challenges and Opportunities of EU Enlargement* (pp. 256–269). Wallingford: CABI Publishing.

McGehee, N.G. and Santos, C.A. (2005) Social change, discourse and volunteer tourism. *Annals of Tourism Research*, 32(3): 760–779.

Moore, K., Cushman, G. and Simmons, D. (1995) Behavioral conceptualization of tourism and leisure. *Annals of Tourism Research*, 22(1): 67–85.

Pearlman, M. (1990) Conflicts and constraints in Bulgaria's tourism sector. *Annals of Tourism Research*, 17(1): 103–122.

Puczkó, L. and Rátz, T. (2006) Product development and diversification in Hungary. In D. Hall, M. Smith and B. Marciszewska (eds), *Tourism in the New Europe: The Challenges and Opportunities of EU Enlargement* (pp. 116–126). Wallingford: CABI Publishing.

Rathkey, P. (1990) *Time Innovations and the Deployment of Manpower*. Aldershot: Avebury.

Rhodes, M. (1995) 'Subversive liberalism': market integration, globalization and the European welfare state. *Journal of European Public Policy*, 2(3): 384–406.

Richards, G. (1999) Vacations and the quality of life: patterns and structures. *Journal of Business Research*, 44(3): 189–198.

Ryan, C. (2002) Equity, management, power sharing and sustainability – issues of the 'new tourism'. *Tourism Management*, 23(1): 17–26.

Samuel, N. (1986) Free time in France: a historical and sociological survey. *International Social Science Journal*, 107, 47–63.

Samuel, N. (1993) Vacation time and the French family. *World Leisure and Recreation*, 35(3): 15–16.

Sandu, D. (2005) Emerging transnational migration from Romanian villages. *Current Sociology*, 53(4): 555–582.

Schor, J. (1991) *The Overworked American: The Unexpected Decline of Leisure*. New York: Basic Books.

Seaton, A.V. (1992) Social stratification in tourism choice and experience since the war. *Tourism Management*, 13(1): 106–111.

Seaton, A.V. (2002) Tourism as metempsychosis and metensomatosis: the personae of eternal recurrence. In G.M.S. Dann (ed.), *The Tourist as a Metaphor of the Social World* (pp. 135–168). Wallingford: CABI Publishing.

Sharpley, R. and Sundaram, P. (2005) Tourism: a sacred journey? The case of ashram tourism, India. *International Journal of Tourism Research*, 7(3): 161–171.

Singh, S. (2009) Spirituality and tourism: an anthropologist's view. *Tourism Recreation Research*, 34(2): 143–155.

Sin, H.L. (2009) Volunteer tourism – 'involve me and I will learn'. *Annals of Tourism Research*, 36(3): 480–501.

Sinn, H-W. (1998) European integration and the future of the welfare state. *Swedish Economic Policy Review*, 5(1), 113–132.

Smith, M. (2003) Holistic holidays: tourism and the reconciliation of body, mind, spirit. *Tourism Recreation Research*, 28(1): 103–108.

Smith, M. and Hall, D. (2006) Enlargement implications of European tourism. In D. Hall, M. Smith and B. Marciszewska (eds), *Tourism in the New Europe: The Challenges and Opportunities of EU Enlargement* (pp. 32–43). Wallingford: CABI Publishing.

Smith, V. and Hughes, H. (1999) Disadvantaged families and the meaning of holiday. *International Journal of Tourism Research*, 1(2): 123–133.

Sunoo, B.P. (1996) Vacations: going once, going twice, sold. *Personnel Journal*, August: 72–80.

Teuscher, H. (1983) Social tourism for all – the Swiss Travel Saving Fund. *Tourism Management*, 4(3): 216–219.

Tokarski, W. and Michels, H. (1996) Germany. In G. Cushman, A.J. Veal and J. Zuzanek (eds), *World Leisure Participation: Free Time in the Global Village* (pp. 107–112). Wallingford: CAB International.

Turnock, D. (1999) Sustainable rural tourism in the Romanian Carpathians. *Geographical Journal*, 165(2): 192–199.

Wearing, S. (2001) *Volunteer Tourism: Experiences That Count*. Wallingford: CABI Publishing.

Williams, A.M. and Baláz, V. (2001) From collective provision to commodification of tourism? *Annals of Tourism Research*, 28(1): 27–49.

Case Study 7: Polish Tourist Country-Lovers' Society (Polskie Towarzystwo Turystyczno-Krajoznawcze, PTTK)

Paweł Zań *Senior Specialist, Management Office*

Polskie Towarzystwo Turystyczno-Krajoznawcze (PTTK)
ul. Senatorska 11
00–075 Warszawa
Poland
Telephone: +48 22 826 22 51
Fax: +48 22 826 25 05
Email: mail@pttk.pl
http://www.pttk.pl

Aims/Mission

PTTK's mission is to promote domestic tourism in Poland, to disseminate ethical values in society and to develop citizens' interest in their homeland. The Association serves persons whose passion is hiking and travelling, and who show a great interest in their country.

History

PTTK is Poland's oldest tourist association. It was established as a result of merger of the Polish Tatra Society (founded in 1873) and the Polish Sightseeing Society (founded in 1906). PTTK is a successor of the two organisations, both in legal terms and in terms of the tradition, ideology and property it has inherited from them.

Since its foundation in 1950 PTTK has developed and promoted sightseeing and so-called active tourism of all forms: hiking in mountains and lowlands, canoeing, sailing, cycling, horse riding, motor tourism and skiing.

The Association has developed and popularised a tourism and sightseeing programme related to domestic tourism, Poland's nature conservation and protection of landscape and historical monuments. PTTK is focused on facilitating tourism and sightseeing, both in

Poland and in other countries. It supports individual and group travellers. The Association has developed and implemented a system of tourist 'badges' with the aim of generating interest in the development of various forms of tourism and sightseeing.

PTTK promoted information about the most attractive tourist regions of Poland and promotes its own tourist product, active tourism, both domestically and abroad.

In 2010 we had 61,715 members, including 18,625 children and young people. In 2010 we organised over 30,000 projects in the field of social tourism. The overall number of participants was nearly 1 million, including nearly 450,000 children and young people.

Location

PTTK operates through a network of 309 branches established across Poland. The head office is in Warsaw.

Current Activities/Programmes

Throughout the year PTTK organises, on a not-for-profit basis, guided walks, rafting trips, canoeing rallies and rallies for children and youths. During the summer holidays, walking camps and training camps focused on specific types of active tourism are organised. All PTTK initiatives combine the recreation function with educational and teaching aspects.

Beneficiaries

The activities undertaken by individual branches of the PTTK are addressed to all age groups, starting from children up to seniors.

Funding Sources

The Association has some income from its operations, through participation fees, but also receives grants from local and national government, as well as the EU.

Role in Social Tourism Provision

Specific activities in local communities are conducted by local branches of the PTTK. The vast majority of the initiatives are low-cost projects addressed to the general public, but taking into account the needs and limitations of low-income groups. There are grants available in projects specifically targeted at children and young people from low-income families at risk of social exclusion, and for children and young people with different types of disabilities. The activities are mixed and the participants in the activity are not made aware who has received a grant and who has paid the full price.

Depending on the season, certain branches of the PTTK organise one-, two-, or three-day events as well as one-week or two-week events.

Projects lasting several days or more are usually organised close to the place of residence of the participants. This reduces the costs of the programme. These initiatives have an important educational function: children and young people are able to learn about the region in which they live, and develop a sense of attachment to their homeland. The multi-day trips and rallies also have a recreational function.

One-week and two-week trips are organised to places that are attractive in terms of their natural environment and cultural heritage. These are: national parks, natural land-scape parks and historic sites. The trips are educational and are focused on learning about the home country, its history and beauty.

For many of the participants, PTTK initiatives are the only possibility of travelling and discovering their home country.

Areas and Examples of Best Practice

Active tourism badges. PTTK has popularised in Poland a system of active tourism badges. The first badges of this type were introduced in 1930s. The metal badges are accompanied by a paper certificate and record the achievements of their holders in the field of tourism and sightseeing. The system of collecting the badges encourages tourists to improve their skills, such as the ability to use a map and compass, as well as their cycling skills, canoeing skills, etc. The hierarchical levels of the badges encourages people to broaden their knowledge and skills. The badges can be collected across Poland and through all branches of PTTK. The regulations on the badges contain the requirements which have to be met for each badge to be awarded. The requirements indicate detailed information such as distances in kilometres required for a specific badge, types of objects to visit, or tasks to be performed, as well as time limits within which the achievements have to be completed to get the badge. Membership of PTTK is not a requirement in order to participate in the scheme. The most popular badges include the Mountain Tourism Badge, Hiking Badge and Cycling Merit Badge. Kids Tourist Badge, introduced in 2009, is also gaining in popularity. Many teachers use the system of badges as a complementary tool for the school education programme.

Kids Rally is an event organised by the PTTK branch in Prudnik. It has been held annu-ally for 31 years, and each year the number of participants increases. In 2010, over 2000 children with their parents or carers took part in the rally; the total number of the partici-pants was over 6000. The participants are not only Prudnik residents, but also visitors from all over Poland and from other European countries. In 2010 we had participants from the Czech Republic, Germany, Norway, England and Austria. Each year, after a walk of several kilometres, including a difficult ascent to Góra Kapliczna (Chapel Hill), 320 metres above sea level, the participants take part in an open-air festival with a number of attractions. The event takes place at a horse stable. The children have the opportunity to participate in competitions, games and other activities, such as first-aid demonstrations, costume contests, the award of the title of the youngest participant of the rally or a participant coming from the most distant place in relation to Prudnik. All participants receive an award for completing the route. The participation fee for the event is nominal.

Youth Main Rally in Palmiry is a PTTK event organised annually since 1959. It combines tourism and sightseeing with a tribute to commemorate those who lost their lives in vari-ous conflicts. The rally is held in October and is addressed primarily to children and young people from across Poland. In 2010, the event attracted nearly 2500 persons. Every year the rally has a different theme and starts at a different place connected with Polish history. The 2011 rally focused on the Polish–Russian War of 1830–31 and, in particular, the victory in the battle of Iganie. The rally has several routes which differ in terms of time limit and difficulty. All the routes are planned to form a star shape. There are five routes, taking one to five days, each starting from a different part of the Mazowsze region. All the routes end at the Palmiry Military Cemetery at Kampinos National Park. During the rally, young people with their teachers and guides walk across the Mazowsze region, the central part of Poland, learning about its history and current status. Moderate and balanced exercise during the rally helps the participants to maintain fitness and good health. Young people learn how to be self-dependent by preparing their meals; they also learn about themselves and make friends with other participants. In the closing part, there are demonstrations by historical re-enactment groups. The rally ends with an evening march with torches to the Second World War cemetery in Palmiry, where the reading of the roll of the dead takes place, with solders assisting the ceremony.

8 The Family Factor in Social Tourism

Elizabeth Such and Tess Kay

Tourism has become such an integral component of modern lifestyles that to be outside tourism is to be outside the norms of everyday life. Non-participation in tourism makes a deep contribution to exclusion that goes beyond the immediate experience of being deprived of participation in tourism activities. This loss is particularly significant when viewed in the context of family life, because of the central role that shared tourism activities play in our notions of what a family is – or should be. Tourism provides opportunities for family members to spend time together away from the demands of employment and everyday domestic labour, creating shared experiences, expressing common interests, building and rebuilding intimate relationships – and thus fulfilling personal and societal expectations of what family life should be like. Tourism is therefore a key domain in which families seek to be 'proper' families.

It has of course been well recognised that tourism has this significance to family life. There has been a tendency, however, for tourism research to treat 'family' as a given, underplaying its diverse and dynamic character. Families vary in their size, structure and ideology, and in post-modernity have undergone particularly rapid change. The resulting complexity of family forms requires tourism researchers to adopt a more critical approach to how 'family' is conceptualised. Consideration of family is particularly important in relation to social tourism, given the importance of families in positioning individuals within the social structure and giving or limiting access to the material resources that facilitate tourism. While in theory family tourism can enhance quality of life, many families struggle to fulfil such functions: in most Western states, 'family' is so problematic that it has become a central social policy concern. Tourism research may benefit from giving fuller recognition to these more challenging aspects of family.

The purpose of this chapter is therefore to bring into focus the complexity of family, and to consider the significance of this for tourism research.

We argue here that contemporary families are characterised by diversity, and this has implications for how we analyse tourism choices, constraints and behaviours in the family context. As Smith and Hughes have argued, tourism research has tended to 'assume the homogeneity of the tourist experience without allowances for differences in gender, sexuality, ethnic background, social living circumstances, employment status, domestic situation, etc.' (Smith & Hughes, 1999: 123). In this analysis we suggest ways to redress this deficit in the study of family and tourism. We start with an exploration of the representation of family diversity in tourism research and look to the broader leisure literature to establish the significance of free-time activity in family life. We go on to establish some of the parameters of diversity in contemporary families in the UK and identify ways in which tourism research can benefit from recognising the structural, cultural and internal diversity of families.

The Representation of Family Diversity in Tourism Research

Contemporary families vary considerably – in their position in the social structure, in their cultural practices, and in the relationships that are developed within them. As well as being diverse, they are also dynamic: over time, family units change in their structure and membership, sometimes from natural progression through the traditional family lifecycle, but often as a result of established households breaking down and new ones being formed. Understanding the relationship between tourism and family life requires fuller recognition of these complexities.

This is especially so when the focus is on social tourism, as experiences of deprivation are so closely and selectively connected to family character-istics. Research by the Joseph Rowntree Foundation (2000) into subjective measures of poverty found that an annual holiday away from home (not staying with relatives) was considered a necessity by most respondents (55%), but was one of the activities most likely to be curtailed by lack of money. (For comparison, 56% classed a television as a household necessity and 71% a telephone). As Table 8.1 shows, more children (22%) forego an annual holiday because their parents cannot afford it than miss out on any other necessity. Overall, the Joseph Rowntree research found that it was around four times more common for those living in poverty to be unable to afford a holiday than for those who were not in poverty (Joseph Rowntree Foundation, 2000: 81, Table A4). Similarly, Palmer et al. (2008) reported that well over half of families in the poorest fifth of incomes could not afford a one-week annual holiday away from home, compared with just over a quarter of families with average incomes. Being deprived of an annual holiday is therefore a strong marker of low income and is subjectively experienced as exclusion from prevailing social norms.

Table 8.1 Holidays as a necessity and holiday deprivation

'Necessity'	% of parents regarding item as 'necessity'	% of children who lack item because their parents can't afford it
Holiday away from home at least one week a year	63	22
Celebrations on special occasions	92	4
Hobby or leisure activity	88	3
Swimming at least once a month	71	7

Source: Adapted from Joseph Rowntree Foundation (2000: 34, Table 9).

In the UK, national tourism statistics provide some indication of the relationship between families' socio-economic status and their access to tourism but do not directly measure whether tourism activity is lower among families with low income. Aggregate figures show that in 2007, when people with children in the household accounted for a third of the 123 million tourist trips made by UK residents (VisitBritain et al., 2008: 17, Table 1), higher socio-economic groups accounted for substantially more trips than lower ones: in 2007, 35% of trips were made by people in socio-economic group AB (professional and managerial), compared with 16% of group DE (unskilled, state pensioners) (VisitBritain et al., 2008: 18, Table 1).

Other data sources provide some additional evidence. The Family Expenditure Survey (FES) shows that holidays are an important element of family spending: they are the largest single item in spending on recreation and culture, itself the second largest category in family expenditure. Holiday spending varies markedly, however, across family income levels. In 2007, when aggregate household expenditure on package holidays averaged £13.40 per week, the poorest 10% of households were spending only £1.10 per week while the highest 10% were spending £37.40 per week (ONS, 2008a: 104–105, Table A8). Although package holidays are only one element of family tourism activity, these data do indicate substantial differences in tourist activity between families of different income levels.

The relationship between family characteristics and tourist activity is inadequately recorded in official tourism statistics (Hazel, 2005) but features in some commercial sector data (e.g. Mintel, 2005) and has also been addressed in broader studies of family behaviour. Haezewindt and Christian's (2004) analysis of the Family and Children Study provided a useful example of how family income levels are associated with family structures, with the two interacting to produce differentiated patterns of tourist activity. They found that in lone-parent households, 55% of children were likely to be deprived of a one-week annual holiday, compared with 22% of children in couple-parent households. Tourism analysts can, however, call only on piecemeal evidence of the relationship between families and tourism, often relying on the inclusion of some elements of tourism within broader behaviour studies. This provides only a very partial picture of how tourist activity relates to family characteristics and circumstances.

It is nonetheless evident that many poorer families struggle to access tourist activities. As low income correlates with family characteristics, certain types of families are particularly likely to be excluded from tourism – for example lone-parent families, and families who are members of an ethnic minority group. Tourism is therefore likely to feature in family life to varying degrees, according to certain family characteristics, which raises a number of questions for tourism researchers. What role do holidays, for example, play in the lives of different types of families? How do they contribute to family life for different family types, at different stages of the family life course? How is family diversity reflected in tourist practice and meaning?

The Significance of Free-Time Activity in Family Life

Tourism and other forms of family leisure are valued because they allow family members to enjoy each other's company, share activities and build collective experiences. Spending 'free' time together is important to family life: it offers escape from the everyday stresses of paid and domestic labour and provides opportunities for family members to focus instead on nurturing relationships with each other. Research into *leisure* in family contexts has a stronger academic tradition than research into family tourism, and shows that free time is a central component in 'creating' families: it is actively used by parents to meet their aspirations for family life, for example when they spend 'quality time' at leisure with their children to build a sense of 'togetherness' and 'family', or use goal-oriented or 'purposive' leisure to foster children's development (Shaw & Dawson, 2001; Hilbrecht et al., 2008). Recent debates about how 'fathering through leisure' allows men to meet societal expectations of involved fathering (e.g. Coakley, 2009; Harrington, 2009; Jenkins, 2009; Kay, 2007, 2009; Shaw, 2008; Shaw & Dawson, 2001; Such, 2006, 2009) provide further evidence of the importance of shared free time activity to family life.

Focusing on free time can reveal aspects of contemporary family relationships that might otherwise be undetected. The emerging picture is not necessarily positive. Within leisure studies, several authors (e.g. Deem, 1986; Green & Hebron, 1988; Green et al., 1987, 1990; Kay, 1996a, 1996b, 1998; Shaw, 1992; Such, 2002) have shown that women have more limited access to leisure within families than men do, and that the demands of creating family leisure may themselves be work-like, requiring planning, organising and the micro-management of intra-family relationships. Coakley (2009) has drawn attention to the high expectations imposed by prevailing ideologies of 'child-centred parenting' in Westernised societies, which puts pressure on parents to fill every minute of their child's time with 'constructive' activities.

The body of work into family tourism is smaller but has revealed similar issues (e.g. Davidson, 1996; Haldrup & Larsen, 2003; Hilbrecht *et al.*, 2008; Smith & Hughes, 1999). As in the field of leisure studies, one of the key findings from family-related tourism research has been that family holidays have the potential for strengthening family bonds and relationships. This forms one of the core arguments for promoting holidays as a social right through social tourism (see Corlyon & La Placa, 2005; Hazel, 2005; Minnaert *et al.*, 2009). Holidays have been shown to help bring families together outside of the stresses of everyday life and the normal routines of employment, education, domestic work, care obligations and so on. Nurturing relationships has been shown to be both a motivation for and outcome of family holidays. These include relationships between partners and between parents and children (Davidson, 1996; Hilbrecht *et al.*, 2008; Smith & Hughes, 1999). Smith and Hughes (1999) reported that for families with sick or disabled children, relationships between siblings also improved. Research shows, however, that holidays are not always experienced so positively. Even pleasurable family holidays are likely to involve parents in work-like responsibilities for planning, facilitating and managing the experience (Anderson, 2001; Shaw & Dawson, 2001), which may detract from their personal enjoyment and may affect the benefit for the family unit as a whole.

Tourism research has also shown that family tourism activity contributes to meaning and ideology in family life. As in leisure studies research, tourism academics have shown how family tourism can function as means of recreating the family in an idealised form. Haldrup and Larsen's study of family holiday photography describes how 'Much family tourism is fuelled by the desire to find a "home" where families imagine themselves as being a *real* loving family' (Haldrup & Larsen, 2003: 31; see also Löfgren, 1999). When couples spend time with each other at leisure or when the whole family comes together in shared activities – such as holidays – they are enacting the idea that being with each other should be pleasurable and constitute a part of 'good' family life. Tourism is therefore an arena in which families can 'perform' or 'live out' their ideas of familiality:

> Photography is ... a performance that displays the unity and love of the family and that produces its cohesion and intimacy.... Families partly travel in order to make photographs that can help them to construct pleasing family narratives and lasting memories of blissful family life. (Haldrup & Larsen, 2003: 25–26)

Haldrup and Larsen go on to assert that tourist photography centres on re-producing social relations – in this case familial relations – rather than merely providing opportunities to 'consume places'. This leads them to conclude that the 'tourist gaze' (Urry, 1990) expands beyond the material world and into intimate social worlds. They introduce the concept of the 'family gaze', whereby the family tourism experience provides family members with the opportunity to gaze upon one another, recreating an image of the family that, while not perhaps representing a daily reality, offers an image of what the family *should* be. Media representations of 'happy families' at leisure or on holiday both reflect and reinforce this ideology in the public consciousness.

As the above examples illustrate, tourism research highlights how the time families spend together, in activities of their choice, has a central significance in creating opportunities to 'be' the family they aspire to. Tourism within the family unit can be said to reproduce and construct family ideologies and practices that represent current expectations of 'good' family life in late modernity. Studying tourism therefore allows us to examine how families behave and interact during tourism experiences, what expectations they bring to them, and to what extent these expectations are fulfilled. This can make an important contribution to our wider understanding of contemporary families.

As we have seen above, however, contemporary family life is charac-terised by diversity. At an objective level of analysis, families vary in size, structure and the relationship of family members to each other; taking a longitudinal perspective, they differ also in their histories and experiences of transitions. Underpinning these differences are ideological differences, varying by culture and class and mediated by individual experience. When researchers consider family tourism as a way of enacting 'family', they must also address the issue: what type of family is being enacted?

The Parameters of Diversity in Contemporary 'Family'

Social policy analysts refer to 'family' as both an economically productive and a socially reproductive entity. This recognises that the family performs economic as well as relationship functions, providing for the welfare of its members. Extensive statistical data tell us much about the dynamic nature of families and households in respect of both of these roles. They paint a picture of a diverse social institution that has altered considerably over time, changing in size, composition, in its relationship to the labour market, and in the number and types of transitions it undergoes. In the UK, as in most Western states, the key trends of recent decades have included the following:

- *Changes in the structure of households, especially the increase in one-person households.* Time series data show that the number of households in the UK grew by about a third between 1971 and 2006, from 19 million to

25 million (Smallwood & Wilson, 2007: 3, Figure 1.1). This has been fuelled not by significant growth in the population but by increases in the number of smaller, particularly one-person, households. In 2008 there were 7.5 million people living alone in the UK (ONS, 2009: xxvii, Table A.2).

- *Changes in patterns of marriage and partnership.* There have been several changes in patterns of household formation, leading some critics to talk about the 'decline' of 'traditional' family life. The main trends have been the fall in marriage rates, the rise in (unmarried) cohabitation and the rise in rates of divorce. Despite the increasing incidence of relationship breakdown, the old patterns nonetheless hold sway: most people, including those who cohabit, marry; and most who divorce or separate re-partner, forming new ('reconstituted') households.

- *Changes in parenting arrangements.* Female lone parenthood has become increasingly common, in large part owing to increases in the divorce rate: nearly 3 million dependent children were in female lone-parent households in the UK in 2008. In comparison, 8.3 million children were living in married-couple family households, and a further 1.6 million were living with non-married cohabiting parents (ONS, 2009: 16, Table 2.4). In reconstituted families, parenting responsibilities may be shared by adults now living in different households, with children dividing their time between two separate homes.

- *Less stability in family life.* Many of the above changes contribute to an overarching trend – the increased tendency for families and their members to experience transitions. Higher levels of divorce, separation and re-marriage all point to less permanence in family relationships. At the aggregate level, this means that the profile of family types represents a fluid population. Lone parenthood, for example, is rarely a permanent state: the majority of lone-parent families have emerged from the breakdown of former couple households, and most go on to re-partner or re-marry. At the micro-level, more individuals will experience particular family situations at some point than cross-sectional data reveal.

Families have experienced extensive change in how they fulfil their economic functions as well as their reproductive ones. In the UK, the pattern of household labour market activity, and therefore income distribution, has changed in several ways in the last three decades:

- *Polarisation in the distribution of employment.* As single-earner family households have declined, the proportions of dual-earner and no-earner family households have both increased. The rise in dual-earning has been fuelled by sharp increases in women's employment, which rose from 59% in 1971 to 73% in 2005, reflecting changing gender roles and parenting patterns. Many women with children work part-time, especially when children are young (Cabinet Office & Department for Children, Schools and Families, 2008: 42).

- *Polarisation of the distribution of income.* The increase in no-earner households has contributed to the growth of income inequality and increased child poverty. Workless households roughly quadrupled from 4% in 1968 to over 17% in 1996 (Cabinet Office & Department for Children, Schools and Families, 2008: 62). At the same time, household income inequality grew, particularly during the 1980s, plateauing at a higher level of inequality during the 1990s and 2000s. Lone mothers are at particular risk of economic inactivity and low income. In 2008, 58% of lone mothers with at least one child aged under five years were economically inactive, compared with 34% of equivalent married or cohabiting mothers (ONS, 2009: 48, Table 4.3). Around one-third of all children in lone-parent families live in households with less than 60% of median income (Department for Work and Pensions, 2008). Children in reconstituted families are also vulnerable to reduced income, especially in the short to medium term. In total, 2 million children fall below thresholds of low income and material deprivation in the UK (Department for Work and Pensions, 2008: 76, Table 4.5tr).

The above broad trends and patterns in family structure and income can mask considerable variation between social groups.

- *Many aspects of family life are differentiated by social class.* Families headed by parents from lower socio-economic groups are more likely to experience difficult situations in both the 'productive' and 'reproductive' spheres. On the economic side, they are more likely to be no-earner households and to experience low income and/or poverty. It is particularly notable that the growth in maternal employment has been strongly class differentiated: women with high educational qualifications are much more likely than less well educated women to maintain a continuous employment record and to work full-time while their children are young. There are also class differences in patterns of family formation, with parents from lower socio-economic groups more likely to have families of above average size, to have them at a younger age, and to experience divorce and/or separation.
- *There are strong differences in family situations across cultural groups.* Ethnic minority families are at a greater than average risk of living in a household with low income. In 2006/07, 54% of Pakistani and Bangladeshi households were in the bottom fifth of the earnings distribution (ONS, 2009: 75, Table 5.16) and the majority of children in this group were growing up in low-income households. Black, black British and African households are similarly overrepresented in low-income groups, with around one-third of all households being low income (ONS, 2009: 75,

Table 5.16). There is a correlation between the incidence of low income and family structure in the case of many black and black British households. In 2008, nearly half (48%) of all black/black British households with dependent children were headed by a lone parent, compared with less than a quarter (23%) of all white families (ONS, 2009: 16, Table 2.5). Such structures place families at higher risk of poverty, although this is somewhat mitigated by the relatively high levels of maternal employment among black mothers. Analysis of the Millennium Cohort Study reveals that nearly two in five black Caribbean mothers have continuous employment from pregnancy through early childhood, although a large proportion of these families nonetheless live on a low income (Equal Opportunities Commission, 2007: 3).

Statistical profiles such as these provide tangible indicators of how complex, diverse and dynamic contemporary family situations are. This diversity is underpinned by corresponding variety in ideologies and expectations, which both influence and are influenced by behavioural change. Changing patterns of parental employment, for example, have partly driven, and have partly been driven *by*, changing ideas about gender roles and family life. The rise in mothers' employment levels has not only increased the total amount of time parents are spending in paid work, but also required change in ideas about the division of domestic labour and parenting responsibilities. To some extent, men and women have become less differentiated in their adult roles: both are now more likely to combine earning with domestic labour.

In some respects, these ideological shifts of recent decades have been contradictory. Clearly, ideas about partnership have broadened: cohabitation now has widespread acceptance, the stigma attached to divorce has reduced, and a broader recognition of partnerships has evolved. This has included moves in many countries to grant greater rights to families headed by same-sex couples, reflected in the UK in legislation governing issues such as civil partnerships and adoption. Although affecting a relatively small proportion of families, these changes are an important indication of how concepts of 'family' have shifted. But although these developments may appear liberating for individuals, in some areas ideologies have become more demanding, especially in relation to expectations of parenting. Fathers are now expected to perform 'involved fathering' – while nonetheless retaining their role as primary providers (Kay, 2009). Mothers are 'expected' to work – the state requests this even of those who are lone parents. Overarching these changes, many social scientists argue that the numerical decline of the 'traditional' family is a manifestation of the core tension in our society – the implications of individualisation.

Change and diversity in contemporary families are not simply structural changes that can be captured in statistical measures. At the heart of family life lie the relationships and experiences within the family unit, and the expectations that individual family members bring to their own and others' roles. As several writers have shown, the significance of tourism to families lies in its contribution to these relationships (e.g. Haldrup & Larsen, 2003; Hilbrecht et al., 2008). Several qualitative studies have addressed this, and later in the chapter we review this research, examining in particular what it tells us about how diversity plays out in different family tourism contexts.

Responding to Diversity in Family Research in Tourism Studies

In this section we try to flesh out in a more tangible way why diversity has specific implications for the study of family and tourism. We demonstrate this by comparing family ideologies and structures across different cultural (ethnic) groups in the UK, to highlight how much the basic concept of 'family' varies between different communities. Ethnicity provides a particularly useful focus for illustrating this, for three reasons: because of the centrality of 'family' to ethnic identity; the relevance of multiculturalism throughout Europe; and the vulnerability of members of minority groups to low income, which restricts access to tourism. Through this example we aim to explain why, when researchers examine how families use tourism to 'be' an 'ideal' family, they need to recognise how diverse concepts of an 'ideal' family may be.

Diversity in Family Ideologies: 'Family' and Culture

The relationship between 'family' and culture is very strong: Elliott (1996) places family at the heart of cultural identity and depicts different family arrangements and values as crucial distinguishing characteristics of ethnic, racial and cultural groups. 'Families' therefore play a central role in the production and reproduction of culture: it is through family arrangements that many minorities seek to preserve their distinctive traditions, practices and values. Thus, cultural identity is a significant influence on family structure and practice, and attitudes and beliefs about what 'the family' is or should be vary considerably between different socio-cultural groups, and indeed between cohorts within those groups. This has implications for practices of 'doing family' by engaging in tourism experiences.

Cultural differences in families are evident in national statistical data. Table 8.2 shows how the profile of family structures varied across ethnic groups in the UK at the time of the 2001 census (the most recently available national dataset). It distinguishes between three family structures for households with dependent children: those headed by a married couple, a cohabitant couple, or a lone parent. Across all ethnic groups, most households with children are headed by a couple who are either married (63%) or cohabitant (11%), while one in four (26%) is headed by a lone parent. There are strong variations across ethnic groups however, and we have drawn attention to this here by ranking the data according to the level of attachment to the 'traditional' model of a family headed by a married couple. This shows that the strongest attachment to marriage is found in Indian communities, among whom 85% of households are headed by a married couple, and the lowest among 'other black' groups, among whom only 27% are. The white British (majority) group closely mirrors the aggregate national profile, with 63% of families headed by a married couple, 12% by a cohabitant couple and 25% by a lone parent. In the UK, ethnic minority groups therefore provide both the strongest and weakest attachment to the traditional model of family, and as Table 8.2 shows, there is quite a noticeable contrast in this respect between communities with an Indian/Asian heritage and black groups. Most noticeably, Indian–Asian groups show particularly strong attachment to marriage, low levels of cohabitation (2–3%), and rates of lone parenthood below the national average. In contrast, black groups show almost the reverse profile: much lower attachment to marriage (less than 45%) and high levels of lone parenthood. Lone parenthood is a prominent family structure among all black groups, and the majority structure for some: lone parents head 47% of black African family households, 57% of black Caribbean ones and 64% of other blacks households.

Table 8.2 Proportions (%) of UK families with dependent children by ethnic group and family type (April 2001)

	Married couple	Cohabiting couple	Lone parent
Indian	85	2	13
Other Asian	81	3	16
Chinese	79	3	18
Bangladeshi	79	3	18
Pakistan	78	3	19
White	63	12	25
Black African	44	8	47
Mixed	42	12	46
Black Caribbean	32	12	57
Other black	27	10	64
Other ethnic group	74	4	22
All ethnic groups	63	11	26

Source: ONS (2008b), Census Commissioned Table M502; Data from Census, April 2001, Office for National Statistics; Census, April 2001, General Register Office for Scotland; Census, April 2001, Northern Ireland Statistics and Research Agency.

These differences in family structure signify markedly different underlying ideologies. As Harvey (2001) has shown, minority groups attach importance to 'maintaining their differences' and actively protect and reproduce their cultural identity by preserving the traditions of 'family' of their country of origin. In practice this means that families with Indian–Asian cultural origins tend to be oriented towards an ideology of family which: emphasises collective interest rather than individual development; expects respect and obedience by children; is underpinned by strong religious faith; and is often socially conservative in its values, including differentiated gender roles. In contrast, black families draw on the 'social' (as opposed to 'biological') model of parenting that is prevalent in many non-Westernised global regions, in which family units are fluid, biological relationships are given less significance than in Western culture, and parenting roles are therefore performed by many adults – a communal concept of family captured, for example, in the saying 'It takes a village to raise a child' (Kay, 2009). In the UK, both these orientations are evident in the corresponding minority ethnic communities, while the white British majority lies somewhere between these approaches.

Cultural diversity in family structures is evident in parenting practices (Equal Opportunities Commission, 2007). In a study of parents and young people with Muslim and Christian backgrounds, faith was considered an important part of parenting. 'Good' parenting was equated with being warm and loving, while also setting boundaries and standards for children (Howarth *et al.*, 2008: 1). In these families, parents viewed the family as a mutually supportive unit under the direction of an 'authoritative' model of parenting. In other cultural family settings, styles of parenting are likely to vary.

Studies by Kay (2006a, 2006b) of leisure and parenting in two contrasting cultural groups illustrate this. The first was conducted with Muslim families of Bangladeshi origin living in the East Midlands, and investigated family influence on daughters' participation in sport. The second involved white British families living in the same location, and focused on fathers' involvement in their sons' football. Contrasting family arrangements and ideologies were encountered throughout. In the study of Muslim families, family life was very much reflective of South Asian practice, in terms of: collectivism (daughters' sport participation was judged according to its impact on the family's standing in the community); gender differentiation (daughters' leisure behaviour was subject to more stringent controls that sons', and was circumscribed by higher levels of domestic duties); and high levels of parental authority and child obedience. In contrast, the study of white UK fathers' involvement with their children through sport revealed a very different ideology of parenting, in which the emphasis was on the individual development of the child and on 'democratic' relationships between adults and young people. Disciplining children was, if anything, contrary to the ideal fathers felt they had to live up to. As one said:

And with children, directly with children, I think in a way you're expected to be like a kind of father angel, you know this perfect guy, who
never shouts at his children, never smacks them, encourages absolutely
everything they do, never gets cross when he's absolutely knackered and
all he wants to do is collapse in front of the TV, and the children have
got demands for whatever. And there is that expectation there, and it's
obviously an unrealistic one. (Kay, 2007: 78)

The examples of Kay's studies are in some senses almost diametrically
opposed: the first emphasising parental authority and the collective nature
of family; the second emphasising responsiveness to children, the father 'on
call' to meet his children's needs. They have in common, however, that they
both highlight the central influence of ideology – made explicit by the father
in the above quote referring to 'that expectation there'. Our understanding
of what a family *should* be is a very immediate and strong influence on how
we conduct our family life.

Haldrup and Larsen (2003) are therefore right when they talk about
families trying to reproduce an ideal family in their photographs – but we
need to recognise that that ideal may vary. There are very different ideas of
what a family should be and what roles individuals should play within it.
Differences do not occur only between culturally distinct groups, but they
are particularly easily observed among them and also particularly relevant in
today's increasingly multicultural societies.

Tourism researchers could usefully develop issues of structural, cultural
and ideological diversity in their work and highlight to policy makers in
social tourism the importance of family difference in provision. While some
social tourism providers have recognised these factors (for example, one-
parent families are provided for by organisations such as HELP Holidays),
policy makers have yet to fully acknowledge that inequality in participation
goes beyond issues of affordability and consumer choice. Family structure
and family ideology, informed by cultural diversity and attitudes, crucially
shape tourism behaviour. Given this diversity in family structures, it is
always difficult to envisage a one-size-fits-all approach to policy making
of provision.

Conclusions

Families are a key mechanism for inclusion or exclusion: they position
individuals socially and economically; they develop or undermine skills in
building productive social relationships; and they come in almost infinite
combinations of structure and ideology. Tourism research that reflects this
diversity can illuminate the relationship between families and exclusion in a
variety of ways. To do this requires:

- *Researching diverse family forms.* This means avoiding being too narrowly focused on the 'traditional family'; addressing cultural and ethnic diversity; and extending the scope of such work beyond the stereotypical child-rearing phase to other stages of the family life course. There is a particular need to redress the omission of older and younger people in their family context, to consider intergenerational relationships, and to examine how early family experiences may shape individuals' later tourism choices.
- *Unpicking how family relationships are played out in tourism experiences.* Family tourism puts family relationships under the spotlight: it shows them in all their glory and, quite probably, in all their horrors. In a relatively unconstrained context, it highlights the different expectations individuals bring to 'family'. By exposing the workings of family so starkly, it has a significant contribution to make to our understanding of why our pivotal social institution is so 'unstable' in the post-modern period.

In conclusion, this chapter has argued that because tourism is such a significant family activity, it offers great potential to illuminate the dynamics, and also the tensions, across diverse forms of family life. Tourism provides opportunities to bring family members together to 'be' a family and to develop skills in sustaining the productive social relationships on which inclusion is based. It also, however, requires family relationships to be acted out in unfamiliar environments away from the reassurance of established routines. Tourism research is uniquely positioned to highlight the tension between what we believe families should be, and how in practice we live out family life.

References

Anderson, J. (2001) Mothers on family activity holidays overseas. In S. Clough and J. White (eds), *Women's Leisure Experiences: Ages, Stages and Roles* (pp. 99–112). Eastbourne: Leisure Studies Association.

Cabinet Office and Department for Children, Schools and Families (2008) *Families in Britain: An Evidence Paper.* Online at https://www.education.gov.uk/publications/standard/publicationDetail/Page1/DCSF-01077-2008.

Coakley, J. (2009) The good father: parental expectations and youth sports. In T. Kay (ed.), *Fathering Through Sport and Leisure* (pp. 40–50). London: Routledge.

Corlyon, J. and La Placa, V. (2005) *Briefing Paper for Policy Makers and Services Providers: Holidays for Families in Need – Policies and Practice in the UK.* London: Policy Research Bureau and FHA.

Davidson, P. (1996) The holiday and work experiences of women with young children. *Leisure Studies,* 15(2): 89–103.

Deem, R. (1986) *All Work and No Play? The Sociology of Women and Leisure.* Milton Keynes: Open University Press.

Department for Work and Pensions (2008) *Households Below Average Income: An analysis of the Income Distribution 1994/5–2006/07.* Online at http://research.dwp.gov.uk/asd/hbai/hbai2007/index.php?page=contents.

Elliott, F. Robertson (1996) *Gender, Family and Society*. Basingstoke: Macmillan.

Equal Opportunities Commission (2007) *Ethnicity and Patterns of Employment and Care*. London: EOC. Online at http://www.cls.ioe.ac.uk/core/documents/download. asp?id=920&log_stat=1.

Green, E. and Hebron, S. (1988) Leisure and male partners. In E. Wimbush and M. Talbot (eds), *Relative Freedoms: Women and Leisure* (pp. 37–47). Milton Keynes: Open University Press.

Green, E., Hebron, S. and Woodward, D. (1987) *Leisure and Gender: A Study of Sheffield Women's Leisure Experiences*. London: Sports Council and Economic and Social Research Council.

Green, E., Hebron, S. and Woodward, D. (1990) *Women's Leisure, What Leisure?* Basingstoke: Macmillan.

Haezewindt, P. and Christian, V. (2004) Living standards. In Office of National Statistics, *Focus On: Social Inequalities* (pp. 55–68). London: The Stationery Office.

Haldrup, M. and Larsen, J. (2003) The family gaze. *Tourist Studies*, 3(1): 23–46.

Harrington, M. (2009) Sport mad, good dad: Australian fathering through leisure and sport practices. In T. Kay (ed.), *Fathering Through Sport and Leisure* (pp. 51–72). London: Routledge.

Harvey, C. (ed.) (2001) *Maintaining Our Differences*. Aldershot: Ashgate.

Hazel, N. (2005) Holidays for children and families in need: an exploration of the research and policy context for social tourism in the UK. *Children and Society*, 19(3): 225–236.

Hilbrecht, M., Shaw, S., Delamere, F.M. and Havitz, M.E. (2008) Experiences, perspectives and meanings of family vacations for children. *Leisure/Loisir*, 32(2): 541–571.

Horwath, J.L., Sidebotham, P., Higgins, J. and Imtiaz, A. (2008) *Findings: Religion, Beliefs and Parenting Practices: A Descriptive Study*. York: Joseph Rowntree Foundation.

Jenkins, J. (2009) With one eye on the clock: non-resident dads' time use, work and leisure with their children. In T. Kay (ed.), *Fathering Through Sport and Leisure* (pp. 88–105). London: Routledge.

Joseph Rowntree Foundation (2000) *Poverty and Social Exclusion in Britain*. York: Joseph Rowntree Foundation.

Kay, T. (1996a) Women's leisure and the family in contemporary Britain. In N. Samual (ed.), *Women, Leisure and the Family in Contemporary Society: A Multinational Perspective* (pp. 143–159). Oxon: CAB International.

Kay, T. (1996b) Women's work and women's worth: the leisure implications of women's changing employment patterns. *Leisure Studies*, 15(1): 49–64.

Kay, T. (1998) Having it all or doing it all? The construction of women's lifestyles in time-crunched households. *Society and Leisure*, 21(2): 435–454.

Kay, T.A. (2006a) Where's dad? Fatherhood in leisure studies. *Leisure Studies*, 25(2): 133–152.

Kay, T.A. (2006b) Daughters of Islam: family influences on Muslim young women's participation in sport. *International Review for the Sociology of Sport*, 41(3–4): 339–355.

Kay, T.A. (2007) Fathering through sport. *World Leisure Journal*, 49(2): 69–82.

Kay, T.A. (ed.) (2009) *Fathering Through Sport and Leisure*. London: Routledge.

Löfgren, O. (1999) *On Holiday: A History of Vacationing*. Berkeley, CA: University of California Press.

Minnaert, L., Maitland, R. and Miller, G. (2009) Tourism and social policy: the value of social tourism. *Annals of Tourism Research*, 36(20): 316–334.

Mintel (2005) *Holidays – Popular Destinations, Special Report*. London: Mintel.

ONS (2008a) *Family Spending: A Report on the 2007 Expenditure and Food Survey*. Basingstoke: Palgrave Macmillan.

ONS (2008b) *2001 Census: Commissioned Tables*. Online at http://www.statistics.gov.uk/census2001/downloads/com_tab_finder.xls.

ONS (2009) *Social Trends 39*. Basingstoke: Palgrave Macmillan.

Palmer, G., MacInnes, T. and Kenway, P. (2008) *Monitoring Poverty and Social Exclusion 2008*. York: Joseph Rowntree Foundation/New Policy Institute.

Shaw, S.M. (1992) Dereifying family leisure: an examination of women's and men's everyday experiences and perceptions of family time. *Leisure Sciences*, 14(4): 271–286.

Shaw, S.M. (2008) Family leisure and changing ideologies of parenthood. *Sociology Compass*, 2(2): 688–703.

Shaw, S.M. and Dawson, D. (2001) Purposive leisure: examining parental discourses on family activities. *Leisure Sciences*, 23(4): 217–231.

Smallwood, S. and Wilson, B. (2007) *Focus on Families*. Basingstoke: Palgrave Macmillan.

Smith, V. and Hughes, H. (1999) Disadvantaged families and the meaning of the holiday. *International Journal of Tourism Research*, 1(2): 123–133.

Such, E. (2002) *Leisure in the Lifestyles of Dual-Earner Families n the United Kingdom*, unpublished thesis, Loughborough University.

Such, E. (2006) Leisure and fatherhood in dual-earner families. *Leisure Studies*, 25(2): 185–200.

Such, L. (2009) Fatherhood, the morality of personal time and leisure-based parenting. In T. Kay (ed.), *Fathering Through Sport and Leisure* (pp. 73–87). London: Routledge.

Urry, J. (1990) *The Tourist Gaze: Leisure and Travel in Contemporary Societies*. London: Sage.

VisitBritain, VisitScotland, VisitWales and Northern Ireland Tourist Board (2008) *UK Tourist 2007*. Edinburgh: TNS Travel and Tourism.

Case Study 8: The Family Fund, UK

Clare Kassa *Network Development Manager*

helping disabled children

The Family Fund
Unit 4, Alpha Court, Monks Cross Drive
York YO32 9WN
UK
Telephone: 0845 130 4542
Email: info@familyfund.org.uk
http://www.familyfund.org.uk

Aims/Mission

The Family Fund helps families with severely disabled children and young people aged 17 and under to have choices and the opportunity to enjoy ordinary life. We give grants for things that make life easier and more enjoyable for a disabled child, young person and their family such as washing machines, driving lessons, computers and holidays.

History

The Family Fund was set up by the UK government in 1973 to offer practical help to families who had children affected by thalidomide. It was then expanded to help severely disabled and seriously ill children under the age of 16. For over 20 years the Fund operated under the wing of the Joseph Rowntree Foundation but in 1996 became an independent charity. Since 1998 the Family Fund has been funded by the four governments of the UK.

Location

The Family Fund operates throughout the whole of the UK with staff and advisers working regionally and locally. The head office is based in York.

Current Activities/Programmes

In the year April 2009 to April 2010 the Family Fund gave over 24,000 holiday grants to families caring for severely disabled children. Grants are given to families to take their children and young people on holiday. For many of the families who apply to the Fund, this is the first opportunity they have had to take a holiday; for others, the grant is their only means of financing a holiday each year. The Fund provides its holiday grants in the following ways:

- *A payment to Haven Holidays*. This offers families self-catering packages at a choice of 35 Haven Holidays parks in the UK.
- *Vouchers for Thomas Cook*. This offers families holidays in the UK or abroad through Thomas Cook, the third largest travel group in the world. Thomas Cook can arrange flights, ferries, train and coach travel for the holiday destination, as well hotels, holiday parks, self-catering accommodation, campsites and caravan sites.
- *Cash grant*. The Fund can make a cash grant for holidays that cannot be made through either of the above, such as a specialist holiday being arranged by a local parent group.
- *Outings grant*. For those families unable to take a holiday because of their child's disability or care needs, a grant can be given for families to take days out nearer home.

Beneficiaries

The Family Fund provides all of its grants to families who are on the lowest of incomes caring for a severely disabled child. In England, this means a family applying to the Fund must have a net income of less than £25,000 per year and in Wales, Scotland and Northern Ireland a net income of less than £27,000.

Funding Sources

The Family Fund is a registered charity helping around 53,000 families in the UK, with around £31 million in grants each year. The national governments of England, Northern Ireland, Scotland and Wales provide the Fund's income as part of their commitment to disabled children and young people.

Role in Social Tourism Provision

We know from what families tell the Fund that a holiday is critical to their family well-being – for many families it gives the only opportunity of a break and allows them the pleasures that other families take for granted. Families caring for a severely disabled child report that the impact of caring places great strains on mental health, physical health and relationships. In being able to take a break, it affords families positive experiences with their children and fun for the whole family. Holidays can be particularly beneficial for siblings, who often miss out on everyday experiences because of the impact of their brother's or sister's disability. It also gives disabled children the chance to have a break away from the home environment, to develop their social skills and to widen their recreational opportunities. Lots of families tell the Fund's staff that because of the financial strains of caring, without this help it would be impossible to take a family holiday – indeed, many families applying to us for the first time say that they have never had a holiday and often view this as a distant dream.

Over the years, the Family Fund has built positive relationships with both Haven and Thomas Cook to provide a range of holiday options for families. Many families, because of the challenges of caring, find it difficult to make the arrangements, so giving specific options makes taking a holiday easier. Contract arrangements with large companies means that the Fund can offer more generous packages for families and make the budget go further, so that more families overall can be helped.

Areas and Examples of Best Practice

The Family Fund has been working with a small number of local authorities in a pilot project to assist families to take a break. Money has been allocated from central government to local authorities under the Aiming High for Disabled Children agenda to help more families have a break from caring or to access recreational activities. The Fund's work with local authorities has meant that families have been able to take a holiday with both accommodation and care hours provided, which enables families who could not go away without extra physical help to take a break as a family. The Fund has worked with care providers to ensure that the holiday can be as flexible as possible to meet the family's needs. The Family Fund has administered this project and been able to pass on its discounts with holiday providers to local authorities, allowing their budgets to go as far as possible, while ensuring that the families have the holiday which meets their needs. Here is how it worked for two families:

Family A had two workers assigned during their holiday. Mum could not praise them enough, saying that they slotted in amazingly and it was like having a family friend around to help out. Mum wasn't sure how it would go being on holiday but now feels really confident about going away and would like to do it again – and next time would even consider heading 'up north' to the Yorkshire site please!

Family B had an amazing time. It was a surprise for the kids after a difficult year and they all loved it. Mum found it impossible to put into words how much they had gained from it as a family and they did all sorts of wonderful things like day trips to Butlins and both children loved the swimming pool.

9 Disability, Representation and Access to Tourism

Gareth Shaw and Sheela Agarwal

The rights of disabled people to accessible tourism and travel have been increasingly recognised by policy makers across Europe (European Disability Forum, 2001) and they are now of major concern to the European Union (EU) (European Network for Accessible Tourism, 2010). However, the fight for equality for the disabled traveller is far from won. Indeed, it is currently marked out in a range of well meaning top-down policy initiatives and publications that in many instances do very little to improve access to holidays and travel (European Commission, 2010). Of course, legislation is of critical importance, as evidenced by the impact of the passing of the Disability Discrimination Act 1995 (DDA) in the UK, which focused the attention of the tourism industry on developing more accessible products (Shaw, 2007). In 2010 the Equality Act replaced the most of the DDA and set discrimination on grounds of disability in a wider setting. The 2010 Act similarly stipulated that those with disabilities must not be treated unfavourably unless that treatment can be objectively justified. It prompted an increased interest in disability among tourism researchers, as reflected in the growing number of publications (see Darcy, 2005).

But policy alone has not been responsible for stimulating debate concerning the disabled traveller. Other major important changes in the way disabled people are viewed have been brought about through action by people with disabilities themselves. Of particular significance is the shift from the medical model of disability to that of the social model, which emerged in the UK following the activities of the Union of Physically Impaired Against Segregation. In contrast to the medical model of disability, which views illness and disability as being the result of a physical condition intrinsic to an individual and which may reduce their quality of life, the social model, which has become an important if sometimes contested paradigm (Shakespeare & Watson, 2001), argues that 'people with impairments are disabled/excluded by a society that is not organised in ways that take account of their needs' (Thegaskis, 2002: 458). In other words, it emphasises the existence of barriers, negative attitudes and exclusion by society (purposely or inadvertently), meaning that society itself is the main contributory factor in disabling people. Thus, rather than using medical solutions to normalise a disabled person's participation in society, as in the case of the medical model, the social model of disability espouses that society should identify all barriers confronted by people with disabilities and formulate strategies to mitigate them (Daruwalla & Darcy, 2005).

Clearly, there are a number of policy-driven changes which have been introduced with the specific intention of improving tourism participation among people with disabilities. It is within this context that this chapter is couched, as it aims to explore the reality of access to tourism and travel for disabled people. In doing so, we look at a number of key aspects, including the policy contexts within the EU. In particular, attention is given to the increasing policy domain accumulating around the issues of disability rights, access and tourism, before going on to consider current practices. Here we see a gap between policy intentions and the experiences of many disabled people in relation to the tourism products on offer, along with difficulties of access. This chapter then moves on to examine the experiences of people with disabilities and the response from tourism providers. In terms of the latter, we focus on how people with disabilities are represented by the travel media, along with the tourism products they are offered. We draw on European-wide studies where possible, but our points are illustrated by examples from the UK.

Policy Contexts: Empowering the Disabled Tourist

Social policy regarding disability rights in general has largely followed the development of the social model of disability. Thus, the EU has increasingly viewed disability 'as the result of the dynamic interaction between a person and their environment' (Qatrain, 2007: 2). Moreover, the momentum for change has been driven by aspects of anti-discrimination policies set within the EU (European Commission, 2000). The EU adopted a policy framework for developing a strategy towards equal opportunities for people with disabilities with the New Community Disability Strategy (1996), expanded upon in 1999 (Living Research and Development, 2001). Aspects of the social model are part of the two main perspectives impacting on policy, namely: 'Why accessibility?' (rights to equality) and 'How accessible?' (creating a better environment). The notion of access is seen in the context of barriers to mobility, and includes areas such as education, healthcare, leisure and tourism (Living Research and Development, 2001).

Surrounding these policy initiatives are a plethora of organisations concerned with the agenda of access and disability. These include the High Level Group of Disability (HLGD), established by the European

Table 9.1 European Action Plan for Disability and Equal Opportunities (2004–07)

Action phases	Key actions
2004–05	Creating conditions to promote employment for persons with disabilities, based on four main areas: • access to, and remaining in, employment • lifelong learning • harnessing the potential of information technology • accessibility to the built environment (links with European transport policy)
2006–07	Active inclusion, independence and increased participation in four priority areas: • encouraging activity • promoting access to quality support/care • fostering accessibility to goods and services (tourism) • increasing the EU's analytical capacity

Source: Europa (2006).

Commission in 1997 as a policy forum for knowledge exchange. These organisations in theory should help inform the policies of member states as well as monitoring progress. In addition, there is the European Network for Accessible Tourism (ENAT), established in 2006. Furthermore, the EU, following the European Year of People with Disabilities in 2007, introduced the Disability Action Plan (DAP), aimed at 'mainstreaming disability issues in the relevant community policies' (Europa, 2006: 1). Table 9.1 shows the key strategic stages in the DAP, covering 2004–10. As can be seen, tourism is only indirectly mentioned, although other policy initiatives via ENAT and the One-Stop-Shop for Accessible Tourism in Europe (OSSATE) project are much more specific to tourism (Buhalis *et al.*, 2005).

The European Commission has now launched the European Disability Strategy (2010–20) to replace the current DAP. This strategy aims to make it easier for people with disabilities to go about their daily lives like everyone else and to enjoy their rights as EU citizens. Emphasis is placed on ensuring access to funding, raising public awareness about disability and encouraging group members to work together in removing obstacles to inclusion. Its implementation will also fulfil the EU's commitment to the United Nations' Convention on the Rights of Persons with Disabilities, which the member states signed in 2007. The Commission's strategy encompasses a broad remit; its key objectives and actions over the 2010–20 period are summarised in Table 9.2, but the strategy's targets for the first five years include:

Table 9.2 The European disability strategy, 2010–20: Key action areas and objectives

Key areas of action	Key actions
Accessibility Prevent, identify and eliminate obstacles and barriers to accessibility through the possible development of a European Accessibility Act	Explore the possibility of completing the legal framework addressing the rights of persons with reduced mobility by covering all relevant modes of transport Address accessibility to the built environment Make full use of all existing legal instruments and address disability matters in their revisions following the UN Convention in the area of the information society, in line with the Digital Agenda for Europe Support research on new technologies addressing assistive technology and accessible mainstream solutions
Participation Ensure equal opportunities for persons with disabilities and their families to fully participate in all aspects of social and economic life, namely: • to exercise all their EU citizenship rights, in particular the right to free movement and residence • to be able to choose where and how they live • to have full access to cultural, recreational, leisure and sports activities	Address the obstacles that persons with disabilities face in exercising their rights as individuals, consumers, students and professionals, and political actors Address problems related to intra-EU mobility Enhance the use of the European model of disability parking card Enhance member states' efforts towards the transition from institutional to community-based care Optimise the use of Structural Funds and the Rural Development Fund to support the development of community-based services Improve the knowledge base on the situation of people with disabilities living in residential institutions Promote the participation of people with disabilities in sports Promote the access of people with disabilities to cultural materials and events
Equality Promote and protect the inherent dignity of persons with disabilities, combat all forms of discrimination on the basis of disability, and ensure that persons with disabilities enjoy, on an equal basis with others, all fundamental rights and freedoms	Support the negotiation in Council of the draft Directive on equal treatment beyond the field of employment Monitor the application and impact of Directive 2000/78 EC for improving employment of persons with disabilities Promote attention to disability matters in equality bodies, notably through Equinet Provide guidance on reasonable accommodation for people with disabilities, addressing employers and service providers Promote exchange of good practices on legal capacity Raise awareness among trade unions of the concept of reasonable accommodation Use the existing Progress programme (until December 2013) to support national activities aimed at combating discrimination and promoting equality Address disability issues in awareness-raising seminars in the areas of non-discrimination and equality targeted at civil society organisations Address disability discrimination in annual calls for proposals aimed at supporting national authorities in their fight against discrimination and their promotion of equality Introduce a disability-specific focus in the 'What Can Social Europe Do For You?' campaign

Employment

Improve the employment situation of women and men with disabilities through recognition of their right to work, including the right to the opportunity to gain a living by work, freely chosen or accepted in a labour market and work environment that is open, inclusive and accessible

Increase knowledge on employment situation of people with disabilities, identify challenges, propose remedies

Optimise the use of the new strategy for jobs and growth, 'Europe 2020', for the benefit of people with disabilities

Focus on what people can do and persuade potential employers with convincing arguments and support to employ people with disabilities

Give special attention to difficulties of young people with disabilities in transition from education to employment and address intra-job mobility, including for those working in sheltered workshops (access to and retention in employment)

Address the issue of quality of jobs, such as salaries, working hours and career advancement of people with disabilities

Fight prevailing disability benefit cultures and help to integrate persons with partial work capacity into the labour market, develop active labour market policies and tackle benefit traps

Education and training

Ensure that people with disabilities receive the support required within the general education system to facilitate their education, and that individualised support measures are provided in environments that maximise academic and social development, consistent with the goal of full inclusion

Increase knowledge of education levels and opportunities of people with disabilities

Support policy developments towards the goal of inclusive and quality education and training within the framework of the Youth on the Move initiative

Increase the mobility of people with disabilities through enhancing their participation in the Lifelong Learning Programme and the Youth in Action Programme

Social protection

Ensure decent living conditions for people with disabilities through access to social protection systems and poverty-reduction programmes, disability-related assistance, public housing programmes, and retirement and benefits programmes

Optimise the use of the European Platform against Poverty and the European Social Fund

Assess the adequacy of social protection systems with respect to people with disabilities

Health

Ensure that people with disabilities have equal access to healthcare, including prevention, and that quality and affordable specific health services are provided

Support policy developments to improve equal access to healthcare

Support policy developments to improve quality of healthcare and rehabilitation for people with disabilities

Promote actions in the field of health and safety at work to reduce risks of disability during working life

External action

Promote the rights of people with disabilities within a broader non-discriminatory approach in the EU's external actions, including the enlargement process and development programmes, taking due account of the common EU and member states' approach to development

Ensure that EU development cooperation reaches persons with disabilities, both through projects/programmes specifically targeting persons with disabilities and by improving the mainstreaming of disability concerns

Ensure that infrastructure financed in the framework of EU development projects meets the accessibility requirements of people with disabilities

Ensure that progress is made by candidate and potential candidate countries in promoting the rights of persons with disabilities and that accession funds are used to improve their situation

Source: European Commission (2010).

- devising policies for inclusive, high-quality education;
- ensuring the European Platform Against Poverty includes a special focus on people with disabilities;
- working towards the recognition of disability cards throughout the EU to ensure equal treatment when working, living or travelling in the region;
- developing accessibility standards for voting premises and campaign material;
- taking the rights of people with disabilities into account in external development programmes and for EU candidate countries.

Perhaps more importantly and directly relevant to tourism, in their commitment to creating a barrier-free Europe, the Commission is also considering proposing an European Accessibility Act which would set EU standards for products, services and public buildings.

Much of the policy agenda is being driven by the European Commission and so it is hardly surprising that some common perspectives with UK institutions may be identified in relation to disability and access to tourism (English Tourist Board, 1989; English Tourism Council, 2000). These concern the key issues of selling the idea of a so-called barrier-free Europe for People with Disabilities (European Disability Forum, 2001: 4). These issues are:

- tourism as a social right;
- accessible tourism making commercial sense, given the large number of disabled people and their families;
- improving training to develop skills within the tourism industry to cope with disabled tourists;
- improving information for disabled tourists, using information technology, for example;
- improving the quality of tourism products, partly by developing a European Accessibility Label scheme.

While few would disagree with this agenda to help provide equality of access to tourism, it does raise the question of whether this policy framework delivers real benefits to people with disabilities. Have disabled tourists been empowered by such high-level activities and the many reports on access?

The question of empowerment can be viewed at a number of levels. At its most basic, it clearly concerns raising awareness via policy statements of the EU and the individual member states. Such awareness impacts on the provision of accessible holidays. In this context, the early campaigns of the English Tourism Council demonstrated the business case to tourism providers to encourage them to consider meeting the needs of disabled holidaymakers (English Tourism Council, 2001). Similarly, more recent studies by the German Federal Ministry of Economics and Technology

(European Commission, 2010) estimate that improving access to tourism for people with disabilities would yield between €620 million and €1.93 billion for the German tourism industry. The development of such business cases is important to help raise awareness and support any legislation. There is a pitfall, however, as we shall argue below, in that to see such provisions as a niche market (Ray & Ryder, 2003) is a form of economic (as well as social) segregation.

A second area of empowerment is through direct anti-discriminatory legislation, which is only partial at the EU level and is lacking in many member states (Living Research and Development, 2001). The UK and Germany are leaders in this context, in the case of the former through the passing of the DDA in 1995 and subsequently the Equality Act in 2010 (Hurstfield *et al.*, 2004). However, even within the UK the degree of empowerment brought about through the legislation is often difficult to determine, although it clearly raised expectations and gave a set of legal rights to people with disabilities (Shaw, 2007).

A final aspect of empowerment, and arguably the most critical, is how people with disabilities themselves view progress towards accessible tourism. Once again there are difficulties in assembling evidence, certainly across the EU, where data are rather patchy. It is this latter aspect that we focus on now by drawing on some recent EU-wide surveys. The first of these was a small-scale survey of stakeholder consultations to help support the European Disability Strategy 2010–20 (European Commission, 2010). Between 2009 and 2010, a public online consultation was implemented on the Commission's website, 'Your Voice in Europe'. The web-based questionnaire was completed by just 336 respondents, of whom 101 were from organisations for people with disabilities. The characteristics of individuals within the sample are shown in Table 9.3. This highlights the bias of the sample towards the UK and Germany – two member states that have largely led the way in anti-disability legislation. Despite this limitation, however, it does demonstrate the effectiveness of such legislation in raising awareness and empowerment.

Interestingly, only 49% of the participants were people with disabilities, although a further 16% were family members. This also highlights the disadvantage that many disabled people experience in gaining access to the internet (Lee *et al.*, forthcoming; Shaw & Veitch, 2011). Studies within the UK have shown that online access for people with disabilities is often limited by cost factors, together with a lack of knowledge, with 25% claiming they could not afford internet access, and 40% of those who had it not being able to use it effectively due to a lack of training (Pilling *et al.*, 2004). The European Commission's (2010) survey asked for reactions to a series of themes covering the role of the EU and member states concerning employment, accessibility, education, healthcare, standards of living and recreation and leisure. Table 9.4 shows the highest agreement categories

Table 9.3 Sample of respondents in the EU-wide survey 2009–10

Profile	Percentage
Country	
Germany	23
UK	23
Belgium	7
France	5
Ireland	5
Italy	5
Age	
18–24	8
25–49	55
50–64	32
65+	3
Gender	
Male	43
Female	57

Source: European Commission (2010).

for selected themes. This shows an overwhelming importance attached to legislation, along with aspects of physical access, cost factors and related employment opportunities, better education, and the avoidance of stigmatisation through the process of institutionalisation. All of these were rated by 90% or more of the sample. Moreover, as illustrated, a whole range of other related factors were seen as being in need of attention (Table 9.4) by a large proportion of the sample.

Other survey data of a more limited type are provided by two special Eurobarometer surveys in 2006 and 2009, which focused on the problems of discrimination in the EU (European Commission, 2007, 2009). Both surveys found that discrimination based on disability was the most widespread and, in contrast, awareness of anti-discrimination legislation in the EU was low, recognised by around just 33%. However, comparison across the two surveys shows some slight signs of change. Thus, in 2006 53% of respondents thought that disability-related discrimination was widespread, compared with 43% in 2009. In both surveys, France was perceived to have a high level of discrimination: 66% in 2006 and 74% in 2009, and well above the

Table 9.4 Disabled consumers' views of their representation in holiday literature

Percentage agreeing	Views
92.9	Believed disabled are under-represented within tourism marketing
66.7	Found television advertising campaigns of little relevance to the disabled holidaymaker
57.1	Felt not valued by mainstream holiday providers
33.3	Felt under-valued by specialist providers
53.8	Felt including images of people with disabilities in mainstream tourism marketing would show they were valued and add to the feeling of inclusion

Source: Modified from White (2010).

EU average. As another measure of the way disabled people are treated in general, the 2009 survey found just less than 33% of able-bodied Europeans felt totally comfortable with having a disabled person in high political office.

Clearly, in many parts of society people with disabilities are still viewed as 'different'. Unfortunately, we know little about how such feelings on the part of the able-bodied stretch into the holiday environment, although Pearn (2009) and Shaw *et al.* (2005) raise these issues. Pearn investigated the detailed reactions of the able-bodied to changes in historic sites to enable better access for people with disabilities. This demonstrated a relatively high degree of tolerance of such modifications. In contrast, Shaw *et al.* found from a study of holiday destinations in the UK that large numbers of disabled visitors were often seen as a negative feature by able-bodied visitors.

A third EU survey was conducted by Buj (2010), who gathered data (again using an online questionnaire) on disabled tourists as well as suppliers of holidays. The data gathered from tourists was based on a convenience sample of 222 respondents drawn from a range of nationalities, including many non-Europeans, though once again the data were biased. As Buj (2010) explains, wheelchair users were the most active respondents, but at least in this case the author recognised the limitations of the online approach. In this survey, attention was given to rating perceived obstacles to travel. The results showed that the highest rating factors were: no accessible accommodation, no accessible transport at the destination, no accessible transport to get to the destination, and inaccurate information on accessibility.

Taking all the results from these surveys together, even though the evidence is limited, a number of important aspects concerning the lack of empowerment become apparent. First, in spite of the various EU strategies intended to improve access, for many disabled people physical access to transport and accommodation remains a key problem. This is obviously the case for wheelchair users. Secondly, there are wide variations across the EU in the empowerment of disabled tourists. Unfortunately, detailed evidence is still lacking on the extent of such variations. Thirdly, there is a sense that the able-bodied are becoming more aware of their fellow citizens who have disabilities. One of the major problems with current EU strategies is the need to engage more fully with the needs of people with disabilities, not just in gathering data from surveys but also to actively co-create better, more inclusive tourism products. The notion of co-creation is of increasing importance in marketing, as highlighted by Vargo and Lusch (2004) (for a discussion of this in a tourism context, see Shaw *et al.*, 2011). Within the context of disabled tourists, Shaw and Veitch (2011) argue that these ideas may help understand the processes of co-creating more inclusive tourism products by involving people with disabilities in the design and marketing of such products.

Consideration of the disabled traveller provides the focus for the remainder of this chapter, in which we turn our attention to three key themes: the experiences of people with disabilities; their representation within the travel and tourism media; and finally aspects of co-creation. Drawing mainly on research and information relating to the UK, it is contended that these are critical areas for the policy makers to consider, at both national and EU levels.

The Holiday Experiences of People with Disabilities

Much has been written on the travel constraints confronted by people with disabilities (Israeli, 2002; McKercher *et al.*, 2003; Shaw & Coles, 2004; Smith, 1987; Turco *et al.*, 1998; Yau *et al.*, 2004). When taken together with the evidence from surveys of disabled people's holiday experiences in the UK, it is clear that they have different experiences from able-bodied tourists. The majority of complaints from disabled tourists concern difficulties in travelling to destinations (57%), along with problems of getting insurance (22%), according to surveys by Leonard Cheshire (2005), a disability charity in the UK.

A more widespread and systematic survey has been conducted by Visit-Britain (2007), which highlighted the factors that disabled tourists thought made a 'perfect' holiday. These included accessible accommodation, as well as detailed information about access to the surrounding attractions in the destination. Carers were also concerned that their dependants had an enjoyable time and were not being treated poorly by insensitive and uncaring staff, leading to a process of de-humanising people with disabilities. In this respect, the survey found that most positive experiences were associated with a high level of customer awareness from staff (VisitBritain, 2007: 4).

Meanwhile, in 2010, Co-Operative Travel, part of Europe's largest consumer cooperative, in conjunction with the UK charity Tourism For All surveyed 215 people with disabilities about holiday arrangements, and found that 84% of respondents did not believe high street travel agents understood the needs of disabled travellers. The survey also found that 78% did not think that they were catered for by the high street, and that 93% found their choice of holidays restricted due to their disability (Co-Operative Group, 2010).

Smaller surveys have also highlighted the fact that people with disabilities tend to be offered poor-quality holidays, or indeed no suitable holidays at all (Shaw et al., 2005). According to Eichhorn et al. (2008) and Kozak (2001), the level of satisfaction involves attribute and information satisfaction. This in turn relates to the quality of information about a particular tourism product, which partly depends on the search process in helping decisions to be made. This is seen by many disabled people as a problem area, given the need for information on accessible facilities (Lee et al., forthcoming; Shaw et al., 2005; Stumbo & Pegg, 2005). It is this context that the OSSATE project (One-Stop Shop for Accessible Tourism in Europe) was funded by the European Commission. VisitBritain was part of the project and Lane et al. (2008) argue that the provision of accessibility information should be incorporated into destination management schemes. Clearly, such information on accessibility is important, but there is no clear evidence of its impact in improving the holiday search experiences of the vast majority of disabled consumers.

One other key factor regarding the experiences of tourists with disabilities is that it is important to remember that they are a diverse group who have differing concerns about access. Their levels and types of disability vary (Shaw & Veitch, 2011), as do their expectations. The emphasis on wheelchair access, critical though that is, focuses the issue of accessibility on impairment rather than disability, and as a result often tends to ignore the needs of others. In addition to this difference, it is also important to recognise that, on the whole, people with disabilities face a multitude of differences in their lives that impact on their holiday patterns. This has been recognised both by the European Commission and by numerous reports within the UK (e.g. Leonard Cheshire, 2008; Office of Disability, 2008). Within the UK, such studies have highlighted that people with disabilities are twice as likely to live in poverty as the able-bodied. Furthermore, they face extra costs because of their impairments and on average these costs are 25% above the normal expenditure of the non-disabled (Leonard Cheshire, 2008). In this respect, their holiday choices are more likely to be limited on financial grounds, which may in turn condition their expectations. Set against this, however, is the evidence that to people with disabilities and their families, holidays hold a special significance (Shaw & Coles, 2004). Studies have also highlighted the role of holidays in providing respite for other members of the family (often the carers) alongside pleasure for the person with the disability (VisitBritain, 2003).

Furthermore, it is also imperative to take account of the fact that the decision to travel on the part of people with disabilities is based on a complex array of intrinsic variables, such as motivations, values and lifestyles, personality and socio-economic characteristics. In particular, assessment of an individual's capabilities plays an important role in the decision to participate in tourism (Alegre *et al.*, 2010; Lee *et al.*, forthcoming). Such a view is supported at least by two theories: negotiation theory and the theory of learned helplessness. According to the theory of negotiation (Jackson *et al.*, 1993), when confronted with leisure barriers, people do not simply give up participating or enjoying leisure. Rather, they seek out solutions which enable them to overcome any constraints. The learned helplessness theory suggests that as individuals make unsuccessful attempts to control their environment (due to their disabilities), they may come to view negative outcomes as inevitable and subsequently discontinue efforts to engage in future participation (Nicassio *et al.*, 1985; Schiaffino & Revenson, 1995). This notion is supported by Smith (1987), who suggested that although tourists with disabilities might face various constraints which influence their tourism-related decision making, the impact of these barriers on their final decision to participate in travel depends on a range of personal characteristics, including perceptions of helplessness.

The Embodiment and the Representation of People with Disabilities in Tourism Marketing

Perceptions of self are also of relevance to debate surrounding the embodiment and representation of people with disabilities in tourism marketing, the second key theme considered in the remainder of this chapter. Shakespeare and Watson (2001) in their critique of the social model of disability argue that, in addition to viewing disability through the lens of social barriers, it is important to recognise further complexities which involve embodiment, a line of thought which considers the role that the body plays in shaping the mind. In this respect, they put forward the notion of 'embodied ontology', claiming it is not possible to separate the physical body from particular lived experiences, such as holidays. Such a view in turn links the social model of disability to structures and agencies in society. These structures create the barriers – physical, economic and social – that constrain access for those with disabilities. Within travel and tourism, one of these major areas of importance is the structures and agencies that create the 'images' of holiday experiences and destinations. This brings us to a neglected and yet major topic of concern, namely how people with disabilities are represented in the travel media.

As argued above, presenting people with disabilities as a market segment via the business case rather misses the point that they mostly want to be included in mainstream society. Existing disability legislation is aimed at creating 'inclusive access' to holidays but such inclusivity needs to embrace the marketing media. Early work in the US by Burnett and Paul (1996) following the passing of anti-disability legislation found that there were significant differences in the use of media, attitudes towards the media, and needs between disabled and non-disabled consumers. More recent work in the UK using online media and the BBC's web magazine *Ouch*, produced by people were represented in this magazine and in mainstream media (Thoreau, 2006). This analysis found that, in contrast to other media, people with disabilities in *Ouch* were represented as multidimensional people with varied interests and issues. Moreover, the study concluded that 'there is still a gap between how disabled people are represented in the media and how they wish to be represented' (Thoreau, 2006: 466).

Indeed, Drake (1999) states that the representation of disability in the media is clichéd, stereotyped and archetypal, and focuses on impairment as opposed to disability. Moreover, he believes disability political correctness to be responsible for such representations, as it has resulted in the use of images of disabled people that normalise and sanitise impairment, as opposed to developing ideas that support the social model of disability, thereby enhancing understanding of the wider societal issues underlying disability. Thus, he contends that representations of disability largely consist of a certain kind of valued disabled person who looks, according to Western ideals, beautiful, is educationally competent and who is striving to achieve a normal wealthy lifestyle. Drake's (1999) arguments are extremely compelling, particularly given the long-standing debate surrounding the use of disabled models in advertising campaigns. While for some, the decision by Debenhams in conjunction with the Channel 4 television programme *How to Look Good Naked* to become the first high street retailer to feature a wheelchair user in its campaign photography, was a major step forward in furthering the rights and access of people with disabilities, others are less convinced. Commentating on the campaign, one wheelchair user, for example, criticised the campaign for focusing on the wheelchair and not the model, stating that 'this kind of marketing makes me feel like I'm different, which is totally the wrong direction you should be taking' (Debenhams Blog, 2011).

Within some disabled communities, there is a general desire to be treated as 'normal' (Burnett & Baker, 2001). In this way, studies suggest that they believe positive portrayals within the media will make people with disabilities visible (Horowitz, 1993; Williams, 1992). More specifically, Frost (1998: 57) states that 'people with disabilities are very sensitive to being portrayed as dependent, vulnerable, or objects of pity', preferring rather to be seen as 'overcoming these difficulties, transcending their limits, and living life as other people do'. However, according to Drake (1999), it is exactly these notions of normality which are responsible for the nature of representations of impairment, or what he terms the mainstreaming of disability. This is because they entrench the belief that there is an essentially correct way to have been born, to look like and to be. In contrast to these views, Maloff and Wood (1998) claimed that the able-bodied tended to respond to people with disabilities in three main ways: (1) indifference; (2) fear (or discrimination); and (3) patronisation. Legislation is eroding discrimination in many cases, but despite the DDA in the UK, the charity Leonard Cheshire (2007: 15) found that 89% of disabled people sampled 'felt there was discrimination and prejudice towards disabled people'. Other studies have found that while the able-bodied want to attempt to be accepting and helpful towards disabled people, there is typically a low level of internal comfort (Burnett & Paul, 1996).

Specific studies of the representation of people with disabilities in the travel media are more restricted, and the few studies that do exist have examined the role of travel agents (Eichhorn et al., 2008; McKercher et al., 2003). One small-scale study has, however, attempted to cover some of these aspects of the media representation of tourists with disabilities (White, 2010). In this research, the focus was on how people with disabilities felt about their image/representation in the media along with how the able-bodied reacted to such representations. The survey was based on a convenience sample of 42 respondents drawn from the readership of two disability magazines: *Able* and *Disability Now*. It is difficult to draw generalities from this small sample but it seems that the majority thought that they were under-represented in the travel media (92.9%). As Table 9.4 shows, there was a general feeling that, across all types of media, they were under-represented and that travel providers tended to 'take the view that one size fits all' (White, 2010: 17), and failed to provide specific information concerning accessibility. Furthermore, 57.1% believed they were not valued by holiday companies in general, while a relatively large proportion (33.3%) also felt the same about specialist tour providers.

In the smaller number of in-depth interviews undertaken by White (2010), it was also found that people with disabilities reacted negatively to any form of tokenism. As one respondent stated:

> I think that [inclusion] would be positive, as long as they weren't a token disabled person in like a setting, … if they weren't there because they were disabled, but because they were just there … then I would say that was very positive. (White, 2010: 18–19)

The idea of representing disabled tourists in natural holiday settings is clearly seen as important but is difficult within the mainstream holiday literature. However, such inclusive representation can be achieved through the holiday industry at all levels, including destination marketing, utilising the concepts of co-creation embedded within the 'service-dominant logic' (Vargo & Lusch, 2004). This marketing paradigm in essence views consumers as operands in a process of co-creation between producers and customers (Shaw et al.,

2011), and brings us onto consider the third aspect of the disabled traveller in this chapter, this being the co-creation and co-production of holidays for disabled travellers.

Travellers with Disabilities, Co-creation and Co-production

A key premise of the service-dominant logic is that the consumer is an empowered entity who wants to be part of not just service consumption but also service production. In this respect, a service provider is merely a proposer of value and customers have to decide if they wish to engage with the provider and consume the services offered to them. Thus, the customer is always a co-producer, and both service providers and clients share resources and effort to co-create value and ultimately service experience. It is this co-creation of value which appears to be the key driver of customer service quality evaluation (Vargo & Lusch, 2004).

Given the emphasis placed on the customer, the service-dominant logic draws attention to the need to fully understand the role customers play in co-producing the experience they want, the extent to which they are empowered to co-create and co-produce, the processes that lead to feelings of empowerment, and the extent to which customers feel in charge of their consumption. The chief implication of these issues for the development of more inclusive holiday products, including the representation of people with disabilities within the mainstream media, is that disabled consumers need to be involved in all aspects of the co-creation process. This involvement may encompass ensuring that destinations are accessible, the production of detailed accessibility information (albeit at a site and/or destination level), the production of a range of different types of holidays which meet the needs of people with disabilities, and the generation of images of disability which for use in the marketing of holidays. In addition to placing the disabled traveller at the centre of the production and consumption process, however, it is also imperative that their individual needs and requirements are catered for, alongside those of their able-bodied family and friends with whom they may want to holiday.

Conclusions

This chapter has attempted to explore the EU and UK policy contexts surrounding disability rights, access and tourism, and in doing so has highlighted a number of gaps between policy intentions and the experiences of disabled people. There is increasing evidence that the travel industry is not doing enough for disabled travellers in terms of: ensuring accessibility and access to accessibility information; the range of products on offer; and how these products are marketed. Although an increasing number of specialist travel providers exist, the available evidence suggests that people with disabilities still encounter difficulties due to a lack of knowledge about accessibility at a destination-specific and site-specific level, as well as the limited flexibility in catering for their diverse needs and the needs of their companions who may or may not be able-bodied. Moreover, the representation of people with disabilities in marketing is clearly a highly contentious issue, particularly regarding the seeming mainstreaming of disability, and the resulting dominance of normalised and sanitised disabled imagery which highlights impairment as opposed to elucidating the underlying societal factors which create and entrench disability.

Given these shortcomings, this chapter has emphasised the importance of involving people with disabilities in the co-creation and co-production process of all aspects of the travel experience, including the production, marketing and consumption of holidays; only by doing so will the gap between policy and practice be addressed. In addition, this chapter has also highlighted several key areas which would benefit from further research, which, in turn, would substantially improve the tourism industry's responsiveness to the disabled market. These areas primarily revolve around empowerment, and include examinations of: how people with disabilities view progress towards accessible tourism, within member states and across the EU, of their holiday preferences, needs and requirements; the selection of imagery used in the marketing of holidays; and how they may be more integrally involved in the co-creation of the holiday experience.

References

Alegre, J., Mateo, S. and Pou, L. (2010) An analysis of households' appraisal of their budget constraints for potential participation in tourism. *Tourism Management*, 31(1): 45–56.

Buhalis, D., Eichorn, V., Michopoulou, E. and Miller, G. (2005) *Strategy for Commercial Exploitation, Branding and Promotion (eService Exploitation Plan)*. One-Stop-Shop for Accessible Tourism in Europe (OSSATE) Project Report under the European Commission eContent Programme. Athens: OSSATE.

Buj, C. (2010) *Paving the Way to Accessible Tourism*. Leeds: Leeds Metropolitan University.

Burnett, J.J. and Baker, H.B. (2001) Assessing the travel related behaviour of the mobility-disabled consumer. *Journal of Travel Research*, 40(1): 4–11.

Burnett, J.J. and Paul, P. (1996) Assessing the media habits and needs of the mobility disabled consumer. *Journal of Advertising*, 25(3): 47–60.

Co-Operative Group (2010) Co-Operative Travel rolls out custom holidays for the disabled. *Co-Operative News*. Online at http://www.thenews.coop/news/Retail%20 Societies/1726.

Darcy, S. (2005) *Disability and Tourism: A Bibliography*. Online at http://www.business. uts.edu.au/lst/downloads/07_Disability_Tourism.pdf.

Daruwalla, P. and Darcy, S. (2005) Personal and societal attitudes to disability. *Annals of Tourism Research*, 32(3): 549–570.

Debenhams Blog (2011) Meet Shannon, our first disabled model. *Debenhams Blog*. Online at http://blog.debenhams.com/meet-shannon-our-first-disabled-model/womens-fashion.

Drake, P. (1999) Introductory essay on normality theory. *Outside Centre*. Online at http://www.outside-centre.com/.

Eichhorn, V., Miller, G., Michopoulou, E. and Buhalis, D. (2008) Enabling access to tourism through tourism information schemes? *Annals of Tourism Research*, 35(1): 189–210.

English Tourist Board (1989) *Tourism For All*. London: English Tourist Board.

English Tourism Council (2000) *People With Disabilities and Holiday Taking*. London: English Tourism Council.

English Tourism Council (2001) *Holidays For Disabled Travellers*. London: English Tourism Council.

Europa (2006) *Equal Opportunities For People With Disabilities: A European Action Plan (2004–2010)*. Online at http://europa.eu/legislation_summaries/employment_and_social_policy/disability_and_old_age/c11414_en.htm.

European Commission (2000) *Establishing a General Framework for Equal Treatment in Employment and Occupation*. Council Directive 2000/43/EC. Brussels: EC.

European Commission (2007) Discrimination in the European Union. *Special Eurobarometer*, 263.

European Commission (2009) Discrimination in the European Union. *Special Eurobarometer*, 317.

European Commission (2010) *European Disability Strategy 2010–2010: A Renewed Commitment to a Barrier-Free Europe*. Brussels: EC.

European Disability Forum (2001) *EDF Position Paper on Tourism: Framing the Future of European Tourism*. Brussels: EDF.

European Network for Accessible Tourism (ENAT) (2010) *Paving the Way to Accessible Tourism –Survey Report*. Athens: ENAT. Online at http://www.accessibletourism.org/?i=enat.en.reports.1014.

Frost, D. (1998) The fun factor: marketing recreation to the disabled. *American Demographics*, 20(3): 54–58.

Horowitz, B. (1993) Caught in a delicate balance. *Los Angeles Times*, 22 May: p.A1.

Hurtsfield, J., Ashton, J., Mitchell, H. and Ritchie, H. (2004) *Monitoring the Disability Discrimination Act (DDA) Phase 3*. London: Disability Rights Commission.

Israeli, A.A. (2002) A preliminary investigation of the importance of site accessibility factors for disabled tourists. *Journal of Travel Research*, 41(1): 101–104.

Jackson, E.L., Crawford, D.W. and Godbey, G. (1993) Negotiations of leisure constraints. *Leisure Sciences*, 15(1): 1–11.

Kozak, M. (2001) Repeaters' behaviour at two district destinations. *Annals of Tourism Research*, 28(3): 784–807.

Lane, M., Sillito, A. and Veitch, C. (2008) Making access easy. *Tourism Insights*, July edition. Online journal at http://insights.org.

Lee, B., Agarwal, S. and Kim, H. (2011) Influence of travel constraints on people with disabilities' intention to travel: an application of seligman's helplessness theory. *Tourism Management*.

Leonard Cheshire (2005) *Disabled People's Holiday Experiences*. London: Leonard Cheshire.

Leonard Cheshire (2007) *Disability Review 2007*. London: Leonard Cheshire.

Leonard Cheshire (2008) *Disability, Poverty in the UK*. London: Leonard Cheshire.

Living Research and Development (2001) *Accessibility Legislation in Europe*. Brussels: Living Research and Development.

Maloff, C. and Wood, S.M. (1998) *Business and Social Etiquette With Disabled People*. Springfield, IL: Charles C. Thomas.

McKercher, B., Packer, T., Yau, M.K. and Lam, P. (2003) Travel agents as facilitators or inhibitors of travel: perceptions of people with disabilities. *Tourism Management*, 24(4): 465–474.

Nicassio, P., Wallston, K., Callahan, L., Herbert, M. and Pincus, T. (1985) The measurement of helplessness in rheumatoid arthritis: the development of the Arthritis Helplessness Index. *Journal of Rheumatology*, 12(3): 462–467.

Office of Disability (2008) *Experiences and Expectations of Disabled People*. London: Department for Work and Pensions.

Pearn, M. (2009) The attitudes of disabled and able-bodied visitors to heritage sites: a case study of Devon and Cornwall. Unpublished PhD, University of Exeter.

Pilling, D., Barnett, P. and Floyd, M. (2004) *Disabled People and Their Internet Experiences, Barriers and Opportunities*. York: Joseph Rowntree Trust.

Qatrain (2007) European Policy on Disabled People and the Position of Disabled People. Online at http://uk.qatrain2.eu/european-policy-on-disabled-people-and-the-position-of-disabled-people.

Ray, R.M. and Ryder, M.E. (2003) 'Ebilities' tourism: an exploratory discussion of the travel needs and motivations of the mobility-disabled. *Tourism Management*, 24(1): 57–72.

Schiaffino, K. and Revenson, T. (1995) Why me? The persistence of negative appraisals over the course of illness. *Journal of Applied Social Psychology*, 25(7): 601–619.

Shakespeare, T. and Watson, N. (2001) The social model of disability: an outdated ideology? In B. Altman and S. Barnartt (eds), *Exploring Theories and Expanding Methodologies: Where We Are and Where We Need To Go* (pp. 9–28). Research in Social Science and Disability, Volume 2. Bingley: Emerald Group Publishing.

Shaw, G. (2007) Disability, legislation and the empowerment of tourists with disabilities in the UK. In A. Church and T. Coles (eds), *Tourism, Power and Space*. London: Routledge.

Shaw, G. and Coles, T. (2004) Disability, holiday-making and the tourism industry in the U.K: A preliminary survey. *Tourism Management*, 25(3): 397–403.

Shaw, G. and Veitch, C. (2011) Demographic drivers of change in tourism and the challenge of inclusive products. In D. Buhalis and S. Darcy (eds), *Accessible Tourism: Concepts and Issues*. Bristol: Channel View Publications.

Shaw, G., Veitch, C. and Coles, T. (2005) Access, disability and tourism: changing responses in the UK. *Tourism Review International*, 8(3): 167–176.

Shaw, G., Bailey, A. and Williams, A.M. (2011) Aspects of service dominant logic and its implications for tourism management: Examples from the hotel industry, *Tourism Management,* 32(2): 207–214.

Smith, R.W. (1987) Leisure of disabled tourists: barriers to travel. *Annals of Tourism Research*, 14(3): 376–389.

Stumbo, N. and Pegg, S. (2005) Travellers and tourists with disabilities: a matter of priorities and loyalties. *Tourism Review International*, 8(3): 195–209.

Thegaskis, C. (2002) Social model theory: the story so far. *Disability and Society*, 17(4): 457–470.

Thoreau, E. (2006) Ouch: an examination of self-representation of disabled people on the internet. *Journal of Computer Mediated Communication*, 11(2): 442–468.

Turco, D. M., Stumbo, N. and Garncarz, J. (1998) Tourism constraints for people with disabilities. *Parks and Recreation*, 33(9): 78–84.

Vargo, S.L. and Lusch, R.F. (2004) Evolving to a new dominant logic of marketing. *Journal of Marketing*, 68(1): 1–17.

VisitBritain (2003) *Holiday Making and Planning Amongst People With a Disability*. London: NOP.

VisitBritain (2007) *Access Consumer Research*. London: VisitBritain.

White, S. (2010) An investigation into the representation of the disabled community within tourism marketing. Unpublished MSc dissertation, Business School, University of Exeter.

Williams, J.E. (1992) Fear of the disabled cripples us all. *Wall Streeet Journal*, 23 July: p. A13.

Yau, M.K., McKercher, B. and Packer, T.L. (2004) Traveling with disability: more than an access issue. *Annals of Tourism Research*, 31(4): 946–960.

Case Study 9: Cooperative Social Society (Consorzio Sociale, COIN), Italy

Anna-Grazia Laura *COIN Project Coordinator*

Consorzio Sociale COIN – Società Cooperativa Sociale
54/A Via Enrico Giglioli
00169 Rome
Italy
Telephone: +39 06 5706036
Fax: +39 06 23289417
Email: segreteria@coinsociale.it
http://www.sociale.it/

Aims/Mission

COIN's principal mission is the development of professional employment opportunities for disadvantaged people (those with physical disabilities and learning difficulties, and those at risk of social exclusion) through social cooperation, and more broadly it aims to create conditions that are favourable to the full establishment of citizenship rights for the weaker strata of the population. Activities undertaken by COIN have led to wide range of services for all citizens, in the fields of the environment, tourism and local development, and have contributed in a significant way to the quality and enhancement of social cooperation in Italy.

History

COIN is a non-profit organisation set up in Rome on 30 May 1995 by a number of social cooperatives. The group now brings together 28 social cooperatives that aim to improve the working opportunities for people with disabilities. Together they employ more than 3000 people full-time, 50% of whom are disabled.

Location

The head office is in Rome. The large majority of the member cooperatives are based also in Rome and the Lazio region, with a few exceptions in northern and southern Italy.

Current Activities/Programmes

COIN has acquired long-standing experience and know-how in the field of tourism, by carrying out specific projects, organising mobility services, conducting surveys, and organising special events and meetings at both national and international level. COIN is not, though, a travel agency or tour operator: rather, it provides support services to the tourism sector, to better meet the needs of tourists with disabilities.

By appointment of the former national Department of Tourism, COIN has worked on the project 'Italy For All', which was set up in 1997 with the aim of creating better tourism conditions for people with disabilities (see below).

COIN is fully aware that information is a essential for people with disabilities to fully enjoy their holiday destination:

- People with specific needs do not always have the possibility to adapt to the unexpected circumstances they find themselves in. They need, therefore, prior information that is reliable and allows them to plan first and then realise their stay and their travelling experience in optimal comfort.
- Tourists with disabilities have personal needs that are not easy categorise; consequently, an appropriate information system should allow them to make choices based on their personal situation.

In view of the above, COIN has set up an office for accessible tourism that can provide information to people with reduced mobility (both disabled and older people) concerning accessibility in a wide sense (accommodation, sights of interest, transport and assistance) through call centres staffed by expert operators. Three services are provided:

- Roma per Tutti, financed by the Municipality of Rome, has been active since 1966. It employs 17 people, of whom 14 are people with disabilities. It has processed more than 50,000 requests for information and advice (20% in English).
- Presidio del Lazio, financed by the Social Affairs board of Lazio Region, has produced several guides with information for tourists with disabilities. On its website (http://www.presidiolazio.it) the section 'Accessible itineraries' provides information and descriptions in Italian and English, while the section 'Tourism For All' contains online free training modules for tourism operators.
- Superabile, financed by INAIL, the Italian Workers' Compensation Authority, offers an information portal with 10 thematic areas, 20 regional sites and a mobile version, 'Superabile MOBILE'. It has received more than 200,000 enquiries since 2001 on work, legislation, tourism and leisure time, schooling and training, architectural barriers, social care and assistance.

As a pilot service, promoted and funded by the municipality of Rome, COIN is also organising free guided tours of Rome for residents and tourists with disabilities. This, though, is to be seen more to do with social inclusion than a tourist product.

Beneficiaries

The primary target audience for COIN are people with disabilities wishing to go on holidays. Their key requirements are:

- specific reliable and updated information on the level of accessibility and usability of the tourist facilities at the destination and during the journey (transport systems);
- the availability of accessible facilities;
- the availability of accessible services, along the entire service chain of tourism.

Funding Sources

The activities, centralised at consortium level, are financed mainly by public funding, at local, national and international level (EU-funded projects). A small amount is provided via member cooperatives' yearly contributions. The member cooperatives are funded via contracts with the public or private sector.

Role in Social Tourism Provision

COIN provides assistance to tourists with disabilities, and emphasises the promotion of a form of tourism that is inclusive of all citizens. It does so via:

- training on accessible tourism;
- consultancy on eliminating architectural barriers, based on the principles of 'design for all';
- networking at national and international level;
- the provision of specialised information.

Areas and Examples of Best Practice

The 'Italy For All' project was the first to define quality criteria for accessible tourism for the whole of Italy. Concluded in 2001, the project is still considered one of the largest and most thorough of its kind in Europe. It brought together tour operators, administrators and people with disabilities to develop ways to overcome travel barriers, and the influence of this project is still visible today in the training sessions, information provision and strategic planning of several tour operators. A key output of the programme was the handbook *Quality in Welcoming Tourists With Special Needs*, intended for tour operators. This included guidelines for service provision for people with different types of disability. More than 55,000 copies were printed, with a reprint of 5000 copies a few years later. The printed version was updated in 2009 with an online version, which includes the most recent developments in legislation, disability and inclusion concepts.

10 Social Tourism and Sustainability

Christian Baumgartner

This chapter deals with the ways in which the concepts of social tourism and sustainable tourism have become increasingly connected. Although the origins of both concepts go back to the 19th century, the links between them have only recently been made the focus of policy making within the European Union (EU). The European Economic and Social Committee (2006), in its *Opinion on Social Tourism*, proposes that social tourism is a key measure to increase and maintain the economic, social and environmental sustainability of destinations. This raises the question of whether the two concepts are inherently different, or whether sustainable tourism is the logical consequence of social tourism, and whether that would make the concept of social tourism redundant. Is sustainable tourism the logical new step in the historical development of social tourism, or are there aspects of social tourism that cannot fully be covered under the ambit of sustainability? This discussion is rendered more complex by the fact that both social and sustainable tourism are fluid, adapting to changing environments, and both have contested definitions. Although sustainable tourism can thus be seen as a fairly recent concept in the academic literature (really being articulated only after the Brundtland report in 1987 – see Hunter, 1997), this chapter will show that sustainable tourism practices existed long before the conceptualisation of the phenomenon. In these early practices, it will be shown that the divisions between social and sustainable tourism cannot always be readily made.

This chapter will then discuss the conceptualisation of sustainable tourism in the 1980s. It will propose that sustainable tourism, rather than being a separate form of tourism, is an approach to tourism that may have been practised prior to its inclusion in academic debates. The chapter highlights the links between social and sustainable tourism, based on the three sustainability pillars – ecological, economic and socio-cultural. But it also tackles the challenges and contrasts between the two concepts, and concludes that sustainability should indeed be a concept underlying all discussions

166

about tourism development, but also highlights political limitations that may hinder this approach. The case of Naturefriends (Austria) is provided as an example of an organisation that has aimed to link environmental and social concerns since its inception in the late 19th century. This example demonstrates the inherent complexities and issues that need to be addressed in policy making that seeks to further integrate the two concepts.

Sustainable Tourism

Sustainability and sustainable development came to prominence in 1987, when the United Nations World Commission on Environment and Development, chaired by Norwegian Prime Minister Gro Harlem Brundt-land, published its report *Our Common Future*. The central recommendation of this document, usually known as the Brundtland report, was that the way to square the circle of competing demands for environmental protection and economic development was through a new approach: sustainable development, defined as development that 'meets the needs of the present without compromising the ability of future generations to meet their needs' (Dresner, 2008: 1). Further United Nations conferences on the environment and development have included the 'Earth Summit' in Rio de Janeiro in 1992, where Agenda 21 was produced. The 40 chapters of Agenda 21 offer an action plan for sustainable development, integrating environmental with social and economic concerns, and articulating a participatory, community-based approach to a variety of issues, including population control, transparency, partnership working, equity and justice (Blewitt, 2008: 17).

The term 'sustainable tourism' has come to represent and encompass a set of principles, policy prescriptions and management methods which chart a path for tourism development such that a destination area's social and environmental resource base (including natural, built and cultural features) is protected for future development (Lane, 1994). Sustainable tourism policies thus aim to balance the economic, social and environmental aspects of tourism development. The concept has received considerable attention in the tourism literature since the 1980s, and diverging views exist on how the concept should be defined, what forms sustainable policies should take and how sustainable tourism relates to other forms of tourism that aim to reduce negative impacts on the host community and environment (such as eco-tourism, responsible tourism and community-based tourism).

Sustainable development in tourism can be portrayed as a pentagonal pyramid (see Figure 10.1), with 'economic prosperity', 'intact nature', 'intact culture', 'wellbeing of the local population and the staff' and 'satisfaction of visitors' needs' at its base, while the top represents the intergenerational approach to sustainable development (Müller *et al.*, 1999).

The framework outlined in Figure 10.1 is aligned with other, more general models of sustainable tourism in that it aims to show the linkages between

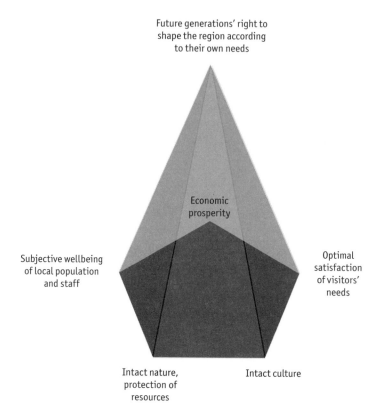

Figure 10.1 Sustainable development in tourism (based on Müller & Flügel, 1999; adapted according to Baumgartner, 2000)

economic, socio-cultural, environmental dimensions, which are focused on identifying solutions for the challenges of sustainability. However, this model shows the relationship between these in a tourism context and the need to balance the three pillars in safeguarding future developments at the tourism destination level, including the satisfaction of visitor needs. Key aspects are:

- respect for the natural environment via public policies or private sector self-regulation;
- the embedding of tourism within a sustainable, regionally specific, networking economy;
- respect for the social wellbeing of the local population and the employees in the tourism sector, and for the culture of the destination;

- participation of the host community in the decision-making and planning process;
- the implementation of environmental management systems in intensely visited destinations;
- accountability of the public sector as the main stakeholder in maintaining the sustainability of tourism in the region.

While this model seems simple, the reality of sustainable tourism is more complex. For example, there are different views on how these pillars of sustainability can be implemented at the destination level. Robert Jungk (1980) distinguishes between 'hard' and 'soft' approaches to sustainable development with regard to the environmental, economic and socio-cultural impacts of tourism. He supports the hard approach to sustainability: sustainable tourism can only be a niche activity, and destinations where the burdens of tourism become too large should be stopped from further development. However, this seems to be becoming a minority view, as sustainability concepts are frequently now embedded in development policies and strategies at destination level, including as a consequence of increasing demand from tourists.

These issues are compounded by the different levels at which sustainable tourism is implemented in the destination. Planning and implementing sustainability measures at the destination level are often in the hands of or coordinated by local government. This is also the level of government local residents are most likely to engage with in either opposing or supporting tourism development. In democratic political systems, the local residents may expect to be able to influence or guide political decisions in this area, and have ways to voice their disagreements (see Baumgartner, 2009). Public participation in sustainability planning at an early stage can avoid decisions being opposed by residents once they have been implemented. The success of citizen participation, however, often depends on the presence and willingness of local individuals and pressure groups to coordinate public concerns. Currently, destinations are more likely to implement government-driven (statutory) measures than voluntary actions to allow tourism development in a more sustainable fashion. Many tourism operators have sustainability policies of their own, and there are public guidelines available (for example Agenda 21).

Social Tourism and Sustainability

There are several links that can be identified between sustainable and social tourism. These links refer to all three pillars of sustainability:

- The first link is social sustainability, as the practices of both sustainable and social tourism can be understood to be oriented towards a reduction of social inequality, or at least to foster social inclusion. The sociologist Stefan Hradil (2001) defines social inequality as differences in access to the means of consumption between social groups that lead to one group appearing superior to others. Holidays can be argued to be such a source of inequality in advanced economies. However, holidaying, mainly because of high cost factors associated with participation, is almost by definition a socially exclusive activity. An important implication here is that as holidays have now become a significant part of contemporary social life in many EU member states, involuntary non-participation has become a common indicator of relative income poverty (Dawson, 1988; see also Minnaert et al., 2010).

- The second link between the two concepts addresses the economic aspects of sustainability. Social tourism can help to spread tourism spatially and temporally, extending the tourism season and contributing to employment in tourism destinations. While, traditionally, the development of a 'tourism for all' policy would have focused on benefits such as promotion of intercultural understanding and tolerance, there is a growing literature which suggests that viable economic operations and thus economic benefits to all stakeholders can result from 'tourism for all' initiatives (Griffen & Stacey, 2011; see also Chapter 3 in this volume).

- The third link refers to environmental aspects of social and sustainable tourism. Originally, sustainable development principles were developed out of a concern for protection of the environment, and to some extent this perspective remains at the forefront of tourism policy – as with the sustainable tourism 'labels', which are often focused on environmental measures/indicators. Font and Buckley (2001) describe one of the key aims of eco-labelling as 'to guide consumers in the choice of more environmentally friendly product choices'. And in terms of social tourism, almost coincidentally, many aspects of these activities are inherently more environmentally sustainable. Examples include the fact that much social tourism is domestic tourism, leading to fewer CO_2 emissions; participants in social tourism often use public transport; accommodation in social tourism is often at the forefront of environmental conservation practices (e.g. Ethique Etapes in France, youth hostels across Europe, caravans in the UK).

Indeed, the links between social tourism and sustainability have also been recognised at the level of the EU. The three key objectives of the EU Sustainable Development Strategy are: economic prosperity; social equity and cohesion; and environmental protection. In this regard, 'making holidays available to all' is explicitly identified as one of eight key sustainability challenges facing the tourism sector (European Commission, 2007). This challenge is primarily identified on the basis of social equity and cohesion, including public health and wellbeing, with the challenges of physical disability and economic disadvantage specifically highlighted. 'Making holidays available to all' is also linked to the economic benefits which 'tourism for all' may confer, helping to address two other sustainable tourism challenges, namely reducing the seasonality of demand and improving the quality of tourism jobs. Thus, the European Commission explicitly acknowledges accessibility to tourism for all EU citizens as a key sustainability issue currently facing the European tourism sector (Griffen & Stacey, 2011).

According to the European Commission (2007) there are eight key challenges for the development of sustainable tourism in the EU:

1   reducing the seasonality of demand;
2   addressing the impact of tourism transport;
3   improving the quality of tourism jobs;
4   maintaining and enhancing community prosperity and quality of life, in the face of change;
5   minimising resource use and production of waste;
6   conserving and giving value to natural/cultural heritage;
7   making holidays available to all;
8   making tourism a tool for global sustainable development.

It can be seen that social tourism is an integral aspect of sustainability and something that is intrinsic to the competitive future of the tourism sector.

Naturefriends: Origins in Social and Sustainable Tourism

One example integrating the different links between both concepts is the socialist hiking organisation Naturefriends, founded at the end of the 19th century. Its main objective was to motivate industrial workers in Austria to spend time in the open air. The organisation also played a political role, and was one of the pressure groups that strived to establish the right of the underprivileged working class to have Sundays free. One of the key activities of Naturefriends was to take workers who lived in Vienna to the city's 'home mountains', the Schneeberg and Rax. Many of the accommodation facilities of Naturefriends at mid-altitude, near former industrial towns, still exist today.

The ethos of Naturefriends was to provide access to relaxation and recreation for the working classes, without the religious ideological and organisational framework of many comparable Christian organisations working in this field when it was established. Being able to spend time in the 'natural environment' was presumed to lead to a range of health benefits, and was seen as beneficial, particularly for those with pulmonary problems. The activities of Naturefriends were banned during the fascist era, but were taken up again in the 1940s and 1950s. The holidays the organisation provided were once again popular with the working classes and, as such, social tourism was becoming an integral part of the organisation's objectives. This resulted in social tourism becoming an explicit part of Naturefriend's statutes.

The popularity of Naturefriends in the post-war years had two main drivers. Firstly, the greater part of the Austrian population had little money to spend on holidays and leisure pursuits. Secondly, hikers were dependent on the generosity of big landowners, as there was no right of way or free access to forests and mountains. In 1951, Naturefriends demanded that 'social forest and meadow belts' be laid out around the towns as recreation areas for both blue-collar and white-collar workers. Through the organisation's lobbying activities, the Austrian Federal Railways also granted a 25% reduction to members of Alpine clubs on most railway lines.

Naturefriends also developed its first international tourism product at this time. Mediterranean holidays became increasingly popular and in 1950 Eze Village, near Nice (France), opened its doors to its first 165 guests, for whom this was most probably the first seaside holiday. The camp offered basic accommodation, with tents for up to 10 persons, sleeping on straw bedding. There was an open cast-iron fireplace for cooking and all guests had to share in the kitchen duties. Eze Village marked the beginning of a democratisation of seaside tourism for low-income families. Naturefriends holidays had two main characteristics: the holiday had to be affordable for blue-collar workers, yet had to include cultural and educational elements. As early as 1956, 'sustainable' was the term used to define this aspect, which was interpreted as:

> Even if socially oriented, travel formats must not make do with superficial impressions, e.g. of the architecture of magnificent buildings. The formats in question must be designed to leave lasting impressions that educate and prepare the inner being for the global society of the future. (Winterer, 1956: 28; translation by present author)

Sustainability Challenges for Social Tourism

Although social and sustainable tourism thus have a number of potential overlaps, there are also areas where there are contrasts between the two concepts and practices. A number of questions need to be answered:

- Do the disadvantaged social groups who are targeted by social tourism actually wish to travel and to natural or protected areas? If not, is demand for tourism created where none would have existed, thus making the practice less environmentally sustainable?
- If so, how is the destination chosen? Is international travel more or less appealing than domestic travel?

- Is the on-going discussion in Europe about social tourism driven by an interest in improving the social conditions of specific target groups? Or is it driven by the industry, mainly to create new markets, and thus oriented towards economic viability rather than balanced, sustainable, long-term development?

There is certainly a lack of data about the travel preferences of non-travellers. It is unclear whether, given the choice, they would prefer support in the form of a holiday or in the form of another commodity. The possibility exists that, because of social tourism initiatives, at least some people are enabled to participate in tourism who would otherwise not have chosen (or been unable) to do so.

There is also a lack of studies on the preferred destinations of disadvantaged groups. International exchanges play an important role in the European Commission's Calypso project (European Commission, 2010), a project aimed to stimulate cooperation between different member states in the area of social tourism. During its first year, the main objectives were:

- to catalogue the main (most representative) good practices as a means to encourage tourism, particularly during the off-peak season, thus generating employment opportunities when tourism demand is traditionally low;
- to identify the existing measures at European and national level allowing the exchange of persons from the following target groups: senior citizens, young people, disabled citizens and families facing difficult social circumstances;
- to examine the difficulties related to such exchanges while proposing the most appropriate solutions;
- to propose one or several mechanisms in the tourist low season enabling particular target groups (senior citizens, young people, disabled citizens and families facing difficult social circumstances) to go on holiday in other member states or candidate countries on the basis of themed programmes and accommodation offers coordinated by national, regional or local public authorities, on the basis of initiatives from stakeholders, including municipalities, charitable organisations, parishes, unions, social partners, cooperatives or any not-for-profit associations.

International travel via social tourism is thus a clear central objective of the project – it is open to conjecture, however, whether international travel is always the preferred option for disadvantaged groups: aspects such as a difference in language and the complexity of the holiday preparations may deter the target groups from international holidays. Domestic holidays are often more sustainable, due to the reduced need for transport, as mentioned above.

This may indicate that the primary aim of some social tourism projects that have recently been proposed in Europe is the economic revival of destinations during the off-peak season via the attraction of new customer groups. If this is the case, the sustainability claims could be seen as justifications for the introduction of stimulation measures for one particular industry sector – a practice that would not be politically acceptable otherwise.

The European Commission, when describing the aims of the Calypso project in a leaflet, equates sustainability with economic permanence (or an increase in demand) (European Commission, 2010) and as a way of securing jobs:

> Create more and better jobs in the tourism sector (respect for tourism sustainability challenges; strengthening full-time employment prospects as opposed to seasonal part-time work; improving employment conditions by stressing the importance of a qualitative work environment throughout the entire tourism supply chain). (General information about the CALYPSO preparatory action, online at http://ec.europa.eu/enterprise/sectors/tourism/calypso/general/index_en.htm)

Although increasing the quality of employment opportunities could be seen as achieving a social sustainability objective, the improvement of the performance of and demand for a specific service or product is not a sustainability objective per se. The economic sustainability of the destinations is not linked to their environmental sustainability, although limited links with social sustainability are established (increase in citizenship and improved wellbeing, for example) (European Economic and Social Committee, 2006). The Calypso preparatory studies refer only to environmental sustainability, with references to eco-labels and farm holidays (Ramboll, 2010a). This is a very limited view of environmental sustainability, and does not question the encouragement of international travel and the ecological impacts this would have. The following quote highlights that environmental sustainability is not a priority for the project:

> At the supply side, it will be necessary to have criteria in place for assessing the quality and sustainability of offers, as well as to ensure that information on accessibility for example is correct and coherent. The verification of these criteria would need to be undertaken by participating Member States, and today the mechanisms to undertake or organise verification do not exist at the Member State level in most countries. (Ramboll, 2010b)

Social sustainability criteria are more prominent; however, this could be seen as motivated by economic rather than social considerations. The economic benefits of social tourism tend to be discussed in much more detail than the social benefits, as shown in this quote:

The EU is addressing these issues through the promotion of a concept known as 'social tourism', which is not only good for specific target groups but can also help promote off-season travel and develop the tourism sector in Europe's regions, especially those that are off the regular tourism map. (Stärkung des europäischen Tourismussektors, online at http://www.ec.europa.eu/enterprise/e_i/news/article_10573_de.htm, translation by author)

Without a more explicit emphasis on sustainability and clear sustainability criteria, the tourism sector may regard government subsidies to social tourism primarily as a welcome new source of income. In a panel discussion at a world congress of the International Social Tourism Organisation, for instance, the President of the Italian Federation of Tourism – Assoturismo – suggested that underprivileged social tourists would be welcome to fill the less popular accommodation and destinations during low seasons. In this interpretation, social tourism leads to social segregation – an outcome that is wholly opposed to the conceptualisations of both social and sustainable tourism. This discussion has shown that social tourism is not sustainable tourism *sui generis* – most particularly not when it is interpreted as a mainly economic measure designed to mitigate seasonal fluctuations and to ensure greater demand for declining destinations and facilities. Unless both social and sustainable tourism are more clearly defined, and the links between them made clear, they run the risk of becoming vague terms that can be used to serve any political purpose whereby some social and/or environmental benefits are achieved.

Conclusions

This chapter has shown that the concepts of social and sustainable tourism have a number of features in common, and that in early examples of nature-based social tourism the two aims often converged. It is, however, important to highlight that there are also differences between the two concepts, and that social tourism is not automatically sustainable – sustainability factors needs to be explicitly built into social tourism initiatives. This chapter has suggested that in current discussions on tourism, sustainability should be included as a matter of course, as it is an approach to tourism rather than a particular form of tourism. Social tourism, with its particular focus on disadvantaged persons in the generating region and the host community, is a particular form of tourism that can be approached in a sustainable way.

Social tourism can be a particularly suitable vehicle to achieve the aims of social sustainability, an aspect of sustainability that is often overshadowed by purely environmental interpretations of the concept. Examples of the benefits of social tourism that promote social sustainability include the improved wellbeing of the beneficiaries, the cultural contacts between the host population and the visitors, the working conditions in the host community and greater accessibility.

Conversely, there is a need for the public decision makers as well as the private and voluntary operators to focus more explicitly on sustainability in social tourism initiatives. This includes the following aspects:

- The term 'social tourism' should not be given to initiatives whose main aim is to increase demand for a product or service. Social tourism initiatives should have as their primary concern the social benefits for the beneficiaries and/or the host community.
- Social tourism must not lead to social segregation, whereby lesser-quality products are offered to disadvantaged groups. Instead, social tourism should lead to greater social integration and inclusion.
- Finally, social tourism, just as any other form of tourism, needs to pursue the aim of sustainable tourism development.

References

Baumgartner, C. (2000) *Nachhaltigkeit im österreichischen Tourismus. Grundlagen und Bestandsaufnahme*. Vienna: Studie für das BMWA.

Baumgartner, C. (2009) *Nachhaltigkeit im Tourismus. Von 10 Jahren Umsetzungsversuchen zu einem Bewertungssystem*. Innsbruck: Studienverlag.

Blewitt J. (2008) *Understanding Sustainable Development*. London: Earthscan.

Dawson, D. (1988) Leisure and the definition of poverty. *Leisure Studies*, 7(3): 221–231.

Dresner, S. (2008) *The Principles of Sustainability*. London: Earthscan.

European Commission (2007) *Action for More Sustainable European Tourism*. Brussels: European Commission DG XXIII.

European Commission (2010) Calypso widens Europe's travel horizons. Leaflet. Brussels: European Commission.

European Economic and Social Committee (2006) *Opinion on Social Tourism. Barcelona Declaration: Social Tourism in Europe*. Brussels: EESC.

Font, X. and Buckley, R. (2001) Tourism Ecolabelling: Certification and Promotion of Sustainable Management. Wallingford: CABI.

Griffen, K. and Stacey, J. (2011) Towards a 'tourism for all' policy for Ireland: achieving real sustainability in Irish tourism. *Current Issues in Tourism*, 14(5): 431–444.

Hradil, S. (2001) *Soziale Ungleichheit in Deutschland*. Opladen: Leske und Budrich.

Hunter, C. (1997) Sustainable tourism as an adaptive paradigm. *Annals of Tourism Research*, 24(4): 850–867.

Jungk, R. (1980) Wieviel Touristen pro Hektar Strand? Plädoyer für sanftes Reisen. *Geo*, 10: 154–156.

Lane, B. (1994) Sustainable rural tourism strategies: a tool for development and conservation. *Journal of Sustainable Tourism*, 2(1,2): 102–111.

Minnaert, L., Quinn, B., Griffen K. and Stacey J. (2010) Social tourism for low-income groups: benefits in a UK and Irish context. In S. Cole and N. Morgan (eds), *Tourism and Inequality: Problems and Prospects* (pp. 126–143). Wallingford: CABI International.

Müller, H.R. and Flügel, M. (1999) *Tourismus und Ökologie: Wechselwirkungen und Handlungsfelder* (Berner Studien zu Freizeit und Tourismus no. 37). Bern: Forschungsinstitut für Freizeit und Tourismus.

Ramboll (2010a) *Calypso Study on Social Tourism. Country Study Austria*. Online at http://ec.europa.eu/enterprise/sectors/tourism/files/docs/calypso/country_reports/calypso_country_report_austria_en.pdf.

Ramboll (2010b) *Calypso Study on Social Tourism. Compendium of Good Practices*. Online at: http://ec.europa.eu/enterprise/sectors/tourism/files/docs/calypso/calypso_compendium_of_good_practices_en.pdf.

Winterer, F. (1956) Zum Kongress der Naturfreunde Internationale. *Der Naturfreund*, 1–2.

Additional sources

Böll, H. (1977) *Einmischung erwünscht. Schriften zur Zeit 1973–1976*. Köln: Verlag Kiepenheuer und Witsch.

Esser, H. (2004) *Soziologische Anstöße*. Frankfurt: Suhrkamp.

Hachtmann, R. (2007) *Tourismusgeschichte*. Göttingen: Vandenhoeck & Ruprecht.

Hoffmann, H. and Zimmer, J. (1986) *Wir sind die grüne Garde. Geschichte der Naturfreunde-jugend*. Essen: Klartext.

Hradil, S. (1987) *Sozialstrukturanalyse in einer fortgeschrittenen Gesellschaft. Von Klassen, Schichten zu Lagen und Milieus*. Opladen: Leske und Budrich.

Pils, M. (1994) *Berg Frei. 100 Jahre Naturfreunde*. Vienna: Verlag für Gesellschaftskritik.

Zimmer, J. (1984) *Mit uns zieht die neue Zeit, Die Naturfreunde. Zur Geschichte eines alternativen Verbandes in der Arbeiterkulturbewegung*. Köln: Pahl-Rugenstein.

Case Study 10: European Union Federation of Youth Hostel Associations (EUFED)

Constanze Adolph *Operations Director*

EUFED
European Union Federation of Youth Hostel Associations
Hoogstraat 25, rue Haute
B-1000 Brussels
Belgium
Telephone: +32 (0)2 502 80 66
Fax : +32 (0)2 502 55 78
Email: info@eufed.org
http://www.eufed.org

Aims/Mission

The key aims of EUFED are:

*   sustainability;
*   diversity;
*   mobility;
*   keeping human relations as our focal point.

The mission of the youth hostelling movement clearly focuses on inclusion objectives. Article 2 of Hostelling International, the International Youth Hostel Federation Constitution, gives one aim as:

> To promote the education of all young people of all nations, but especially young people of limited means, by encouraging them in a greater knowledge, love and care of the countryside and an appreciation of the cultural values of towns and cities in all parts of the world and as ancillary thereto, to provide hostels or other accommodation in which there shall be no distinction of origin, nationality, religion, sex, class or

political opinions and thereby to develop a better understanding of their fellow men, both at home and abroad.

In the EUFED 2003 Salerno Declaration, European member associations agreed to aim for 'Access to Europe for all' and to 'contribute to the European Union in the fields of education, social inclusion and environment'.

The EUFED 2005 Toledo Declaration underlined the importance of enhancing cultural understanding in Europe.

Thus, EUFED understands social tourism in its broadest sense, with a special focus on accessibility, social inclusion and sustainability. Following our 'Third Way Strategy' we are committed to offer activities to people who cannot pay a market price for service and who are at risk of social exclusion, while serving people equally.

EUFED's main focus is on working on coordination, strategy building and advocacy for young people, with a special focus on sustainable tourism. We establish dialogue with EU key decision makers to ensure proactive consultation in all fields of policy and legislation regarding youth, sustainable/responsible tourism and non-formal education. We call for access to Europe for all, which means overcoming barriers for youth travel to, and within, Europe. In this context, EUFED appears in several expert and focus groups of the European Commission, for example in the Calypso project, which addresses social tourism in Europe (DG ENTR), and the demographic forum (DG EMPL). We are in contact with seven Directorate Generals of the European Commission and a group of Members of the European Parliament.

History

The youth hostelling movement began in Germany in 1909. The idea of creating a network of youth hostels, each situated a day's walk from each other so as to welcome young hikers, soon proved attractive across Europe. By 1921, the number of overnight stays had already reached 500,000. In 1932, 11 European associations founded the international Youth Hostel Federation, which today is represented in 90 countries. Hostelling International is the biggest member association worldwide for young people: it offers its 3.5 million members a choice of over 4000 accommodation centres.

EUFED was set up as a non-governmental organisation in 1987, when the Single European Act came into force, to represent the views of youth hostels and guests at the European political level. Today, EUFED represents 19 youth hostel associations in 15 countries, operating 1787 youth hostels across Europe, serving about 2.8 million members and achieving 23 million overnight stays a year. Despite their name, youth hostels are open to people of all ages.

Location

EUFED's head office is located in Brussels.

Current Activities/Programmes

Youth hostels offer a place where everybody can feel at home: places to meet and to learn, and places for dialogue. They also offer a remarkably wide range of programmes and activities, which aim to overcome barriers and so further promote intercultural dialogue and European integration. We especially welcome people with disabilities.

Youth hostel associations across Europe host millions of young people every year. These young people work together, whether formally or informally, on a wide range of matters. Principal topics include such issues as sustainable development, environmental protection and biodiversity, social learning and social inclusion, intercultural dialogue and diversity, culture and creativity, sports and wellness (including the promotion of a healthy lifestyle), team-building and conflict management, job orientation and training, history, politics and cultural heritage, new media and technologies. Youth hostels also offer a whole variety of programmes for families; having a break in youth hostels gives families the opportunity to spend quality time together and to rediscover each other.

Beneficiaries

Contrary to what our name suggests, hostelling is not just for young people. We welcome people of all ages, cultures and nationalities. Individuals, families, small and large groups are all welcome and it is this mix of visitors that makes hostelling the unique and interesting experience that it is.

Funding Sources

EUFED's projects are mainly financed by the EU Youth in Action programme, the Comenius and the Leonardo programme. We also cooperate with national ministries and public as well as private partners.

As support mechanisms within the member states differ considerably, so do funding sources for our member associations.

Role in Social Tourism Provision

EUFED's role in social tourism provision is to facilitate exchange of best practices and cooperation between the member associations. In 2010, EUFED was the main partner and multiplier of the DG EMPL EU Campaign 'For Diversity/Against Discrimination', the '112-foundation' to promote the emergency telephone code Europe-wide and multiplier of the 'European Action on Drugs'. Besides planning, applying for, implementing and evaluating numerous projects subsidised by the EU, EUFED's third task is to function as a coordinating link between the member associations, the European institutions and its own network of partners (e.g. the Family Holiday Association and 4motion). Last but not least, EUFED is a member of the experts group of the preparatory action called Calypso, set up by the European Commission, DG Enterprise and Industry. The aim is to facilitate social tourism on a European level by improving tourism's seasonality patterns across

Europe, particularly through the social policy function of tourism (see http://ec.europa.eu/enterprise/sectors/tourism/calypso/general/index_en.htm).

Areas and Examples of Best Practice

Our activities include staff training as our staff – as diverse as our guests – are seen as an important source of inspiration. Specific projects are briefly presented below.

'World Without Boundaries' – Croatian Youth Hostel Association (CYHA)

In recent years, the CYHA has run the project 'World without boundaries' that includes young disabled people in youth activities organised by the CYHA and other youth organisations. Every year, this project allows 10–15 young disabled people to be actively involved in the preparation, organisation and implementation of different events and activities, such as concerts, exhibitions, excursions and the preparation of media information.

The highlight of the project is a five-day seminar at a CYHA youth hostel, which gathers young CYHA volunteers and young disabled people. The objectives are to create an atmosphere of trust and to break stereotypes and prejudices. The seminar involves 50 participants and provides an excellent opportunity for young disabled people to take an equal, active part in the production of future youth activities. One of the outcomes of this project is the production of a brochure providing information on all the youth hostels accessible to people with disabilities.

'Chernobyl Campaign' – Austrian Youth Hostel Association (ÖJHV)

Holidays for children of Chernobyl victims (who are suffering from genetic defects) are arranged by different Austrian regions under different patronage and mixed initiatives. The programme aims to allow young people affected by the legacy of Chernobyl to leave behind their daily routines and social exclusion.

'Summer Holiday Campaign for Large Families on a Low Income' – German Youth Hostel Association (DJH)

Funded by the Rhineland-Palatinate Regional Ministry for Labour, Social Affairs, Health, Families and Women, the campaign represents an auxiliary engagement of the Land in promoting 'leisure time for families'. The programme addresses low-income families with three or more children and single parents with one child or more.

'Out of the Shadow' – Macedonian Youth Hostel Association (MYHA)

This is a summer camp for socially excluded young people living in disadvantaged urban areas in Kosovo, in the region of Skopje and the south of Serbia, displaced by the conflicts in Kosovo and in Macedonia in 1999. Many of them have a Roma background. The objectives of this programme are the advancement of the social integration and empowerment with artistic and sport activities, using intercultural methods as means to encourage creativity and to increase the self-esteem of the young participants.

'IOU Respect': An Intercultural Youth Exchange Programme

Shortly after 11 September 2001, there was a clear need to exercise the Hostelling International mission of building peace by bringing people together in order to close the gap between the cultures of youth from Western countries and those from predominantly Muslim countries.

In 2010, for the sixth time, EUFED member organisations in Germany (DJH) and France (FUAJ) and youth hostel organisations from Morocco, Tunisia, Egypt and the USA organised the 'IOU Respect' intercultural youth exchange. Twenty-four young people aged 18–25 gathered in Morocco for an intensive experience of living, dialogue, sharing and learning together, in an effort to bridge cultural divides. Through a series of engaging, fun, challenging workshops, and time spent in hostels together, participants developed friendships (still alive via Facebook) and respect, and discovered the similarities between people and cultures of different countries.

'Breaks4Kids' and 'Do It 4 Real' Summer Camps – Youth Hostel Association (England abd Wales)

Since 2004 more than 45,000 young people, with funding from the UK government's Department for Children, Schools and Families, have taken part in summer camps run by the UK Youth Hostel Association, with support from other organisations. The programme aims to identify at an early stage children and young people at risk of social exclusion, and make sure they receive the help and support they need to achieve their potential.

The Youth Hostel Association commissioned research into the benefits of attending 'Do It 4 Real' summer camps. Young people who attended the camp took part in the research and their parents were also included. The researchers found that 86% of young people attending camp expected to be more active afterwards, and 92% agreed that they had made new friends from different backgrounds, showing that a long-term impact of going on camp was better understanding of people from different backgrounds.

'FAB Spreads Smiles Across Families Faces' – Youth Hostel Association (England and Wales)

Families' Activity Break (FAB) sets up camps for bereaved family members who have lost someone serving in the armed forces. The camps are designed for families to come together and experience challenging and fun activities, engaging in communication as a family and socialising with others who are in the same position. FAB camps have proved to be a real success, as over 100 families have experienced these breaks. Families are challenged to take part in activities like horse riding, canoeing, mountain biking and abseiling, and to communicate with one another and are encouraged to spend time together.

Families' Activity Breaks is a charity backed by the UK Ministry of Defence that aims to offer holidays to service families with children up to the age of 19.

'Diversity on Tour' – EUFED together with the German Youth Hostel Association (DJH)

The Diversity on Tour project aims to diminish the social exclusion of young migrants and is a common initiative of several youth hostel associations and external partners from Belgium, Luxembourg, Germany, Slovenia, Portugal and Israel. In its context, a three-day seminar is be organised, and participation will be open to all interested European non-profit organisations, such as migration associations and departments for integration. This platform for intercultural exchange, thereby, aims to trigger a multiplying effect and will support the setting up of several follow-up initiatives.

11 Conclusions and Future Research Issues

Scott McCabe, Anya Diekmann
and Lynn Minnaert

This book has examined different conceptualisations and practical implementations of social tourism in Europe from a range of perspectives. Social
tourism is a little-known concept; it is not widely understood either within
the tourism industry, as an aspect of social and welfare policy, or as a subject
or field of study in tourism social science. This is despite the fact that social
tourism has been in existence since the emergence of modern mass tourism, and that there is more recognition of social tourism within the French
language and culture. Our aim in dealing with this lack of knowledge has
been threefold: to develop understanding of social tourism and its position
within the spectrum of tourism phenomena, especially in view of current
developments in European policy, society and tourism economy; to highlight the critical contextual and conceptual links between social tourism,
social science and social policies, with an emphasis on the multidisciplinary
aspects of social tourism; and to highlight the diversity of social tourism
schemes in Europe to illuminate current challenges and opportunities for
the development of a more sustainable, fair and integrated tourism sector.

In achieving these aims, we feel that the main contributions are as
follows. The multidisciplinary perspective has been an innovative aspect
of the book, aimed at integrating different approaches to provide a more
coherent overview of social tourism phenomena and systems. This book
is not only the first of its kind in the English language, but is also the first
to approach the topic from a European perspective. The different chapters
deliver experiences and research from different countries. The case studies
sought to understand practices from Belgium, Ireland, Italy, the UK, Poland
and Denmark. Finally, the book has adopted an innovative approach in that
it combines theory and practice. The combination of theory and practice
gives an integrated overview of social tourism and stimulates mutual
interaction. Having come to the end of this volume, the discussion now
turns to *look back* at how these different perspectives have enriched our

understanding of social tourism in Europe. It is also important to consider how the issues raised present us with an opportunity to propose new ways for social tourism to *move forward*: both in terms of policy, research and the academic sphere, and in its practical implementation.

Looking Back

The evolving definitions and historical development of social tourism (Chapter 2) and the current organisational structures (Chapter 3) high-lighted that social tourism is dynamic, responding to changes in the global context of tourism, but also, in analysing these historical and current con-texts, we can detect a gradual shift in emphasis away from a more social imperative for social tourism within policy, towards its integration into the market-driven tourism economy. At its heart, however, as many of the contributors to this volume have asserted, social tourism is underpinned by two basic concepts: that the right to travel is a human right; and that tourism is an essentially progressive, positive and desirable activity in which all people in society should be able to participate, should they wish to do so.

While tourism statistics have risen steadily over the last 60 years within Europe, the proportion of the population which does not have access to participation has remained fairly stable at around 40–45%. There are well known barriers to participation: inequalities within societies arising from housing, employment, social mobility, education, disability and so on are major causes of unequal access among different social groups, leading to lower participation rates among the lower social classes, which have become entrenched over many years. Therefore while tourism has emerged as a key sector of the market economy in Europe, and more and more people now see tourism as an essential part of life, inequalities in access and participation appear to have widened in some countries. There is an emerging recognition among governments and policy makers of the importance of tourism to the European economy and society of the future and increasingly of social tour-ism's potential in a broad-based market for tourism, having the additional benefits of being able to meet social welfare objectives.

The critique of tourism as solely an industry based on hegemonic lib-eralism principles (Chapter 4), which alongside liberalism more generally have not led to overall increases in quality of life, despite growing economic prosperity (Layard, 2005), was contrasted with the alternative approach in the form of a 'social economy' (Chapter 5). Higgins-Desbiolles argues in Chapter 4 that the fact that tourism has been constructed as purely an 'industry' has not lent credibility to the sector within government policy. She argues that tourism is more likely to meet the challenges and needs of the emerging political economy in the post-capitalist global era through a reconnection to the humanist vision of tourism. The social and personal benefits of tourism need to be highlighted, and particularly social tourism has a great role to play in connecting government agendas for social and other policies. Caire has shown in Chapter 5 how a pluralist approach can yield a successful, mixed system that is built on socially oriented principles.

However, this ideal is not without its challenges. A more discerning and diverse market, greater competition in social tourism supply chains and a reduction in funding place pressures on the French model, yet the ideas of the social economy offer opportunities for the future. There are many issues discussed by Caire which chime with current thinking in the UK about the move towards the 'big society', where community-led organisations, associations and businesses are to be encouraged to develop socially oriented (and perhaps environmentally friendly) programmes to take the strain away from the state in the delivery of some social services. The UK situation, where much social tourism is already delivered primarily through the voluntary sector, offers some potential, not driven by state involvement in provision of services or investment in infrastructure. However, the UK system is highly fragmented, lacks cohesion and is small in scale, and greater coordination would be a benefit. As we have seen, there are many different systems in Europe, too many to be comprehensively described in the context of this book, although we have sought to highlight the main approaches, posing questions which we will address later in this chapter.

The links between tourism participation as an aspect of the welfare rights of individuals were outlined and contextualised in Chapter 7, by Hall and Brown. Differences in the cultural prioritisation of tourism within society, and also differences within countries in orientation to welfare, create an interesting lens through which to explore current trajectories and possible sources of conflict. Hall and Brown identify four models of social tourism in European welfare systems, but focus on the former Eastern and Central European states, which were part of the Soviet state socialist system. The authors identified that the regulated and formalised support of holidaymaking as an intrinsic aspect of workers' rights for health and welfare also included exclusionary practices, in that it favoured urban, industrial classes. In the Eastern and Central European states, tourism was perceived, particularly through spa and health participation, to be critically linked to health improvement and also more generally to recuperation from work. The role of social tourism in the welfare agenda does need to be repositioned as an investment in the wellbeing and fabric of society and yet how this can be achieved in the light of current budgetary constraints requires a leap in innovation in the delivery of services, as well as much greater evidence on the benefits that can be attributed to such an investment.

Some of the major challenges in developing better theory and practice in social tourism stem from a shifting societal context in terms of, for example, access to mobility and demographic structures. In Chapter 6, Hannam charts the development of a new mobilities paradigm emerging in social sciences that has the capacity to link issues of unequal access to and participation in leisure travel to more general theories of the importance of movement and co-presence in everyday social life. Whereas to date the mobilities perspective has largely focused on social elites, theorising their travel practices in relation to globalisation processes, technology, communications and material objects, Hannam argues that the approach is equally relevant to understanding 'immobilities', exclusionary forces and differential mobility empowerments which reflect structures of power according to ethnicity, gender, age and social class. Tourism social science has a lot to learn from leisure studies in this area and Hannam focuses on the particular issues facing children, such that their mobilities are 'patterned', shaped by an increasingly youth-oriented media spotlight and subjected to various forms of control. Given the importance of leisure travel experiences to long-term memories, building family relationships and self-development, it is incredible that tourism social science has virtually extinguished the child from its focus of study (Small, 2008). The relationships between mobility, holiday experiences and social and human capital need to be determined, but similarly the effects of exclusion need to be understood.

Children's issues come again to the fore in a shifting demographic structure of society. The conventional notions of family are not consistent with emerging family structures. With a focus on the UK, Such and Kay in Chapter 8 highlight the diversity of family groupings, and the importance of cultural identity for family structure, attitudes and practices. Families are a key mechanism for inclusion and exclusion, and play a critical role in positioning individuals socially and economically. Tourism research has failed to respond to the diversity in family ideologies and make-up. We need to develop our understanding of different family forms and to unpack how family relationships inform tourism experience and how tourism experiences affect family relationships. In previous research evaluating the needs for and benefits of social tourism, McCabe (2009) has highlighted the importance of the holiday as a chance for family members to spend quality time together, breaking away from routines and familiar places. Social tourism systems need to be flexible enough to accommodate diverse family contexts, but also more evidence is required on the outcomes for families of provision of support.

Perhaps even more complex than shifting family structures are the issues and challenges raised in terms of the inclusion of people with disabilities into the social tourism system, which was the focus of Chapter 9. Shaw and Agarwal argued that although there is an increasing awareness of disability issues among the general population, and also attention to disability issues and improvements in research, this still falls some way short of a full understanding of issues affecting people with disabilities, their experiences of tourism and the barriers to participation and access they feel, highlighting the gap between policy and practice. They argue that these gaps can be bridged by including people with disabilities in the co-creation and co-production of the tourism experience, incorporating the production, marketing as well as consumption of holidays. A more inclusive approach to research in tourism will also enable greater insights to be gained into the needs and expectations of these groups of people.

Chapter 10 turned to the issues raised by the recent drive to associate social tourism with sustainable tourism. There are many possible connections between the two concepts. Much social tourism takes up spare capacity in the low season, thus potentially contributing to continued employment in tourism resorts, increasing the seasonal spread of tourism, and contributing to the tourism economy. There are of course the social benefits to tourists, often overlooked in the context of sustainability. However, Baumgartner reminds us of the critical challenges to the widespread association of social tourism with sustainable tourism. He asks whether social tourists wish to use sustainable forms of travel and accommodation, or appreciate rural, small-scale tourism experiences. Good practice by many social tourism infrastructures (such as holiday centres and other accommodation facilities) in the area of sustainability can provide a good example for the mainstream sector. There is opportunity in respect of sustainability for social tourism but we must not lose the social imperative.

Emerging Themes in Social Tourism

In synthesising the main issues arising from these contributions, a number of overarching themes can be observed throughout the book. A first observation is that even though many different implementations of social tourism exist today, most social tourism initiatives in the European Union (EU) can be traced back to the rise of social movements at the end of the 19th century. Although different countries have gone on to develop divergent approaches and systems of social tourism, some based on the various political and ideological orientations to welfare and the role that holidays play in society, there are some general trends, convergent themes and common issues that emerge that are directly attributable to this common heritage. The mediation system described in Chapter 3 represents the basic approach in most EU countries. This demonstrates that some unifying aspects can be identified that could be brought into a single framework for social tourism across the EU. What this means is that, in order for social tourism to be implemented successfully, it needs to be managed by an intermediary organisation, as the market cannot independently or on its own volition cater for the needs of social tourists. This is because potential beneficiaries may have no experience of tourism. In the UK, for example, generations of families do not prioritise holidays, and thus there is no family background in tourism participation. These families do not understand the benefits that a holiday can bring to all members of the family until they have experience of it; moreover, they usually lack information about opportunities, or require different types of support beyond the capabilities of the mainstream tourism industry.

A second point is the observation that social tourism is reliant on some form of stimulus funding. This has often been provided by the state or the public sector, and yet the contributors to this book have noted that the role of the public sector in the provision of opportunities for tourism participation is on the decrease in most European countries. The financial downturn of recent years has led to public sector spending coming under increased scrutiny. A range of different funding mechanisms have been discussed, from direct state aid, funding via membership organisations, charitable funding, as well as the Danish system, where funding is provided through interest accruing on paid vouchers/stamps. It appears that, in many cases, funding is moving away from investment in physical resources and towards stimulus for collaborative or partnership programmes, in a pluralistic financing model. The fiscal challenges to the public sector make it imperative that: innovative approaches to funding can be developed to ensure social tourism is not dependent on vulnerable sources of funding going forward; the justification for such funding support is not solely evidenced by benefits to health and social welfare but also by the added value to the national/regional economy; shared knowledge about collaborative, public–private funding partnerships demonstrating cost-effective solutions be disseminated across organisations in Europe.

Thirdly, the organisational structure of social tourism is changing in response to a dynamic tourism industry sector, which poses challenges as well as opportunities. In several countries, the social tourism infrastructure has been privatised over recent years, and some social tourism accommodation centres now attract a very different clientele from the one it was originally intended for. In some cases it is not clear whether social tourism facilities actually benefit social tourists. Different authors in this volume have highlighted the growing similarities between, indeed convergence of, social and commercial tourism: in many countries social tourism organisations now have to compete with private competitors. The availability of budget accommodation on a mass European scale has led to pressures on the cost and revenue systems of the social tourism sector in this area. Similarly, social tourism accommodation is often of high quality and in good locations and, as previously identified, meets demanding environmental sustainability criteria. These features make it very attractive to a middle-class clientele. There are positives to be taken from these developments: commercial tourism becomes more accessible to low-income families, who have increasing amounts of choice, and there are opportunities for more inclusive social exchanges between members of different social classes, which can encourage social mobility. However, there is also a need to ensure that provision of services and infrastructure actually meets the needs of social tourists as a primary concern (in the social tourism sector), so that availability, cost and other barriers are not exacerbated. Secondly, the move to privatisation could lead to a loss of focus on social tourism objectives more generally as social tourism moves into a profit/market imperative, which could jeopardise provision and the reputation of social tourism as a positive force in society. A plural approach is to be applauded but, as we have seen in the preceding discussions, a focus on the social role should be at the forefront of activities.

A fourth observation is that while the main target groups for social tourism (low-income families, young people, senior citizens and disabled people) look basically similar across different programmes and countries, these four groups cover a dynamic and evolving market, and the rules about who is or is not part of these target groups can differ greatly between nations. This has led to instances where certain social groups may be in need of social tourism, but their type of disadvantage does not 'qualify'. As shown in Chapter 8, for example, changing family structures have led to an increase in non-nuclear families with specific needs – and these families are not always effectively catered for. Some target groups, such as young to middle-aged adults without children, are excluded from social tourism in many countries. Another exclusionary factor may be labour status. While in some countries the social tourism system is very much linked with workers and their affiliation to trade unions, in other countries it concerns only the most disadvantaged social groups, those without a working parent, and those without affiliation to a membership organisation. There is an urgent need to understand how the market for social tourism is changing in order for policy and provision to be targeted most effectively. Similarly, there are choices to be made in terms of the nature and level of provision. On the one hand, there are the universal systems of benefit, where measures target everyone in society. On the other, are special measures targeted towards specific, marginalised groups.

Moving Forward

Social tourism has a long history and has shown itself to be a dynamic concept that has adapted to social, economic, cultural and technological changes in society. The growth of mass tourism, the decrease in the prices of package holidays abroad, the rising affluence within the developed world and the new types of social disadvantage that have manifested themselves have all made social tourism evolve into the multifaceted concept it is today.

Further challenges are no doubt ahead for social tourism, and this chapter has identified three in particular:

- Social tourism has, until recently, occupied a peripheral position in the academic tourism literature in English. The concept needs to develop greater scientific credibility for it to become the subject of wider research.
- Social tourism faces different prejudices and image problems. In many countries, the term has pejorative connotations. Several alternative terms have been proposed, but none has been universally accepted.

- The EU has shown an interest in integrating social tourism policies and practices across the member states. This leads to a range of challenges. Moreover, the feasibility and desirability of this course of action can be questioned.

The chapter will conclude by examining these three challenges in more detail:

Lack of Recognition of Social Tourism as a Concept in the Academic Sphere

This book has shown that, at present, the term 'social tourism' can refer to a range of practices with very different motivations and outcomes. Social tourism has long been an under-researched area. Now that a research interest in the phenomenon is growing, a 'scientification' of social tourism should take place. Jafari (2001) has explored this process for tourism studies, in itself a relatively new area. He discussed how knowledge and theory in the field of tourism in general have developed around four platforms. These platforms have emerged chronologically, with one platform leading to the next, but one platform does not replace the other: Jafari (2001: 29) claims that all four coexist today. The platforms are:

- The *advocacy platform*, traditionally occupied by those who are attracted by the economic benefits of tourism, highlights the positive aspects of tourism: for example that it is an economic alternative for some countries and regions, that it is labour intensive, and that it generates foreign currency. This platform is mainly represented by the private sector and public development agencies.
- The *cautionary platform* rejects the claims of the advocacy platform, and highlights the negative impacts of tourism: the damage it can do to natural environments, the fact that many jobs are low skilled and low paid, that it mainly benefits big corporations and not local communities. This platform is mainly represented by members of the academic community, public agencies and the media.
- The *adaptancy platform* tries to develop a more nuanced position between the polarised views of the previous two platforms. It suggests that some forms of tourism have more positive/negative impacts than others, and advocates the forms that have more positive impacts. This platform is mainly represented by academics, consultants, community developers and religious groups.
- The *knowledge-based platform* aims to suggest a balanced and objective evaluation of tourism based on a scientific foundation. Studies in this platform are intended to contribute to a holistic treatment of tourism, not just its impacts or forms, but tourism as a whole. This platform

is mainly represented by members of the academic community. Jafari (2001) argues that tourism theory increasingly moved into this last, knowledge-based platform from the 1980s onwards, although evidence continues to be produced for other platforms simultaneously.

This framework highlights how tourism, as a discipline, is fairly young: the first research into tourism phenomena was performed in other disciplines, such as sociology, economics and anthropology. In a relatively short period of time the field has generally evolved through the four platforms described above, but it needs to be emphasised that tourism research is still in a very dynamic phase, with new strands developing continuously. For research areas like urban tourism and tourism policy, for example, the evolution into the knowledge-based platform is very recent – although research may have been carried out by public, private or voluntary organisations in earlier platforms. A similar observation can be made for social tourism: in many countries in Europe, social tourism practices have been in use for many years, and research has been developing in many practitioner or public organisations. Only recently, however – perhaps now the welfare state is under increasing threat due to the economic downturn – has it reached the knowledge-based platform in the English language, with a growing number of academic studies dedicated to the topic. A 'scientification' of social tourism has now begun.

A similar 'scientification' is noted by Hardy (1990), who applied the idea specifically to sustainable tourism. Because the term 'sustainable' has become loaded with a range of values and interpretations, it can be seen that the concept is increasingly subcategorised, critiqued and nuanced. Links have been made between sustainable tourism and eco-tourism, community-based tourism, responsible tourism and alternative tourism, to name but a few; yet each of these concepts commands a specific definition and is developing its own strand in the tourism literature. A similar development can be seen to have started in the case of social tourism, with, as potential aspects, concepts such as the four categories proposed in Chapter 2 of this book: host- and visitor-related social tourism; solidarity tourism; and tourism for all. We have maintained that in our view, the visitor-related forms of social tourism, i.e. those with an overt and primary aim for 'social' outcomes, have been the focus of our discussions, although this does not prejudice the potential of other aspects.

Hardy *et al.* (2002: 490) conclude their discussion of the conceptual evolution of sustainable tourism with the following question:

> Given the reactionary nature of sustainable tourism to current paradigmatic approaches and the difficulties associated with defining it, this leads to the question of whether sustainable tourism will be able to be developed theoretically and practically or is it simply reactionary rhetoric?

The same question may apply to social tourism, but with a different twist. Reactionary rhetoric can be identified within certain sections of the media, but not really within the academic field of tourism. In each case, the reasons could be attributed to a lack of information and awareness, and a lack of integration of social tourism concepts into mainstream public and academic discourses. More research is needed into the different forms social tourism can take, how they have evolved and where the theoretical underpinnings of the concept lie – publications like this book aim to make a contribution to this goal.

One aspect of the scientification process must be the link between research in social tourism and its place within the higher education system. There are currently very few pockets of the European tourism education system where social tourism features at all. There are perhaps a small number of modules available which either focus on or feature social tourism. This we believe is unacceptable, and we propose the integration of social tourism into the curriculum across all levels of the tourism education system. This will improve knowledge about and interest in social tourism among future professionals in the tourism industry more generally, and cement social tourism as an intrinsic feature of tourism knowledge. It will also help to develop and increase research interest among professional researchers and academics in the sector.

In terms of research funding, social tourism offers many attractive prospects for innovative projects and programmes. Social tourism is multidimensional and multidisciplinary; it should provide an interest for researchers across disciplinary communities, including tourism social science, education, sociology and social policy, psychology, politics and policy studies, business and management/marketing. There is an urgent need for joined up research across Europe, especially cross-cultural and comparative studies, and collaborative research programmes. Substantive research is required on the benefits of social tourism, on the economic impacts of social tourism (not only in terms of tourism impact studies on destination economies, but also on any welfare spending and social services support), on the changing market demand, and on the employment and sustainability factors. These are just a few of the most pressing areas of research need; there are many more, including fundamental studies. In times of curtailment of public financing for research and teaching (not across all of Europe but in some countries, including the UK), there is a need to maximise the outcomes or the impact of research. The UK Economic and Social Research Council (ESRC) has set out its priority areas for funding for the period 2011–15 as interdisciplinary research in three key areas: 'Economic Performance and Sustainable Growth; Influencing Behaviour and Informing Interventions; and A Vibrant and Fair Society' (ESRC Delivery Plan 2011–15, available at http://www.esrc.ac.uk). It is evident from the debates and issues discussed in this volume that social tourism could be aligned with any of these subject areas, and so is open to research that could increase the legitimacy and impact of tourism as a valid research field.

Connotations of Social Tourism and Image Issues

While there is already lack of clarity and consistency of the use of the term 'social tourism' in Europe, there are also semantic problems associated with the general notion of provision of holidays for disadvantaged people as part of the welfare remit of society. In the UK, it is not acceptable in some cases to talk about the provision of 'holidays' for disadvantaged groups, as this proves contentious to the media and the public. Many organisations have found it more appropriate to use the concept of a 'short break' as a defining category for their activities, because this is recognised as a legitimate aspect of government intervention, particularly in respect of provision of services to carers (people who are looking after a sick, disabled or older family member) – and in fact may not actually mean a holiday short break, but could include a break for the carer from caring within the home, sending the cared-for person on a short break, or the provision of other forms of respite care. This is a problem that may be peculiar to the UK and not the majority of mainland European countries; however, the issue points to the general problem of a misperception or a lack of understanding about the role and value of holidays to individuals and the positive impacts holidays can have on families, relationships and health, perhaps especially for those who are disadvantaged in society for one reason or another.

A key issue for future research is the image and perception of social tourism. This is partly a consequence of the diversity of delivery systems and levels of understanding about social tourism in Europe as we have outlined in this book, and partly a consequence of different perceptions and expectations among consumers. In the UK, social tourism is widely charity based, the majority of charities working with social services, education and healthcare professionals, where knowledge and perceptions about what social tourism is and about how social tourism can benefit people is extremely limited; as mentioned in Chapter 2, a large majority of welfare agents currently referring families for a holiday to the Family Holiday Association had never heard the term 'social tourism'. The problem here is a lack of awareness of social tourism among key professionals. Also, there is always the danger that social tourism could get misinterpreted by the media in a negative sense, as a taxpayer subsidy of 'holidays' for the 'idle poor'. In Belgium, social tourism addresses the whole of the population in a spirit of social cohesion, and there is a much wider appreciation for the concept of social tourism, but it has a fairly poor image nonetheless. The ambiguous or conflicting image that exists in many countries, according to the Belgian stakeholders, is related to a perceived link between social tourism and disadvantaged or excluded sections of society. Furthermore, it is not evident what the general public understands by the term 'social tourism'. As explained in Chapter 2, many definitions and understandings exist in different countries. The term 'social' often leads to confusion, linking social tourism to a social activity benefiting host communities. Partly, this is an issue concerning the fluid position of social tourism within and in opposition to the commercial system of tourism and partly it is connected with a pejorative connotation, which could be associated with a particular neoliberal or individualised political stance, and stems from a lack of general awareness about the role of and benefits accruing from social tourism.

What we must not forget, and as highlighted in Chapter 2, is that social tourism emerged out of an overtly social welfare agenda alongside commercial tourism, although it was not called social tourism at that point. However, 'social tourism' is becoming a more recognised term, and it must now be promoted and explained to a wide set of stakeholders. The image of social tourism needs to be improved and, alongside better research on the outcomes and benefits of activities, there is a need to share knowledge and collaborate on raising the profile to the benefit of all stakeholders. In order for this to happen, social tourism needs coordinated marketing, although this often difficult to justify in difficult financial conditions, where the majority of funding should be directed towards the delivery of programmes.

Social Tourism Policy Perspectives at the European Level

One of the major challenges for social tourism in many European countries is the growing requirement to become independent of state funding and economically self-sufficient, which has often resulted in the adoption of commercialised management systems. The EU has shown an interest in this challenge since 2009 with the Calypso project, which aims to integrate social tourism policies and practices across different member states. At present, social tourism represents across Europe the social democratic ideal of a fair and just society, where equality of access to leisure travel is encouraged because of its benefits to individuals and families; however, in terms of their practical implementation, social tourism policies vary strongly from one country to the other, as highlighted in Chapters 2 and 3.

At a time when public spending is under close scrutiny in most countries, the EU has shown a big interest in the stimulation of social tourism. As highlighted in Chapter 3, this interest was already noticeable in the early 1990s, when social tourism was seen as a social force. It was the first time that, at EU level, the different concepts of social tourism were compared, as well as the levels of funding in the different member states (European Commission, 1994). In 2006, the European Economic and Social Committee recognised in its opinion on social tourism in Europe the right for holidays (article 2.2.2):

Consequently – and without any intention of giving a precise definition of social tourism, but starting from the premise that tourism is a general right which we should try to make accessible to everyone – we can say that an activity constitutes social tourism whenever three conditions are met:

- Real-life circumstances are such that it is totally or partially impossible to fully exercise the right to tourism. This may be due to economic conditions, physical or mental disability, personal or family isolation, reduced mobility, geographical difficulties, and a wide variety of causes which ultimately constitute a real obstacle.
- Someone – be it a public or private institution, a company, a trade union, or simply an organised group of people – decides to take action to overcome or reduce the obstacle which prevents a person from exercising their right to tourism.
- This action is effective and actually helps a group of people to participate in tourism in a manner which respects the values of sustainability, accessibility and solidarity.

The view of social tourism as a force for social change, however, was replaced in that very same year by the 'renewed tourism policy' (European Commission, 2006), which focused more on the economic growth aspects of tourism as an industry; further, with the Lisbon Treaty (2007) the Commission acknowledged the crucial role of tourism for the EU economy for the first time. Yet, along with the shift towards a more economic approach in 2006, the social and environmental objectives were equally integrated, leading to the creation in 2007 of the Tourism Sustainability Group. The Group emphasised in its final report (among others) the need for social equity, cohesion and economic prosperity, preparing to some extent the path to the preparatory action of the Calypso project (Tourism Sustainability Group, 2007). It should be added here, however, that the need for social equity referred mostly to the enhancement of the socio-cultural life of host communities and their involvement in tourism development in their region, and to the provision of a safe or fulfilling experience for all visitors, without discrimination.

The growing interest in social tourism, however, was confirmed between 2006 and 2009, when the Commission's Tourism Unit (DG XXIII) organised three conferences on social tourism issues in collaboration with the International Social Tourism Organisation (ISTO). They focused on issues such as 'tourism for all' (here interpreted as tourism participation for all citizens, and not, as is common in the UK, focusing particularly on tourists with disabilities) and the impact of the Lisbon Treaty on the social tourism market. For the EU, the concept of tourism for all is an aim for social cohesion in European societies, constituting indeed a great potential market, which deserves to be developed and encouraged. From an economic perspective it is considered a response to congestion and seasonality problems. These different events and perspectives led to the current Calypso project. Indeed, the preparatory action in 2010 confirmed the course chosen by the European Commission. Although voices were extremely critical about the outcome, the preparatory action stimulated a joint reflection of stakeholders from many different countries. The communication between the different European stakeholders is one of Calypso's greatest contributions.

As pointed out earlier in this chapter, many social tourism initiatives currently face the challenge that they are forced to reposition themselves to stay competitive, but at the same time feel they need to provide an accessible product to their original target group. This repositioning is encouraged by the European Commission, illustrating a significant shift in orientation towards the economics of social tourism, which is far removed from its roots as a social provision for manual labourers that could lead to individual and social benefits. The tensions between social tourism and the increasing need for competitiveness discussed in Chapter 3 reflects the debates that are bound to take place between different European stakeholders, as the Commission has encouraged a further integration of social tourism with the mainstream commercial tourism sector. There is therefore a range of research questions surrounding the development of policy for social tourism which need to be addressed, including the industrialisation processes and their consequences.

This book is written in a time of transition of the social tourism sector. Although the original orientation of many organisations may be to some extent threatened by these recent developments, there will be benefits attached to a more coherent and European approach, if a balance between social and economic objectives can be struck as a result.

References

European Commission (DG XXIII, Tourism Unit) (1994) *Les différentes notions du tourisme social: L'évolution de l'offre et de la demande*. Luxemburg: UNIPUB, Management Conseil Communication.

European Commission (2006) *A Renewed EU Tourism Policy: Towards a Stronger Partnership for European Tourism* (COM 134 final). Brussels: European Commission.

European Economic and Social Committee (2006) Opinion of the Economic and Social Committee on social tourism in Europe. *Official Journal of the European Union*, C318/12.

Hardy, D. (1990) Sociocultural dimensions of tourism history. *Annals of Tourism Research*, 17: 541–555.

Jafari, J. (2001) The scientification of tourism. In V. Smith and M. Brent (eds), *Hosts and Guests Revisited: Tourism Issues of the 21st Century* (pp. 28–41). New York: Cognizant.

Layard, R. (2005) *Happiness: Lessons from a New Science*. New York: Penguin.

McCabe, S. (2009) Who needs a holiday? Evaluating social tourism. *Annals of Tourism Research*, 36(4): 667–688.

Small, J. (2008) The absence of the child in tourism studies. *Annals of Tourism Research*, 35(3): 772–789.

Tourism Sustainability Group (2007) *Action for More Sustainable European Tourism: Report of the Tourism Sustainability Group*. Brussels: European Commission.

Index